Romanticism and the Materiality of Nature

George Stubbs, 1724–1806. *Freeman, the Earl of Clarendon's gamekeeper, with a dying doe and hound.* Yale Center for British Art, Paul Mellon Collection.

Romanticism and the Materiality of Nature

ONNO OERLEMANS

UNIVERSITY OF TORONTO PRESS
Toronto Buffalo London

© University of Toronto Press Incorporated 2002
Toronto Buffalo London
Printed in Canada

ISBN 0-8020-4863-3

Printed on acid-free paper

National Library of Canada Cataloguing in Publication Data

Oerlemans, Onno, 1961–
Romanticism and the materiality of nature

Includes bibliographical references and index.
ISBN 0-8020-4863-3

1. English literature – 19th century – History and criticism.
2. Nature in literature.   3. Romanticism – Great Britain.   I. Title.

PR447.O33 2002   820.9'36'09034   C2001-902279-4

University of Toronto Press acknowledges the financial assistance to its publishing program of the Canada Council for the Arts and the Ontario Arts Council.

This book has been published with the help of a grant from the Humanities and Social Sciences Federation of Canada, using funds provided by the Social Sciences and Humanities Research Council of Canada.

University of Toronto Press acknowledges the financial support for its publishing activities of the Government of Canada through the Book Publishing Industry Development Program (BPIDP).

Contents

ACKNOWLEDGMENTS
vii

Introduction
Romanticism, Environmentalism, and the Material Sublime
3

I
The End of the World: Wordsworth, Nature, Elegy
30

II
The Meanest Thing That Feels: Anthropomorphizing Animals in Romanticism
65

III
Shelley's Ideal Body: Vegetarianism, Revolution, and Nature
98

IV
Romanticism and the Metaphysics of Classification
123

V
Moving through the Environment: Travel and Romanticism
148

Conclusion
200

NOTES
211

BIBLIOGRAPHY
233

INDEX
247

Acknowledgments

Many people have helped me in the writing of this book. Paul Fry encouraged me to think about the possibilities of ecologically oriented criticism long before it was fashionable, and helped me to see that one could write critically about one's passions. James McKusick, Lawrence Buell, and Alan Bewell have been especially encouraging, and their books have been central in mapping the ground that I re-examine here. Jonathan Bate's *Romantic Ecology* confirmed my sense I was doing something that mattered.

I am deeply thankful to Damhnait McHugh and Ina Ferris for reading portions of the manuscript, giving me valuable feedback, and forcing me to extend my research and knowledge. Steve Lukits provided much-needed trips to Round Lake, as well as bedrock perspectives on Wordsworth. Conversations with Mary Arseneau, April London, and Don Childs have kept me focused. The English Department at the University of Ottawa was a truly marvellous place to develop as a scholar and teacher. This book could not have been written without its collective support.

I also owe a significant debt to the editors. Suzanne Rancourt and Barbara Porter at the University of Toronto Press have helped see the manuscript to print. Judy Williams has done an impeccable job of helping me revise the text.

The University of Ottawa and Hamilton College provided funding for travel to do research at the British Library. A subvention for the publication of the book came from the Humanities and Social Sciences Federation of Canada.

My final and greatest debt is to Sally Cockburn, for it is her form of passionate reasoning on matters moral and intellectual that has been my steady guide in writing the book. I dedicate it to her, with love.

Romanticism and the Materiality of Nature

INTRODUCTION

Romanticism, Environmentalism, and the Material Sublime

Literary criticism of the past decade has begun to define clearly what many students of the romantic period have long assumed: that romanticism is an important origin for environmentalist thought. That many romantic-period writers expressed profound interest in the natural world has always been obvious. Their distinctive passion was marked by the rage for the picturesque tour, a pronounced interest in landscape painting, the celebration and detailed descriptions of natural settings, a seeming rejection of the city and the culture it represented, as well as a notable interest in the physical sciences. We easily recognize too the influence of the *setting* of Rousseau's account of the love of Saint-Preux and Julie, Wordsworth's descriptions of the Lake District, and Gilpin's tours. The work of Jonathan Bate, Lawrence Buell, Alan Bewell, and Karl Kroeber has made explicit connections between romanticism and contemporary versions of the environmental imagination, in each case at least partially as an attempt to rescue romanticism from charges of political and moral apostasy made by new historicist critics in the 1980s. Jerome McGann's definition of romantic ideology as the apparent power of consciousness to recreate itself in apparent resistance to culture seemed to negate, or at least to make seriously suspicious, the romantic interest in nature. In reaction to the chorus of criticism McGann helped to initiate, Buell, for instance, argues that 'the willingness to admit that thick description of the external world can at least sometimes be a strong interest for writers and for readers, even when it also serves ulterior purposes, is particularly crucial in the case of the environmental text ... To give a sufficiently generous account of literature's environmental sensitivity, we need to find a way of conceiving the literal level that will neither peremptorily subordinate it nor gloss over its astigmatisms' (90). It is this 'strong interest' in the external world by writers of the romantic period that I examine, and attempt in part to define, throughout this book.

Specifically, I am interested in tracing versions of the *material sublime*, which seems to me to be a fertile seed for the development of environmentalist thinking in the romantic period. As far as I know, the phrase first occurs in Keats's 'Epistle to J.H. Reynolds.' In the poem, the poet recounts how he has been luxuriating in a discordant but pleasing 'thread / Of shapes, and shadows' (ll. 2–3) produced in a period of pre-sleep dream-play on memories of the day's reading and art-viewing. The speaker shifts suddenly to the wish that

> our dreamings all of sleep or wake
> Would all their colours from the sunset take:
> From something of material sublime,
> Rather than shadow our own soul's daytime
> In the dark void of night. (ll. 67–71)

The desire that Keats expresses here is for the actuality of the physical world, its facticity and material presence, as contrasted to the artificiality of art reflected by both the dreamlike state the poem begins by celebrating and the poet's initial inspiration from explicitly fanciful paintings by Titian and Claude.[1] The material sublime is an effect, not of representation or of an act of the mind itself, but of the presence of the somatic. The poem refers to this presence at first as simply 'the world [in which] / We jostle' (ll. 71–2), but in the well-known final section specifies it through Keats's sudden vision, 'where every maw / The greater on the less feeds evermore ... Of an eternal fierce destruction' (ll. 94–102). The material sublime for Keats is a recognition that the physical world has a reality – including a 'core' characterized by predation and carnivorism – which lies quite apart from the world of beauty and pleasure towards which his art has been aspiring. The material sublime is in this instance not just a sense of awe and fear (those 'horrid moods') but a sudden recognition that it is possible to see at once how thought and existence are estranged from a clear awareness of the physical world, and that they are yet inexplicably rooted in it. It is also, of course, a yearning to recover that rootedness.

My sense of the material sublime in romanticism borrows too from Thomas Weiskel's more broadly defined notion of the sublime, which 'determines the mind to regard its inability to grasp wholly the object as a symbol of the mind's relation to a transcendent order' (23). The material sublime occurs when consciousness recognizes that it cannot fully represent the material order (which is truly 'other'), but that it is the ground for being. This awareness creates, as Burke suggested, a mixture of many emotions – fear, awe, and reverence. An important impetus behind my exploration of this aspect of romanticism's interest in the physical world is a desire to counter the critical revisionism that has seen romanticism as celebrating a falsely isolated and autonomous consciousness, which (as Keats feared too) is idealist and escapist. My aim is to suggest the crucial ways in which nature as material essence was a focus of romantic attention.

While the major books by Jonathan Bate and Karl Kroeber on romanticism and environmentalism have made the romantic interest in the external world a central focus, they have done so, it seems to me, without sufficient regard for the troubling relation between the two terms. While it may seem obvious and necessary to recuperate romanticism in part through a retrospective environmentalist gaze, we need, as Ralph Pite has argued (357–9), to maintain as much as we can a rigorously historical perspective. It is not enough to note the correspondence between past interest and current sympathy. In the first place, contemporary environmentalism, as even a cursory survey of its leading theorists reveals, does not offer a stable platform of values and ideas from which to launch a search for antecedents. We need to explore the form and manner of the strong interest in the material in romanticism and then begin to explore our own environmental imaginations. We could easily argue for what is romantic in contemporary eco-philosophy – the introduction to Michel Serres's *The Natural Contract*, for instance, reads as a modern translation of Shelley, insisting on an abstraction of world history, the power of beauty, and the rationality of idealistic action. Yet, I am looking for something harder-edged, a *ne plus ultra* of our perception of the physical world, rather than an environmentalist ideology.

We need to begin by recognizing that environmentalism (like romanticism) is by now a term, a concept, and a movement, of extraordinary vagueness and multiplicity. Proponents of the movement express their beliefs through such actions as putting bricks in toilet tanks, recycling newspaper, eating low on the food chain, worrying about rain-forests and spotted owls, refusing to invest in oil or nuclear or hydro-electric companies, hiking in the woods, purchasing sport-utility vehicles, or condemning such purchases. Environmentalism includes desires to get closer to nature, to preserve it, to leave it alone, to clean it up, and to pass on stewardship of it to next generations. We alternately feel possessive, defensive, protective, harmonious, and alienated towards what we blithely call the 'environment,' having very little sense of what the environment actually is. We frequently need to be reminded that the term contains no determining sense of what actually does surround us, of what place we find ourselves in, of how we may recognize or define it, and especially of how we come to value it. It is an obvious but troubling fact, for instance, that downtown Toronto and suburban Los Angeles are as much 'environments' as the Galapagos Islands or James Bay. We distinguish them by the degrees and kinds of human involvement in their physical or imaginative construction, rather than by some essential inherent difference. Moreover, we tend to imagine most 'environments' as somehow stable or fixed, leading to what is abstractly a perverse and overwhelming desire for the status quo, both within suburbs, and within apparently natural realms. Fundamentally, perceiving an 'environment' tells us nothing about what our proper attitude towards it should be.

Indeed, the fundamental problem in environmentalist thinking is understanding the place of humanity and consciousness in the physical order of things. The progress of scientific thought has made it increasingly difficult to hold that we are in any material way separate from the natural world, or that we are somehow at the pinnacle of its process of development, although myths of evolutionary *progress*, as Stephen Jay Gould reminds us, seem quite immune to scientific rebuttal (169–75). We are really only a fantastically successful species, if we measure success by population growth and, as we instinctively do, by the ability to transform the world around us through perception and physical intervention. The world is ours by virtue of our desire to survive and conquer it, and not through any teleology inherent or perhaps implicit in the physical processes that have led to the unfolding of life on the planet. We build, we consume, and we reproduce, much as ants so, but on a larger scale. What we have learned about the physical world has mitigated our arrogance; evolutionary biology and geology reveal that it is mere fantasy to believe that the world has been created for our pleasure or use. But the physical sciences have not helped us much in thinking about how or why we should live as we do. As Neil Evernden has argued, there is nothing in the study of nature that can really help us understand how we should value the physical world, our lives in it, or our actions towards it. From an ecological standpoint, humans are entirely as 'natural' as ants. We might imagine ourselves to be aspiring gardeners, tending and preserving and ordering, or we might see ourselves as particularly suicidal parasites, radically transforming our host to the point of our collective demise, at which point other forms of life take advantage of what we leave in our wake. We can find analogues for pretty much all of our behaviour in other organisms.[2]

This is not to argue that we can form no ethic about our relationship to organic and inorganic realms around us. It is, though, to begin to qualify those vague forms of sympathy we broadly term environmental, and to begin to make a case for the need for extreme self-consciousness in the process of their development. Current versions of environmentalism are marked by their moral commitment. Yet how or why these values are produced often remains unexplained or mystified. Mere instrumentalism – that we need to save the earth to save ourselves – is practical but misses the larger point that the natural world exists not simply for our survival or pleasure. Whatever our delusions, humanity is but one species among billions (the vast majority of which are bacteria), and an extremely recent arrival. The 'deep ecology' heralded by Arne Naess and by much ecofeminism, on the other hand, has argued influentially for our recognition of the intrinsic value of all aspects of the natural world. An awareness of this value is produced by what Naess calls a 'relational' ethic, one which allows us to expand our sense of self to include the place in which we exist, and the other beings with which we exist.[3] Yet the 'biospherical egalitarianism' that Naess argues for is, as several philosophers have pointed out, untenable if we see that it nonetheless places humankind at a kind of pinnacle of moral accomplishment; humanity alone, of all species, is required to develop a consciousness of restraint. As Frederick Ferré argues: 'Unless we appeal to the uniquely personal capacities of the human species, we have no leverage for self-restraint, no basis for an ecological ethics. Taking a purely organismic view of nature, including the human as literally no more than one more "plain citizen", our species should be allowed to live out its "destiny" without any more moral censure than is applied to other species that trample and consume' (61).

Ecofeminism wrestles with a similar dilemma. Carolyn Merchant, for instance, has argued that the enlightenment and the scientific revolution succeeded in transforming the way humanity sees the natural world, moving us quickly from nature as a nurturing and 'maternal' to nature as a passive object of our speculation and manipulation.[4] The transformation, Merchant argues, succinctly connects the history of the domination of women with that of nature. Nature is feminized as femininity is made to be a part of nature, and both are made mere objects for manipulation by enlightenment and masculine reason. While the cultural connection of femininity and nature is undoubtedly real, and in much need of deconstruction, ecofeminism seems caught between a desire to reveal and resist the double binding of women and nature, and a simultaneous but contradictory desire to celebrate exactly this connection. Because women *are* historically, culturally, and even biologically closer to nature than men, ecofeminists argue, they are better able to sense its intrinsic values, to be aware of what endangers it and of how to protect it.⁵ I am simplifying a large and complex project, but not, I think, beyond recognition. Patrick Murphy, a more theoretically self-conscious proponent of ecofeminism, argues that ecofeminism's strength lies in its ability to use the powerful sense of being 'other' that women have endured in order to restructure and to make relative all centres of meaning and being in western culture – both to speak for, and to make meaningful, the otherness that the natural world has been invested with in patriarchal culture. As for Naess, reality for Murphy is to be a nexus of porously defined subjectivities, each attempting to speak, with a Bakhtinian heteroglossia, the 'languages' of others. Naess's 'relational' ethics becomes, in Murphy's words, the ability to recognize 'that humans are not only things-in-themselves and things-for-us but also things for others, including the stable evolution of the biosphere' (9–12, 22). Both versions of this deep ecology argue for a radical expansion of self and of the perception of connectedness. For Murphy, this is an expansion of the project which versions of feminism have already committed themselves to; ecofeminism involves an expansion of the boundary of dominated otherness, from race and gender to the more nebulous 'being' of the organic and inorganic realms. As with Naess's version of deep ecology, however, Murphy's and Merchant's ecofeminism has enormous difficulty theorizing the material. Murphy, for instance, sees a locus of value in the virtually oxymoronic notion of a 'stable evolution of the biosphere.' That 'things' include 'humans, animals and ecosystems' also mystifies, since humans are animals, and ecosystems are better understood as processes than as fixed and precisely defined locales with stable inter-species relationships.

Presenting a very different pole of environmentalist thought, in a book that received broad public attention in part because it advocated an environmentalism that does not actually require us to *do* anything very different from what we are doing already, Greg Easterbrook has argued that 'thinking like nature' involves recognizing that our ability to transform the planet is genuinely insignificant when we compare it to a scale of geologic time that reveals the colossal effects of natural catastrophes like volcanic eruptions and asteroid strikes. Seemingly turning the tables on deep ecology, Easterbrook suggests that true humility means not exaggerating the effect or importance of our apparent destructiveness, so that we needn't worry too much, for instance, about our industrial development so long as it does not directly harm us. No cataclysm we could produce can compare with those the planet has already survived. A further source of Easterbrook's optimism lies in his examination of 'natural values,' through which he attempts to transform his anthropocentric instrumental values into something a little more transcendental. His survey of the processes of nature reveals that cooperation, interconnectedness, and self-celebration are inherent goals of evolution and human civilization. The book is philosophically vapid, based on a naïve understanding of evolution as teleological, and the simultaneous deprecation and glorification of anthropocentrism – yet it points to a nearly universal desire on the part of environmental thinkers to root value in the physical world, to give it an objective, material source.

My brief summary of versions of environmentalism reveals a common desire for a firm ethical footing by rooting value *in* the physical world. Even Easterbrook tries ultimately to avoid a projective ethic, one which remains explicitly or implicitly anthropocentric, merely a matter of human consciousness or desire. The goal in each case is the ability to open human consciousness to the possibility of meaning, being, and value in that which seems furthest from mind and its products, that which is in a sense most 'other' – the realm of the physical or phenomenal. It is not surprising, then, that romanticism is so frequently (and vaguely) cast as an impediment to serious thinking about our physical environment, by both environmentalists and critics of environmentalism. Romanticism has frequently been characterized as inherently a movement of Platonism and the isolated self. From anti-environmentalists we hear the charge that sympathy or identification with the natural world is merely sentimental, or hopelessly idealizing – that it imputes to the natural world a spirit (like Lovelock's Gaia, or Wordsworth's 'motion and spirit, that impels all thinking things, all objects of all thought') that is a projection of human consciousness onto the landscape. At worst, the charge that environmentalism is romantic suggests that this projection is in fact a culturally myopic illusion, a kind of willed ignorance in which we cast our own naïve desires for harmony and happiness onto a vague entity we identify with the term nature. We can hear versions of this charge in the political battle waged by ranchers and oil companies in defence of their clearly destructive practices, for instance, and more profoundly in reactions to environmentalists who demand that the preservation of wildlife and forests be made a priority for Third World countries and aboriginal peoples. Amongst environmentalists, romanticism is frequently a pejorative term as well (which the vagueness of the term allows), used to suggest very similar notions of the kind of mistakes they do not wish to make. Patrick

Murphy, for instance, argues that a proper ecofeminism attempts 'to render nature as a speaking subject, not in the romantic mode of rendering nature an object for the self-constitution of the poet as a speaking subject, but as a character within texts with its own existence'(12), and the idea has become a virtual mantra of opposition to a particular understanding of romanticism held by ecofeminists. As we shall see in the next chapter, Murphy here echoes criticism by Margaret Homans and Anne Mellor of William Wordsworth's (ab)use of nature, which is held to be paradigmatic. This in turn is part of the collective charge made by Marjorie Levinson, Jerome McGann, Alan Liu, David Simpson, and others in identifying the 'romantic ideology,' and the idea may be found before that in Geoffrey Hartman's enormously influential and celebratory reading of Wordsworth's use of nature to represent, and then to liberate, his own imagination.

This anti-romanticism might be seen as a deep fear within environmentalism, one we have seen countered in their various attempts to root their own thinking in the material. The 'romantic' impulse that must be resisted is seen to be one of relentless egotism and Platonism, of valuing the culture of self over nature, of mind over matter. The solution, varyingly put, is to expand subjectivity to include all of nature, to make it cease to be fully other, as well as stressing the objective sources of our own consciousness. Ecocritics from Murphy to Karl Kroeber argue that this can be accomplished through an ecological awareness, an ability to see the radical interdependence of beings or objects within an ecosystem. We will then come to recognize the contingency of our own being – that it is never singular and distinct, but wells up from nature and its processes. These arguments are buttressed by recent accounts of 'postmodern science' by Mark Lussier and Philip Kuberski. Taking as literally as possible the insights of twentieth-century physics into relativity, quantum mechanics, indeterminacy, and chaos, these writers argue that the dualism of Newton and Descartes is being replaced in contemporary science by a preference for 'wholeness ... which comes with a marked return of subjectivity, complementarity, indeterminacy and uncertainty.'[6] Yet it is probably impossible finally to avoid the charge that such claims are not 'romantic' in the pejorative sense, that subjectivity is being projected onto the somatic realm in the process of attempting to find meaning in the natural world. Meaning is a product of consciousness, even if consciousness is a product of complex, chaotic processes. The universe and its systems would still exist even if there were no self-conscious entities to perceive them.

In stating that 'there is no nature,' Alan Liu has provided an apt slogan for the apparently thoroughly anti-romantic point of view which argues that there is no conceiving or perceiving the physical world except through pre-existing ideological frameworks.[7] Neil Evernden, arguing in the end *for* an environmental ethic, suggests as well that nature must always begin as a concept, that the pure materiality or otherness of nature passes first through the screen of culture and consciousness, even if these forces are ultimately products of physical, determinate processes (*Social Creation*, 110–24). And Robert Pogue Harrison, similarly concerned with the desire to recuperate the material in human affairs, argues 'that humanity depends on the integrity of the natural world; that human beings belong to the greater network of nature's biodiversity; that we are caught in a forest of interdependencies with the planetary environment; that we are, after all, one species among others – this in itself does not prove that humanity is ontologically continuous with the order of nature' (200). Harrison presents the Kantian argument that consciousness and its tools of perception and representation finally always get in the way of unmediated perception. Kroeber argues that this point is really a 'critical banality ... an idea that was already common-place to Buffon,' which the romantics themselves 'would regard ... as question begging ... because they believed that human consciousness (and the social constructs made possible by it) is a result of natural processes' (*Ecological Literary Criticism*, 17). But this is precisely the point Harrison and others see as profoundly problematic. Knowing that consciousness is itself a construct of natural forces, or even an epiphenomenon of it, does not enable us to overcome the experiential discontinuity that exists between self and the world, consciousness and matter. Although we can know much about the natural world, and can trace our cultural and biological roots to natural objects and processes, we nevertheless experience consciousness and selfhood as distinct. Thus any desire we may also feel for a reunion, for knowing our connection with the world, must be to some degree suspect. This is more than the mere philosophical game that Kroeber suggests; it is the fundamental paradox that lies at the heart of environmentalist thinking, and forms its central conjunction with Romanticism.

As perceivers and users of nature we give value and create meaning. There are certainly degrees of empathy, but all acts of perception leave a trace of the perceiver; our knowledge of the world, whether through direct experience, memory, or the learning of science, always reflects our interest in it, and the growth, as Wordsworth would have it, of our singular or cultural consciousness. We may be materialist enough to acknowledge the certainty that mind is purely the result of physical processes, but this knowledge does little to counter the subjective root of sensation. Jean Baudrillard argues against the tendency in environmentalism to displace this difference, suggesting that we need to be reminded more of what it means for an object to be an object than to be urged to see all the world imbued with subjectivity. Responding to Michel Serres's call to codify the 'rights' of nature in law, Baudrillard writes:

> After having first been matter, and then energy, nature is today becoming an interactive subject. It is ceasing to be an object ... For the ultimate danger is that, in an interactivity built up into a total system of communication, there is no *other*; there are only subjects – and very soon, only subjects without objects ... All our problems today as civilized beings originate here: not in an excess of alienation, but a disappearance of alienation in favor of a maximum transparency between subjects. An unbearable situation, all the more so for the fact that, in foisting on nature the status of a subject in law, we are also foisting on it all the vices of subjectivity, decking it out, in our own image, with a bad conscience, with nostalgia (for a lost object which, in this case, can only be *us*), with a range of drives – in particular, an impulse for revenge. The 'balance' we hear so much of in ecology ('out of balance') is not so much that of planetary resources and their exploitation as the metaphysical one between subject and object. (*Illusion*, 80–1)

The creation of pan-subjectivity threatens our ability to analyse and produce meaning as a result not of decentring or undermining hierarchy but of ultimately erasing the materiality of nature through a kind of ontopomorphism in which human subjectivity and discourse become the sole reality. This is not unlike Heidegger's critique of technology, in which unreflective consciousness has become so dominant that it can no longer recognize its actual connections to other realities, like that of the physical universe, and so has itself been subsumed into systems of its own creation. For Baudrillard, this system allows 'the human race ... to produce itself as waste-product ... Nature – the natural world – is becoming residual, insignificant, an encumbrance, and we do not know how to dispose of it. By producing highly centralized structures, highly developed urban, industrial and technical systems, by remorselessly condensing down programmes, functions and models, we are transforming all the rest into waste, residues, useless relics' (*Illusion*, 78). Evernden similarly argues that environmentalism needs to avoid a 'conceptual domestication of nature' (*Social Creation*, 116), which subdues the world to our imagination. For both Baudrillard and Evernden, resisting such projection results from a necessary recognition of the incommensurate materiality of nature.

The problem is, in part, one of representation and interpretation. As nature writers beginning with the Romantics were fully aware, our experience of the physical world comes through first-hand experience (though that experience is shaped by expectations arising from previous experience of the natural world and from various forms of education), and through recreated experience (memory and its modes of representation). I see an important and mutually beneficial overlap between romanticism and environmentalism in the desire in both that the moment of perception may be more important than the forms of representation, however much we may want them to be intimately connected, in order for writing perfectly to reflect the author's experience and mould the reader's. This desire is an openness to the materiality of the world, to its otherness. It is in part a sense of wonder, a need to take the world in, to try to know it, countered by an awareness that this otherness cannot be made a part of the singular or cultural self. That this desire is, however, not definitive of either romanticism or environmentalism ought already to be clear. We are more familiar with romantic texts that seem to reflect the opposite of this desire – the Platonic pan-subjectivity of Coleridge's 'one Life,' Wordsworth's 'motion and spirit,' and Shelley's 'unseen power,' and the yearning for the transcendence of the material expressed in Keats's 'viewless wings of Poesy.' And we can easily recognize in their poetry the power of language and consciousness over the material, expressed, for instance, in Wordsworth's paradigmatic image of the imagination as 'That awful Power' that rises 'from the mind's abyss / Like an unfathered vapour.' One aim of my book is to defamiliarize this mode of romanticism, to see in its wide range of authors and texts those moments when the material is not transcended, but confronted, and when representation perhaps paradoxically defers to the physical reality that the writers yearn to represent. This will be a 'green' mode of reading, in the vein that Pite suggests, one that regards the field of texts with a care and attention that mirror our regard for actual landscapes, whatever effects these texts may have on our ability to perceive and value those landscapes. Pite argues for the need to preserve the 'wildness' of the text (359), which means resisting an appropriation of the voices of the poets for narrowly ideological ends. More important, it also means attempting to recognize the varying historical and material conditions that helped produce each text, and developing a sensitivity to the diversity contained within a period, an author, a text.

Put another way, it means paying attention to particular moments, to the *particularity* of the moment captured and/or represented by poetry. The 'green' ethic I am espousing may be measured by our ability to take note of detail for its own sake, and to recognize and shift between the scales available to our modes of perception, from the picturesque wide-angle, with the horizon perpendicular to the line of sight, to the macro- and microscopic. The aim may be understood as the desire to resolve individual distinctness, to note the immense complexity and diversity of the physical world, by attempting to see and represent that physical complexity. It is a desire that necessarily encounters paradox. The mode of perception I am interested in characterizing as 'green' and 'romantic' indeed values distinctness and discreteness – the ability to discern units of thingness or being, as it were – as an epistemological and ontological goal. We know the world when we have discovered its primary components. The search for detail is ever the search for the final resolution of discreteness, as we are reminded by Poe's parodic description in *The Purloined Letter* of the police search of D's apartment, or the hunt by particle physicists throughout the past century for the ultimate units of reality. And yet a fundamental openness to the material finds that the discreteness of things in the world is always a kind of illusion (as has been the case in particle physics);[8] that finding a unit or a whole is a matter of arbitrarily limiting boundaries, or, as Drummond Bone has argued, of arbitrarily defining a single scale to be definitive of final depth (3–5). About the ability of language to map categories of nature, Wordsworth says in his *Essay Supplementary to the Preface of 1815* that 'in nature everything is distinct, yet nothing defined into absolute independent singleness' (*Prose Works*, 3:77). Individuality and distinctness seem generally to be reducible into ever-smaller pieces. There will thus always be a struggle, in this process of perceiving the material world, in discerning parts from wholes. I am not arguing, though, for a relentless suspicion of individuality, leading inevitably to a holism that settles upon ecosystems or Gaia as ultimate units of value. For a key feature of this green empiricism is a parallel reluctance to settle upon wholes, or classes.[9] Framing a landscape, a particular organization of life, or a population obliterates the possibility of individuality altogether. While a sense of interconnectedness is clearly an ecological virtue, the openness to the material that I am arguing for is a mode of perception that precedes this contemporary environmental ethic, and which perhaps precedes synchronically environmental ethics in general. Wholeness dissolves before this awareness, as discreteness does.

We develop this openness, as many romantic-period writers did, by going into the world, putting ourselves in nature, which is both a physical and a mental act. It is based on the act of observation and involves striving to make the unfamiliar familiar, which may also be understood as attempting to discover precisely what is unfamiliar. We spend time taking in the infinite variety of the world, and we can perhaps be guided in the significance of this by referring to the accounts of others who have done likewise. In fact, we need to be schooled in an awareness of the particularity of the material, since most of us are only half-hearted naturalists. As the Romantics frequently demonstrate (think of Wordsworth's and Blake's descriptions of children, for instance), our predominant reaction to the external realm is as petty Platonists, searching for essences, tendencies, characteristic qualities, single meanings, totalizing systems of order. It is difficult even to want to see the natural environment 'as it is.' We are easily bored by objects that withhold their meanings, or seem inimical to human being. We characterize entire regions as wastelands when they threaten a sense of our own centrality.

This emphasis on the particularity of the material is a bias of much of the new historicism as well, but there is a different emphasis on the kind of detail. New historicism tends to value the particular in terms of the cultural moment. The material which it is concerned with is still, relatively speaking, Platonic in the sense that it is primarily cultural, economic, and political – entirely the product of human history, of a Foucauldian notion of discourse. It is a particularity that reveals some primary depth, an ultimate, previously ignored or unknown, realm of meaning.[10] Bruno Latour is surely right to argue that cultural criticism has made this version of materiality as absolute, purely objective, and transcendent (in the sense of being impermeable to human will) as nature is frequently deemed to be by science (136–7). New historicism's structuralist roots have thus helped in the reification of discourse, turning consciousness into the effect of an immaterial materialism. If, as Latour argues, we see both the natural environment and our modern sense of discourse as transcendent, then we can perhaps restore a balance by including the physical environment in our growing awareness of the power of the material. This is especially pertinent, it seems to me, in the realm of literary criticism, where an awareness of the power of representation to create its own reality predominates. A green particularity, in contrast, attempts to stress the non-human physical world that romantic writers encountered, and to show their concern for its detail, and its reality.

This version of green criticism must be aware of its own ideological and epistemological negotiations. David Simpson and Alan Liu have presented important critiques of what both identify as the postmodern idealization of the particular, what Liu (following Naomi Schor) terms 'detailism' (Liu, 'Local Transcendence,' 78). Both Simpson and Liu note that valuing the local and the particular is indeed a strong feature of romanticism, and that it is now a characterizing feature of postmodern literary criticism even though that criticism professes to be anti-romantic. Simpson suggests that 'the modernizing generalities that characterize species designation in the utilitarian poetries of such as Dyer and Thomson ... are countered by the microscopically local nomination of romantics like Blake and Clare and by a number of Wordsworthian protagonists who have an eye for every tree and flower and for every minute change in the weather.'[11] Cultural criticism values the particular partly because it enables one to see, and aligns one with, those traditionally at the margins of mainstream discourse. 'Local knowledge' belongs typically to women and labourers; their intellectual and physical mobility is restricted, but they gain an intimate knowledge of a specific place (of work, for example) that is not usually valued. The recent re-examination of the journals of Dorothy Wordsworth, for instance, stresses exactly this particularity. The ability to generalize, Simpson notes, is associated with educational superiority, and thus with the upper class, science, and masculinity. A generalizing imagination is one capable of exploring not a particular environment but a host of them, searching for similarities and essences. Yet for Simpson an ideological alignment with localism as a source of value is naïve. In the first place, criticism is itself a kind of science that seeks explanation, and is thus necessarily aligned with the abstract and general. Moreover, in literature, a representation of the local or particular is frequently either ineffective or false. Simpson finds, for instance, that Clare's localism is only ever nostalgic for what is already lost, and Wordsworth's apparent 'situatedness' (seen notoriously in the opening of 'Tintern Abbey') is based on a contradictory ideological valuing of the particular that is necessarily abstract – a British sense of place to set against the dangerous universalizing of the French Revolution. 'Localism and localization in neither case provide any empirical certainties of being and belonging in place, but instead stimulate uncertainties of meaning and disposition' (158). The real problem for Simpson is that the postmodern valuing of fracturing and piecemeal knowledge amounts to micro-history rather than history. We may recover more texts by formally marginalized authors, or feel that we know more about the detailed history of human society, but without an abstract ideological frame we celebrate them only as individual achievements, as moments within a larger literary or cultural heteroglossia, perhaps. Particularity and localism as ends in themselves get in the way of a holistic and necessarily abstract *historical* awareness that could produce a truly progressive and organized ideological position.

Liu's critique of what he brilliantly reveals to be the postmodern love affair with the particular argues not so much for its ideological problems as its epistemological ones. Focusing on the particular and the local is a 'tenet so elementary, pervasive, and insistent in all the high cultural criticisms that it appears foundational (despite the method's avowed philosophical antifoundationalism). The basis of high cultural criticism is its belief that criticism can, and must, engage with context in a manner so close, bit-mapped, or microbial ... that the critic appears no farther from the cultural object than a cybernetic or biological virus from its host at the moment of code exchange' ('Local Transcendence,' 77–8). Minutely realized context offers a seeming escape from totalizing orders, and from ideology. We will come to know the world or history piecemeal, giving the reader the ability to pick and choose, to create her own connections or narratives. Yet, Liu argues, the current love-affair with the local rests on a rhetorical illusion. It works by allowing cultural critics, empiricists of history, to produce a sense of immanence, the virtual reality of the real, by seeming to have found a kind of information that is at once infinite in supply and yet elemental. Details are 'elementary particles engaged in an overall systemics of combination [and] the atom of detail is a classically hard, discrete unit ... What such empirics projects is a view of cultural matter (economic, social, political, or ideological) so objective that materialism seems to obey the dynamics of literal matter' ('Local Transcendence,' 84, 83). Liu finds in cultural criticism a romantic yearning for objective knowledge through an apparently unpreconceived, or antimethodical, process, a kind of transcendence of subjectivity through an organic connection to the real (reminding one of Coleridge on method and form). It is also the romantic longing for a version of scientific objectivity implicit in much of the humanities, or the yearning, paradigmatically expressed by Wordsworth in his dream of the Arab and the shell, to transform the work of consciousness into something with the permanence and objectivity of the actual material realm.[12]

For Liu, this bind between the local and the real, the empirical and the rhetorical, is inescapable, and points to the continued importance of romanticism. For Simpson, the bind is the result of a misplaced desire to escape ideology, and thus he argues for a positivistic historicism that will enable us to construct ever more powerfully connective narratives. Both critiques can help us place, and see the potential benefits and limitations of, environmental particularism. Clearly an attention to the particular is a predominant and historic concern of many versions of the environmental imagination. Buell's general description of the literary form of the environmental imagination as that which is inclined to produce 'thick description of the external world' gives a clear sense of this value, as does his celebration of Gilbert White, Thoreau, Aldo Leopold, Mary Austin, Barry Lopez, and Edward Abbey as prototypical nature writers because of the sheer detail of their accounts of the non-human environment. Literary representation of specific, precisely delineated locales has indeed been celebrated by a host of ecocritics, from John Barrell's championing of John Clare over Wordsworth to Val Plumwood's argument that an ecofeminist ethic of empathic nurturing explains 'the deep and highly particularistic attachment to place that has motivated both the passion of many modern conservationists and the love of many indigenous peoples for their land' (297). That is, we generate productive emotion not for abstractions (as Burke also argued), but for specific places that are known intimately, as we see in John Clare, Dorothy Wordsworth, and Susan Fenimore Cooper. Similarly, Bate and Kroeber both see William Wordsworth as a prototypical environmentalist for developing a similar kind of attachment to the Lake District, and Bewell celebrates his poetry for its willingness to document, in the vein of enlightenment anthropology, social and environmental diversity.[13]

But what does thick description of the natural world, or close attention to physical detail, get us? What good does it do? What work, cultural or individual, does it perform? Simpson's critique suggests that it may prevent us from seeing a bigger picture, from developing ideological coherence. Like postmodernism, environmentalism also includes a broad range of ideological variation and coherence, from the insipid value-added version of contemporary commercialism (on the order of convincing people that buying a Big Mac in paper rather than foam wrapping is doing something good for the world) to neo-Marxist and libertarian versions. For those versions for which an intimate familiarity with the natural environment matters (such as deep ecology and ecofeminism), Simpson's critique of particularism seems not to hold. As I suggested in the beginning of my discussion, environmental thinkers move with relative ease from perception of nature to a generalized ethical stance. Attention to the particular for environmental theorists typically leads to an awareness of ecosystems, interconnectedness, and deep respect, usually through a sense in which the perceived otherness of the natural world is overcome (though how this may be translated into action is another question). Indeed, in this sense, such environmentalism is distinctly anti-postmodern, offering a vision of nearly sacred wholeness to replace the apparently fractured vision of contemporary being. In spite of the postmodern rhetoric of such ecocritics as Patrick Murphy, their vision of a necessarily dialectical relation between nature and culture, self and other offers a vision of a new plenitude, a surfeit of being. Indeed, Simpson cites Donna Haraway's vision of a dialectics that includes technology/nature as an example of a criticism that takes us out of the postmodern hinterland.[14]

Yet a common ideological critique of environmental thinking (from the Left and the Right) is that it fails to see its own cultural rootedness, and that it varyingly puts the apparent interests of animals and ecosystems (or the interests of environmentalists in them) ahead of the concerns of, or for, specific classes of humanity.[15] Being rooted in particularity, we might say with Liu, can breed an illusion of objectivity or immanence by other means. In observing the grounds of diverse life, surveying vast 'modes of being,' and especially in generalizing from this to the realm of holistic 'super-entities,' like ecosystems or even cyborgs, we assume, or require, an enormous database of facts, or in Haraway's terms, a plenitude of information and information processing. Our awareness, individual and collective, is indeed extended beyond mere culture into the more fundamentally material, and culture is put in a much smaller place. This is very often explicitly a part of the anti-anthropocentric force of most non-'shallow,' or non-instrumentalist, environmentalism. Yet the leap from particularity to ecosystem and the significance of the particulars offered stand, as in Liu's critique of cultural criticism's detailism, with an implicit *etcetera* after them, a large gap between the apparently discrete particulars of observation or documentation and the rather amorphous illusion of wholeness produced by such categories as ecosystems.[16] Here, for instance, is Kroeber's account of the environmental implications of Wordsworth's intimacy with Grasmere: 'Wordsworth's profoundest discovery-creation was that we dehumanize ourselves most perniciously when we use our consciousness to separate ourselves form nature. The separation is disastrous because the natural environment is both the source and the primary sustainer of our singularly human power of consciousness, superbly manifested in our imagination. Because this creative capability of our minds is not transcendent, it is most fully realized when we use it to strengthen and reinforce our participative engagements with our natural environment' (*Ecological Literary Criticism*, 138). The 'participative engagements' that Kroeber speaks of, like deep ecology's notions of depth and identification, ecofeminism's ideal of nurture, or even Linnaean systematics (to move further afield), assume an intense contact with the material that breeds complete familiarity. This is, as Liu suggests, a version of the romantic Platonism that produces and celebrates immanence. The final goal is to reintroduce an essentialism which, although recognizing that nature is in some sense a cultural construction, yet reconnects culture to something deeper and more fundamental than itself. Rediscovering a real and untransformable nature, one that comes before or beside politics, rather than after it, can, as Kenneth Johnston has argued for romanticism's 'idea-elegy,' offer a view of nature 'as that sense of Otherness which seemed to be always there, over against us and any tyrannies which sought to subject us, and could therefore always be invoked as a source of possible liberation.'[17]

Let me stress that I am not finding fault here with the various ethical stances produced by these versions of environmentalism. The openness to the material which I am drawing attention to does not, strictly speaking, contradict these views, but rather precedes them, or stands in productive tension to them. I wish to register, to borrow an apt meaning from an old phrase recently suggested by Stephen Jay Gould, a portion of the full house of romanticism and environmentalism. There are, of course, a variety of environmentalisms within romanticism, and I wish to draw out a thread that seems to me to be crucial to both. The interest in specificity that I will be examining throughout is distinctly not, as in Liu's account of cultural criticism, or my adaptation of it to environmentalism, a matter of quantity producing a sense of the plenitude of being. The modes of perception I aim to describe are not about producing a sheer volume of data (as is the case for much Victorian natural history, for instance),[18] but of striving to perceive distinctness. If anything, it produces an awareness of one's difference from the world, and one's isolation within it. It emphasizes the otherness of the physical as a first step in acknowledging where and how we exist. Rather than breeding familiarity, or creating an illusion of knowledge, it brings us to the limits of what we know. We can construct an idea of nature, make a useful order, but know too that there is a fundamental order that eludes us. Nor is it a vision of a process, a dialectics or dialogics continually promising completion. It is, rather, part of the originary moment of romanticism, a way in which its writers stand against the Platonism that they very often proceed towards nonetheless. It is a resistant step, itself a particular moment for which there are plenty of good examples. The particularism I wish to take note of aims to be consistent with experience and perception, rather than theory or ideology.

It will perhaps appear as something of a paradox that this profoundly experiential awareness can be aided by, or reproduced in, literature. Literary representation is not a necessary complement, since the perception I am arguing for begins prior to representation, but it is perhaps a beneficial one. Language may be seen as in some way parallel to the external environment in that it too shapes and is yet external to subjectivity, so that the act of writing allows one to duplicate the initial interaction with the physical world. The desire to reproduce an experience of the material through an analogous experience with language will indeed be a major focus of this book. In the first place, this desire is a sign of the significance of the experience – that its meaning is indeterminate and in need of reflection and reworking. This follows from the nature of the 'openness' I have been describing, characterized by an unwillingness to project final meanings or to produce a sense of completion. It is frequently characterized by the attempt of the writer and perceiver to stand outside himself, to resist the ready supply of meaning and narrative offered by previous experience and education. This is recognizably a desire for an unmediated access to the material realm, a desire that is moderated but not erased by the inevitable failure to achieve this access.

There is an important overlap between this kind of literary experience and what Paul Fry has recently called the 'ostensive moment' of lyric poetry, which discloses the 'indifference of somatic existence' and 'the underlying unfeelingness of the earth' that 'alienates us from the presence to ourselves of the nonhuman' (*Defense*, 74–5, 37). Fry's analysis of the writing of Wordsworth sees the confrontation with the material as directed towards the recovery of a primary somatic unity that is the ultimate ground for the self. Fry identifies the ostensive moment as profoundly anti-anthropocentric, showing the sense of being produced by language itself to be a kind of illusion before the primary reality of the material (100, 122). With Fry, I want to argue that the complement of literature to the experience I am trying to highlight is its ability to disrupt the rule of consciousness, to open our awareness to something that may be more primary or even essentially other to it. Of course, it is finally impossible to achieve this goal. Language is the medium of consciousness, and thus poetry offers no final escape from the self or consciousness; nor can it make the material transparent. However, lyric is a key form of the exploration of the otherness of the material or the ground of being, precisely because it can allow for the ostensive moment, which I have been calling an openness to the material. It is, as we shall see, crucially a form of incompleteness, of multiple suggestiveness, and perhaps necessary obscurity. In its 'green' mode, it can reveal not just the lacunae with language, which can allow consciousness to see its own activities as other, but also those of the physical world we find ourselves in. In other words, the extraordinary self-consciousness of lyric language reveals the discontinuity, or wildness, of the physical world. It disturbs the illusion that consciousness is somehow pervasive and continuous with what is perceived, and so reveals the physical in relief as the fundamental ground that cannot be reached. This discontinuity we will see romantic writers both engaging, recognizing it as a profound insight in its own right, and struggling to overcome, as Coleridge reveals, for instance, in a letter to Godwin: 'Is *thinking* possible without arbitrary signs? & – how far is the word "arbitrary" a misnomer? Are not words etc. parts & germinations of the Plant? And what is the Law of their growth? – In something of this order I would endeavor to destroy the old antithesis of *Words & Things*, elevating, as it were, words into Things; & living Things too.'[19]

Coleridge returns us to the continually frustrated desire to root consciousness in the physical, which we saw in our brief survey of environmental thinking at the beginning of this chapter, and which readers will remember having encountered as well in the most transcendent moments in Thoreau and Emerson. That we might trace the pathways from nature to consciousness through language has long been a romantic yearning and is vividly displayed in Shelley's explorations of 'Necessity' in *Queen Mab* and *Prometheus Unbound*, in Thoreau's meditation on leaves and language in *Walden*, and, much more recently, in Daniel Dennett's and Richard Dawkins's argument that the Darwinian algorithm must explain the evolution of consciousness and culture in the same way that it explains the evolution of organic life. It is a genuine and plausible desire, produced in part by the fulfilment of scientific narrative. The moment of the material sublime suspends this desire, revealing that the reality of the physical is most keenly felt in a full awareness of its separateness. This is not a Cartesian epiphany, since it does not celebrate the isolation of consciousness but mourns it. The aim of such green writing is still to know what the physical environment is, even as it allows us to feel the limits of consciousness; such awareness does not elevate the soul, but makes us feel a nostalgia for the material world we know we are somehow a part of but yet estranged from. It reminds us, as Drummond Bone argues, that 'the action of thought can be conceived of as an attack on the freedom of the object. It is usual for intellectuals, and possibly especially for those interested in Wordsworth, to put that the other way round, and see the solid object as an impediment to the freedom of thought. But it is perhaps salutary to think of this alternative: thought attacks the freedom of the object.

The desire to explain is close to the desire to transform the specific to the general, the material to the ideal, and indeed it may be identical to it if we exist within such dualist terminology' (10).

My argument needs to be put into a broader context. I am not arguing that the awareness offered by such lyric moments forms either the complete scope or the core of romantic environmentalism. There are clearly other modes of representation, and other kinds of 'green' insight, within romanticism. These other modes tend towards narratives of harmony and completion. They produce accounts of varyingly imagined orders of things, which situate consciousness, or being, within some realm of the material, or, more prosaically, in some actual place. Moreover, the mode of empiricism that I am pursuing here does not operate outside cultural and historical influences, though it may work occasionally to resist them. Thus, in several of the chapters that follow I engage these other modes of green romanticism and their specific historical contexts, and attempt to find elements of this empirical awareness in them, which may be complementary or contradictory. The contexts that I examine most consistently are those in which participants understand themselves to be explicitly concerned with nature as primarily material rather than cultural, often through an awareness of the burgeoning fields of biology, natural history, geology, and medicine. I will examine as well those more obviously culturally oriented discourses concerning the natural world connected with the picturesque and travel writing. The range of my investigations will, I hope, demonstrate the degree to which the physical world is itself an object of intense and sophisticated scrutiny by romantic-period writers.

The variety of topics covered in this book may strike some readers as idiosyncratic or unsystematic. I have not uncovered in the romantic period a sustained and consistent stance towards, or ideology concerning, the natural world. I have rather searched in many different kinds of writing, by different kinds of writers, for what I take to be primarily a resistance to a sense that we can and should be able to come to a complete and comfortable understanding of nature, where a sense of its complexity, intricacy, and otherness is primary and sufficient. Another consistency in my approach regards the importance I place on the ability of literary discourse to engage and reflect this kind of complexity. While literature is only an intermediary in our own relations to the natural world, its ability to reflect self-consciously on the limits of language, representation, and knowledge make it well suited to the kind of questioning that seems to me to be the central interest of each of the broad topics I examine. The value of such writing is both in and of itself (to the degree that the examples I investigate reveal a powerful potential within the literary impulse), and perhaps in our own ability to observe and reflect upon the natural world. Most of the examples I scrutinize can help to get us into the world to observe it by withholding ourselves from it, showing us the possibility that we can reach a point where, in William Carlos Williams's fine phrase, there may indeed be no ideas but in things. That is, these texts attempt to point fundamentally beyond themselves, beyond language, and beyond consciousness.

The first chapter focuses on moments in Wordsworth's poetry where an examination of the material sublime is most in evidence. It seems necessary to begin here because Wordsworth's poetry has so obviously been used already to characterize the romantic period as one that both is, and is not, crucially connected with varying environmentalist conceptions of nature. Moreover, his poetry is most frequently thought of as representing the natural world as organic and as imbued with a human-oriented spirit that makes it 'exquisitely ... fitted to the Mind.' In contrast to this, I examine those moments in his poetry that reflect his ability to confront the materiality of nature, the impenetrable reality of surfaces and appearances. These moments are frequently elegiac, in which the poet sees in meditating on death the overwhelming presence of the physical. The investigation is intended to create 'resonance,' in the sense of the word put forward by Wai Chee Dimock, with currents in environmentalist thinking, allowing us to see ways in which Wordsworth's poetry may both harmonize and seem out of tune with it.[20]

The otherness of the natural world is itself complex and varied, and the next two chapters explore a few of the ways in which thinking about animal life can complicate our sense of what nature could mean to romantic-period writers. In chapter 2, I examine the representation of animals in the romantic period, showing how animal sentience particularly provides a means through which writers could meditate on connections to, and differences from, the natural world. That animal life could be seen as linking and distinguishing human being from the natural world is relatively obvious, but this linking becomes especially important for writers who are commonly thought of as projecting forms of human consciousness onto all of nature. Understanding what is at stake in the process of anthropomorphizing animal being allows us to see the ways in which romantic-period writing (and painting) could pay particular attention to the nonhuman in nature, and how otherness itself could be seen as variegated and nuanced. The chapter examines poetry by a range of poets (including Wordsworth, Clare, and Coleridge) as well as painting by George Stubbs.

The third chapter re-examines Percy Shelley's commitment to vegetarianism. His vegetarianism is in part an ethical stance, and relevant as such, but it is also a way of exploring how consciousness and culture could themselves be materially based, rooted through the body – its health and its appetites – to a world which remains other.

The fourth chapter examines the more abstract issue of what was at stake in the classification and categorization of the natural world, including such fundamental taxonomic divisions as the distinction between the organic and inorganic, and between the individual and the species. The key issue here is the debate over the reality of such divisions, whether they are of and in the natural world or constructs inevitably resulting from the nature of human perception. I argue that though the classificatory sciences achieve a certain dominance during the romantic period (as evidenced by the enormous popularity of Linnaeus, and the work of Lamarck, Erasmus Darwin, Cuvier, and Coleridge), writers such as John Clare, Gilbert White, and Percy Shelley explore the ways in which taxonomy constrains perception, limiting our awareness of the particularity and materiality of the natural world. In a sense, such systems are the most obvious and powerful kind of projection of order and meaning onto the raw material of sensory data.

The final chapter examines how the popular genre of travel writing can be seen to reflect a genuine and widespread interest in the physical as an end in itself. Far from merely aestheticizing landscape, or turning it into an object for touristic consumption, such writing displays a widespread and significant desire in writers and readers for the kind of 'thick description of the physical' that Lawrence Buell identifies as being central to an environmental imagination. I argue here for the complexity of the genre: travel enforces both an awareness of all landscape as in some sense unfamiliar and unknowable, and the desire to see some of the range of complexity in landscape. The chapter begins with a survey that aims to reveal the range of interests that can be incorporated into the genre, and turns to close readings of Dorothy Wordsworth's *Recollections of a Tour Made in Scotland* and some of William Wordsworth's poetry about travel.

In the course of these chapters, I shall be surveying more completely the retrospective environmental visions of the current wave of eco-romanticism presented by such writers as Bate, Kroeber, and Morton. I shall be contrasting my own insights with theirs, and what I have been calling romantic empiricism with other modes of green romanticism, in the chapters that follow. My key contention is that the mode of green empiricism I am highlighting is undervalued and underrepresented within studies both of romanticism and of environmental thinking. Its importance will, I hope, become self-evident from my accounts of it in the following chapters.

To get a more immediate sense of the importance of what I have been calling a romantic empiricism and an openness to the material, and to begin to suggest its relevance to the study of poetry and environmentalism, I will end this chapter with a reading of a poem by Wallace Stevens. Situated as it is roughly midway between Romanticism and the contemporary moment, 'The Snow Man' suggests as well the potential continuity of this mode of environmental awareness within romantic lyricism. Indeed, the poem is nearly a lyric manifesto for the idea I am trying to present. The poem is apt because as I write it is snowing hard outside my window (though it is the last day of March) and I am repeatedly reminded of what it means to be *writing* about what one would much rather be *doing*, which is, as the poem suggests, a matter of being outside, regarding, beholding, and listening to the snow.

Snow is a somewhat peculiar object for empirical scrutiny, in part because one of its distinctive properties is the effect of its accumulation, which is to erase distinctness, to blanket, and slowly to hide from our perception all but the largest features of a landscape. As I watch the snow gather outside, virtually all colour is already gone from my field of view; everything but the underside of tree branches and the east sides of tree trunks has been turned white, and the trees themselves seem but a blurring of the whiteness, rather than things distinct in themselves. It is a minor myth of our childhood that no two snowflakes are alike, but we perceive snow not as flakes or pellets but as an accumulating mass. It may be wet or dry, but unless we wax skis, make snow shelters, or are on guard for avalanches, it is an ephemeral and temporary stuff that always looks the same and yet more radically transforms the landscape than any other 'weather event.' It threatens to reduce the physical world to total blankness, which, as Frost's most famous horse-driven narrator reminds us, is strangely appealing and comforting. An environment that seems to be disappearing under snow gains beauty, and eases consciousness, because there is so little to be conscious of. We are awake and alert; we can see and hear and feel, but sense nothing. Part of the peculiar beauty of snowfall is that is utterly silent, generally producing no sound of its own, and muffling other noises. It allows random experiments in sensory deprivation in which we can become unusually aware of our own consciousness through the frustration of its ability to extend itself through our physical senses. We realize that we do exist apart from our environment, that consciousness actually requires no object other than itself, though it yearns for things.

This is part of the import of Stevens's poem, which I cite now in full.

> One must have a mind of winter
> To regard the frost and the boughs
> Of the pine-trees crusted with snow;
>
> And have been cold a long time
> To behold the junipers shagged with ice,
> The spruces rough in the distant glitter
>
> Of the January sun; and not to think
> Of any misery in the sound of the wind,
> In the sound of a few leaves,
>
> Which is the sound of the land
> Full of the same wind
> That is blowing in the same bare place
>
> For the listener, who listens in the snow,
> And, nothing himself, beholds
> Nothing that is not there and the nothing that is.[21]

The poem is an argument for the ideal of having a 'mind of winter.' Such a mind pays attention to the details of winter, is in some sense constituted only by those details, and, like winter, is still and quiet. The poem represents a desire for a state of perceptive passivity, a wintry and modernist version of the state Coleridge fails to achieve in his poem 'The Nightingale' and despairs of ever achieving in 'Dejection: An Ode.' Having a mind of winter means excluding all that is not of the winter, of the purely physical reality being viewed. The aim is to take in the wintry world with none of the traditional symbolic resonance that winter usually carries (of 'misery,' absence, and death). This requires a fine and still focus on the details that remain, the three kinds of trees, variously crusted, shagged, and glittering; and it involves making absent all that we are mindful of by symbolic and literary association. The ideal for the perceiver, who only watches and listens, is thus 'not to think / Of any misery in the sound of the wind,' subtly alluding to Coleridge's key statement in 'Dejection' of his utterly failed desire 'not to think of what I needs must feel, / But to be still and patient, all I can.' By making himself perfectly empty ('nothing himself'), Stevens's hypothetical perceiver is precisely able to distinguish the real from the ephemeral, perceiving 'nothing that is not there and the nothing that is.' The point is to be able to make the most absolute of distinctions, between presence and absence, to perceive things in themselves, which holds forth the possibility of transcending self. The perfect (and unobtainable) moment of perception is here imagined to be utterly egoless; one becomes what one beholds – not a universal spirit, but part of the 'same wind' 'which is the sound of the land.' One becomes the wintry scene one takes in. This recalls Emerson's account of becoming a 'transparent eyeball; I am nothing; I see all'; but the aims are different. Emerson has no particular landscape in mind – he is 'uplifted into infinite space' rather than a specific place, and his vision is always through the material to a more enveloping mind (what he refers to in the passage as 'the currents of the Universal Being'). The epiphany of the snow man, in contrast, is based on a longing for a materiality that withholds its significance and its being. We can overcome the divide between consciousness and the material only when we can 'behold' the material without an irritable reaching after meaning. Purely to behold in this sense is to be what one perceives, or perhaps to expand the moment of perception into a moment of being. This is, I will argue, a central ideal in much romantic environmentalism. The poem presents a moment of striving for a naturalism that celebrates the act of perception, recognizing that it might be an end in itself, and that forging a connection to the physical environment can rest on confronting materiality rather than dissolving it.

Yet the poem clearly undermines the actual fulfilment of this desire. Having a 'mind of winter,' the poem barely suggests, is itself a deliberate act. One must will oneself into a state in which will is overcome. Moreover, the entire poem is a conditional statement, following from the first line: 'One must have a mind of winter / To regard' winter in this ideal way, but there is no certainty that this state of mind can be achieved. Indeed, that the poem presents us with a kind of formula suggests that the actual experience is either impossible or incapable of being represented. The poem merely presents somewhat cryptic instructions for a purely empirical gaze, and, aided by its extraordinarily calming rhythm, perhaps creates the illusion that such a gaze has actually been achieved. This illusion is enhanced by the subtle rewards of beauty, itself presumably an additive product of conscious desire, found here in the 'junipers shagged with ice, / The spruces rough in the distant glitter' (or our memories of such images). Furthermore, the instructions the poem offers are necessarily associative. The poem must use the symbolic connotations of winter to urge us to a connotation-free awareness. We must come to appreciate the bliss or truth of absence, suggested to us by habitual or cultural reactions to winter, before we can behold what is truly present. Indeed, it is not a stretch to argue (as have several of my students, who in Canada are alert to the reality of hypothermia) that this poem is about an actual death of consciousness – 'One must ... have been cold a long time.' It is, at least, surely an ironic undercutting of the poem's apparent ideal of pure perception that it contains the suggestion that this 'ultimate reality' may be achieved only through one's actual dissolution into nothing but matter. As I suggested earlier, watching snow can have the effect of heightening, rather than reducing or eliminating, our awareness of being in a state of conscious perception. And I think that this is how the poem finally works too. It presents to us the stark possibility of the absence of consciousness, and of transcending into materiality, against which we can see the unremitting presence of our own consciousness. We have never actually seen winter the way the snow man does, though the poem powerfully reminds us of the deep value hidden in our yearning for such perception. An urgent response to the poem ought to draw us out into the snow. The poem, however, teaches us that the material resists being read, that it is not a text. And this ought to inspire awe and respect.

I

The End of the World: Wordsworth, Nature, Elegy

> *It is the uniform effect of culture on the human mind, not to shake our faith in the stability of particular phenomena ... but to lead us to regard nature as a phenomenon, not a substance; to attribute necessary existence to spirit; to esteem nature as an accident and an effect.*
>
> Emerson, *Nature*

Over the past forty years, Geoffrey Hartman has most influentially shaped our understanding of Wordsworth as a poet preoccupied with 'nature.' In *The Unmediated Vision* and *Wordsworth's Poetry* Hartman depicts the poet's struggle between understanding how the external world shaped his consciousness, and liberating his imagination from the essential passivity and materiality of the 'soul' that this influence implies. Though he does not cite Freud in either study, Hartman's account of Wordsworth's development as a poet is Oedipal in so far as it narrates the psychological drama of poetic consciousness freeing itself from the paternal and maternal influences of Milton and Nature. It is a compelling argument which has made many Wordsworth scholars (including myself) feel that they are really just writing footnotes to Hartman's criticism, even as we keep him in the footnotes of ours. Part of the brilliance of his work on Wordsworth is that it has made 'nature' seem both something real and obvious (the rocks, trees, and landscapes Wordsworth actually saw), and something extraordinarily complex and phenomenological – those entities as processed through Wordsworth's consciousness and poetry. Hartman's work has allowed us to see what is at stake for Wordsworth in the act of perceiving the material world, beyond a sense of its beauty and safety and its apparent freedom from blatant human domination. Hartman argues, crucially, that it was necessary for Wordsworth always to personify nature, a trope that Hartman generally repeats. That is, Hartman never attempts to define 'nature' precisely, because the only conception of nature worth talking about is that which enables us to follow the growth of Wordsworth's poetic consciousness. Nature, as far as critics of Wordsworth need be concerned, is what his poetry shows it to be. Indeed, for a long time after *Wordsworth's Poetry*, nature has been discussed primarily, in Wordsworthian criticism, as a literary phenomenon.

Literary critics no doubt deserve credit for their reluctance to pursue conceptualizing nature as material and definite. After all, the *OED* lists fifteen separate definitions for the word, and contemporary environmentalist thinkers rarely do much better with the term 'environment,' which, as I suggested in the previous chapter, is equally vague. Our reluctance has been supported by poststructuralist assertions of the primacy of textual and verbal realities over apparently 'natural' ones, as well as by new historicist suspicions that nature is fundamentally a cultural category of avoidance. A realm of nature *qua* nature that approaches Emerson's common-sense view of it as everything in the physical world that humankind has not fundamentally altered lies beyond the realm of interpretation. For criticism it is moot, profoundly beside the point. We recognize, then, that 'nature' is a term too problematic, too ideologically fraught, to use with equanimity. Within romantic writing and criticism, the word may be taken as a referent for a materialistic fate (what Shelley and Godwin would call 'Necessity'), a transcendent power which may or may not be God, a conservative notion of the proper telos of culture, or the material world itself, often reduced or idealized to mere scenery or landscape. The intrinsic ambiguity of the word has led to numerous facile generalizations over the years about the nature of nature poetry, and partly because we fear treading the same dull path and partly because we now favour hard-edged, truly *critical* criticism, talk of nature has generally subsided.

Indeed, many students of romanticism, having accepted the basic tenets of cultural materialism, assume as obvious that, as Alan Liu has rather notoriously said, 'there is no nature.'[1] Now, this is an interesting notion, and it is worth pondering over because it has become a kind of slogan. Taken in isolation, it may be read in very different ways. A contemporary physicist, for instance, would understand the statement as strictly metaphysical, about how consciousness can perceive, be created by, or create the material world. Berkeley's idealism is the most obvious version of the 'there is no nature' school, though presumably any argument about how perception shapes phenomena (accepted even by empiricists like Locke) might also lead one to this conclusion – that there is no accessible realm of the 'thing-in-itself' about which we can have unqualified knowledge. Contemporary physicists might find Liu's phrase meaningful because of the perplexities introduced by quantum mechanics, including the results of Heisenberg's uncertainty principle, which confirms that the act of measuring subatomic particles clearly affects them, leading to suspicions of a radically relative (subatomic) reality. John von Neumann, who developed much of the mathematics for quantum physics, has proposed that consciousness creates essential properties of the material realm because it appears to be the only way to solve the apparently intractable problem posed by the wave-function collapse that is at the heart of quantum physics.[2]

Of course Liu means something very different from this, but it seems to me worthwhile to contrast two irreconcilable materialisms as a way of grounding my argument and getting our terms straight. We need to examine Liu's statement in more detail. The paragraph where he makes this statement reads in part: 'As is clear in such cases as forests, parks, or dales ... there is no nature except as it is constituted by acts of political definition made possible by particular forms of government. When the governmental understructure changes, nature changes. Each time a nation suffers an invasion, civil war, major change of ministry, or some other crisis, national or international, it must revise its landscape, the image of its own nature' (*Wordsworth*, 104). As is clear from his evidence of 'forests, parks, or dales,' Liu's nature is far more narrowly defined, more idealized, than the 'nature' which is studied by most scientists. For no matter how culturally influenced or ideologically motivated individual examples of science may be, it still begins or ends with an investigation of the objective 'stuff of nature,' from elementary particles to living organisms, which all but the most devoted idealists would say is not, in its existence as part of a vast universe of *things*, influenced by ideas, culture, or politics. Liu and other cultural materialists believe that nature is 'always already' humanized, a product of our peculiar vision – not a Kantian idea, really, but a Nietzschean one, that culture defines and thus produces nature. For instance, Jean Baudrillard has argued for a concept of the environment understood only as a set of signs, and hence 'designed' and open to multiple interpretation, like culture.[3] For these thinkers, 'nature' can never be the pure stuff of the material world, the stuff studied by science or even the more earth-bound notion of an organic and living planet, but is primarily textual and contextual; it is a set of ideas continuously redefined by various cultural struggles.

That nature is fundamentally a system of signs, or a political and economic construct, will seem ludicrously totalizing and self-serving to the more orthodox materialists of science, just as the premise of science that nature is material and yields objective knowledge (producing a muscular and masculine discourse of power) appears totalizing and self-serving to such critics of science as Stanley Aronowitz and Sandra Harding. Interestingly, the idea of nature exemplified in Liu is not, from the point of view of materialist science, very different from the nature of orthodox romanticism or the *naturphilosophie* itself.[4] For both, nature is spiritualized, always primarily an idea rather than an actual physical entity, or an assortment of physical entities. Nature as it is perceived and represented always signifies; it is an entity or a field of entities that must be penetrated and interpreted. In this sense, cultural materialism has not shifted any ground. It is still an idealism in the classic sense, an idea of nature that begins and ends with language, usually texts and the production of texts. It matters little whether this production is the work of a single consciousness or a discourse. Moreover, it essentially differs little from what previous critics of romanticism have been writing about 'nature': that what characterizes romanticism's contribution to thinking and writing about the natural world is the manner in which it supersedes mere empirical description, and becomes about how consciousness finds itself, or a record of itself, in the world. This is what Hartman means in *Wordsworth's Poetry* when he argues that Wordsworth pays a much finer attention to his own mind than to the natural world around him, and that he uses nature to transcend materiality to discover a universal spirituality which the development of his own consciousness exemplifies. What for Hartman (and before him, notably, A.C. Bradley and G. Wilson Knight) is the poet's triumph has become Wordsworth's greatest failing with the near-institutionalization of cultural materialism. Raymond Williams in *The Country and the City* finds that Wordsworth, like all self-conscious observers of 'landscape,' detaches himself from what is actually in nature, through a 'projection of personal feeling into a subjectively particularized and objectively generalized Nature' (133–4). Versions of this argument have been persuasively made as well by Donald Davie and by John Barrell, Jerome McGann, and Marjorie Levinson.[5] Anne Mellor has argued that central to Wordsworth's project of producing a masculine, conquering self is the manner in which he 'deliberately den[ies] his material physicality, even his mortality' in order to represent himself as 'pure ego' (149). For those who admire Wordsworth and those who do not, his 'nature' is a blank canvas, an illusory (though perhaps necessary and worthwhile) space free of received meaning, against and onto which the individual poet paints an idealized version of himself.

Thus Liu's apparently paradigmatic historicist statement counters a position that is virtually non-existent within Romantic criticism. It has never been a question, really, that Wordsworth's idea of nature is malleable, or that he *uses* this fact to produce and represent ideas about his own consciousness. Perhaps Liu seeks to counter the proto-environmentalist readings of Karl Kroeber (*Romantic Landscape Vision*), W.J. Keith, or Edmund Blunden, and anticipates the kind of argument made by Jonathan Bate (*Romantic Ecology*), all of whom make cases for how important it is to recognize that Wordsworth appreciates the natural world in a way that is apparently less self-serving and opportunistic (in crass economic and political terms) than was or is the norm. These readings do assume a realm or entity separate from the poet and poetry themselves, a benign environment and living world in which we as a species may be included and which is self-evidently worth recognizing and valuing. Yet it seems to me that we should ponder Liu's statement more literally, to provide a full-fledged argument for the idea that it may be seen to counter. While it is clear that Wordsworth in his poetry often seeks to transcend and humanize the material world, and can thus make us believe that there is no unmediated nature, it has not been sufficiently recognized that Wordsworth also directly confronts the physical (as opposed to cultural or economic) materiality or otherness of nature in a profound and original way.[6] Indeed, in the terms I set out in my introduction, Wordsworth's openness to the material, his awareness of the 'material sublime,' is paradigmatic. In this chapter I thus propose to take seriously in the poetry of Wordsworth what we might call the most literal definition of nature, the realm of matter, which is essentially or at least initially inorganic, the substance and substantiality of the world.

Why a consideration of this idea of nature in Wordsworth is significant needs briefly to be made clear. An idea of nature as organic, alive and in some sense an entity separate from humanity, is as old as culture itself. It is implied in the very idea that a god created the world, regardless of whether or not humanity is at the centre of it. In any theocentric view, nature is alive because spirit exists first, matter second; matter is derived from spirit. (There are important variations here, of course; like Plato, early Christians saw organic nature as corrupt and ultimately to be transcended because it was fallen, merely and essentially material, while writers such as John Ray and William Derham felt living nature directly reflects, or even contains, God.) From this perspective, the idea of the 'one life' is far from original, either in English romanticism or the *naturphilosophie*. Both argued that all aspects of the natural world were instinct with spirit, an idea taken to its limit separately and not dissimilarly by Erasmus Darwin and Friedrich von Schelling at the end of the eighteenth century. An overwhelming faith in the life of the world was really only shaken by more or less 'strict' materialists like P.D. Holbach and Joseph Priestley (both familiar to Wordsworth). Though Holbach's materialism is a direct precursor of today's scientific orthodoxy, arguing for the entirely material and deterministic origins of life and consciousness, in the late eighteenth century it was a truly radical philosophy (hence Shelley's admiration of it). My argument for Wordsworth is not that he embraces a materialism rooted in lifeless and spiritless matter, but that his understanding of nature is in a critical way based in a response (and not simply a reaction) to it. Far from merely anthropomorphizing nature in the easy and escapist way imagined by some new historicists, Wordsworth may be seen to include an awareness of the indifference, hostility, and inimicalness of material reality to an idea of the 'one life,' or, to cite one of his own formulations of it, of 'A motion and a spirit, that impels / All thinking things, all objects of all thought, / And rolls through all things.'[7] While it is virtually a cliché that Wordsworth imagines spirit and being in the external world of things, it is not fully recognized that his poetry reflects a struggle to ground this imagining in an awareness of the materiality of nature, the impenetrable reality of surfaces and appearances. David Perkins has similarly argued that Wordsworth attempts to overcome the transience of consciousness by linking it to the reality of the physical, a struggle which can reveal that human existence is but 'a brief appearance on the surface, a kind of fungus momentarily clinging to the bleak, immutable rocks' (45). Perkins's examination of Wordsworth's use of nature reveals that the 'grounding' of human consciousness is not nearly as unproblematic as the apparent flight or escape into transcendence, since the former involves confronting a natural reality that seems initially indifferent or even hostile to the possibility of consciousness. This nature is composed frequently of ashes and rocks, rather than forests and ecosystems. As Paul Fry puts it, 'it is finally a question whether the nature poetry of Wordsworth is green or *gray*.'[8]

That recognizing matter matters is reflected in Wordsworth's Fenwick note to the 'Intimations Ode.' In it, one will remember, he explains that as a child (an elastic term for Wordsworth) motivated by both the 'indomitableness of the spirit within me' and the 'stories of Enoch and Elijah,' he was so easily convinced of the possibility of transcendence that he was often forced to '[grasp] at a wall or tree to recall myself from this abyss of idealism.' His difficulty, he writes, stems from his inability 'to admit the notion of death as a state applicable to my own being' (*PW*, 4:463). That idealism is instinctive to Wordsworth and remembered from childhood, and that he has 'deplored, as we all have reason to do, a subjugation of the opposite character,' is one of the central points of the poem. What is more difficult to see in Wordsworth's poetry is what is represented in the note by his grasping at a wall or tree, and only mentioned in the poem as the 'obstinate questionings / Of sense and outward things.' I will argue that these questions signify his broader need to know nature as matter that is not instinct with life or spirit. This impulse is best seen in those poems in which Wordsworth recognizes objects in the natural world that signify blankness and death, since death itself defines our most direct connection to the world through the mortality and materiality of our bodies. Indeed, in his poems on death, Wordsworth seems frequently to be barely repressing, or perhaps rather on the verge of admitting, the idea that our body, and even our being, is an accretion of nature's matter. Elegy, as Liu has recently brilliantly reminded us, forces us to confront not just the ease with which being or consciousness is dissolved, but also that matter remains.[9]

Simply, this case needs to be made because the leap from the relatively easy and familiar idea of the 'one life' to nature simply as the projection of a poet's sentimental desires is not the only one Wordsworth can be seen making. What needs to be resisted, in any case, are blanket generalizations about ideas of nature in both Wordsworth and romanticism in general. For instance, recent claims by some feminist critics of romanticism that nature is typically troped as feminine so that it and women may be made secondary and other, and is then 'regendered' in an '[attempt] to eliminate her other-ness, her difference, her separate being,' are reductive because they too presuppose a more or less continuous anthropocentrism (Mellor, 18–19). The feminist critique of romantic nature also assumes that it is always only ever an idea. It needs to be noted too that the study and admiration of nature increased dramatically during the seventeenth and eighteenth centuries, and the interest this reflects is surprisingly complex and resistant to classification. Characterizing texts or authors as reflecting picturesque, materialist, masculine, or romantic ideology is in fact saying very little, since writing about nature during this century is remarkable for its almost methodical avoidance of singular methods or creeds. There are few, if any, examples of observations of nature which are not both materialistic and idealistic. This is spectacularly the case for travel literature, which I examine in chapter 5, but we may see it in versions of natural history as well. It is instructive, for instance, to contrast the work of Gilbert White and Erasmus Darwin, who represent two very different versions of the eighteenth-century 'naturalist.' The former has been hailed as an important precursor of modern naturalism and environmentalism because his detailed study of the ecology of his native parish shows an open-minded empiricism combined with a sense of awe and wonder.[10] Darwin, on the other hand, like his great hero Linnaeus, is known as a grand theorizer who attempts in each of his works to establish a single idea or history that will account for all the diversity of life that the natural world presents (and is comparatively free of particular fact and observation). Yet the texts of both writers display similar degrees of irregularity in matters of form and subject. In attempting to reveal the extraordinary variety of the natural world, both are meandering and discursive rather than narratival.[11] My point is not that the Darwin and White are basically the same; it is rather to suggest that naturalism goes hand in hand with complexity.

Then as now, thinking about 'nature' is convoluted and contradictory, based on a fundamental inability to define initial terms – what nature actually is, whether and how it includes humanity and its productions, whether it is primarily a realm of matter or spirit. Against this background of diversity and contradiction, which indeed my entire book intends to reveal, I want to situate Wordsworth's notorious 'turn' to nature. This turn is in itself neither new, nor progressive or reactionary. It is, rather, overdetermined. We are very familiar with the arguments which attempt to place Wordsworth's use of nature firmly into the realm of political symbolism: that is, into an idea of nature as a metaphor either of the inevitable history and development of culture (theorized in Burke, and most persuasively presented by James Chandler), or of an instinctive, unvarnished insight into rightness and truth, (theorized by Rousseau and Godwin, and implicit in the arguments of Abrams and Hartman).[12] It ought to be allowed too that nature for Wordsworth may be regarded in a third way, which is literally or empirically, as matter, things that remain unknowable and untranslatable. This idea is at least a recognizable desire in most of the forms of natural history and nature writing that I explore throughout the book, and is thus one which Wordsworth would have been familiar with in his reading of White, Darwin, Bartram, Bligh, all the picturesque guides, Holbach, Priestley, and Newton.[13]

A few recent critics have begun to explore the complexity of understandings of nature, including a consideration of the importance of the materiality of the natural world, though none to my knowledge has focused on this. Nicholas Roe argues that nature as a category was never thought of as ahistorical in romanticism, but was rather a self-conscious means of thinking *about* history. For Roe, regarding nature allowed writers of the romantic period both to imagine an ideal realm (Eden) and to see the real, written into the landscape, as it were, and thus to make progressive historical appraisals. Jonathan Bate has made a case for seeing Wordsworth as an environmentalist, that his concern for preserving and imagining a relationship to the natural world is evidence against 'the proposition that Romantic discourse attempts to seal itself hermetically off from materiality.' Most significant, I think, is the case made by Alan Bewell for Wordsworth's attempt to understand nature as always a local environment, which is altered by, and in an important sense *includes*, the activities of humanity. Thus 'Landscape [is] a historical product of the interaction of human beings with nature; it documents the ways that they have responded to it with labor, government, and domestication and management of plant and animal species.' For Bewell, Wordsworth's empiricist project is that of the enlightenment anthropologist who records our rootedness to specific place, and attempts to understand how each affects the other. He argues how Wordsworth, in *The Recluse* and elsewhere, 'tells the story of how, through the "blended might" of human and natural agency, a certain kind of environment came into being that has allowed the mind and nature to achieve their greatest potential.'[14]

The work of Roe, Bate, and Bewell focuses on specific historical contexts for recognizing the complexity of Wordsworth's understanding of nature; moreover, they include an attentiveness to what we might call a resistance to transcendence in these ideas, an important awareness of the materiality or actuality of the natural realm. My argument differs from theirs in emphasis. All three move easily (for Bate it is explicitly pragmatic) to a more or less fully developed theory about the interaction and necessary interdependence of the material and consciousness. In a sense, the 'nature' they argue for in Wordsworth is still too theoretical, too generalized, and too anthropocentric. Consciousness is still primary, or at least is seen generally to interact easily and harmoniously within the material. It allows us to ignore in his work the full effect of actually being in, or putting oneself into, nature as a material realm that is not immediately malleable to our desires, the kind of particular world documented in part by Dorothy Wordsworth in her journals, by White in his letters, and by John Clare in his poems. These moments are neither obvious nor dominant in Wordsworth, but they provide a sense of the actual experience of confronting materiality, and the intractable problems of representing it.

The arguments of these critics rely on a nature that is already too personified, too much an accommodating 'home' to human thought, and thus maternal and spiritualized. Their arguments are strengthened, I think, by making a case for how Wordsworth's proto-environmentalism is grounded in a realm of perception, rather than theory. Wordsworth can and does 'see' nature more elementally, in its 'thingness,' and this otherness is not ultimately capable of being erased, however we bracket or sublimate this fact in pragmatic assessments of how we may best live our lives as individuals within communities and ecosystems.

I have already cited Wordsworth's letter on the 'Intimations Ode' as one example of the poet confronting the materiality of nature, though it and the poem itself more readily show the relative ease of transcendence, which such a confrontation tests. As I have suggested, elegiac moments in Wordsworth's poetry frequently involve direct confrontations with matter, forming a sub-corpus of unblinkered investigations of the spiritlessness of the external realm. It is here, I think, that Wordsworth is most original. Typically, in the poetry of Wordsworth's productive decade, his examinations of death offer no religious consolation, and nature (as cycles of life, or an emblem of eternity) rarely provides the kind of relief frequently supposed by readers of romantic texts. (It is indeed much more common in Shelley than Wordsworth.) Importantly, imagining and comprehending death for Wordsworth begin by comprehending that matter is primary. The process is, in a sense, an attempt to see our existence as blankly as possible, without or beyond the screens of convention and signification that are inevitably involved with understanding human existence (as consciousness) and nature. Indeed, part of my goal to this point has been to establish how integrally connected thinking about nature and thinking about convention are. Confronting what I have been calling 'elemental' nature is a way too of attempting to think through mediation of all kinds. Thus it is not surprising that elegy should be so closely connected in Wordsworth with lyric. Wordsworth's elegies are typically ones of silence, of being unable to speak or to translate awareness into language. We are presented with images of the speaker standing before things that do not offer up meaning, aware that 'nature's language is mute,' as Adorno has said.[15]

Nowhere in Wordsworth's poetry is this version of elegy more succinctly presented than in the lyric 'A Slumber Did My Spirit Seal.'

> A slumber did my spirit seal;
>   I had no human fears:

> She seemed a thing that could not feel
>   The touch of earthly years.
>
> No motion has she now, no force;
>   She neither hears nor sees;
> Rolled round in earth's diurnal course,
>   With rocks, and stones, and trees.   (*PW*, 2:216)

The two stanzas present the condition of the speaker before and after the death of a loved one. It has frequently been noted that the gap between the two stanzas signifies the death itself. What has been ignored, I think, is how the poem also contrasts an absolute spirit to absolute matter. Alive, the person whom the speaker remembers 'seemed a thing' immortal, a phrase worth puzzling over.[16] The speaker's love for the dead woman or girl, the innumerable bonds formed between two consciousnesses, lead necessarily to a kind of sleep – a forgetting or denial of the materiality and mortality of our existence. There is nothing original in this idea, of course. That love leads one to 'higher' planes, to a sense of the immortality of spirit as seen in the personality of those we love, and grandly personified in God, is traditional. Yet in the poem this movement is seen as a kind of blindness or ignorance (even as it makes this love seem utterly sincere and necessary). The speaker's spirit is 'sealed' to ideas of time and change, and most of all to the mortality of living matter. It is paradoxically as though the girl has already been converted to the seemingly permanent materiality of the final line of the poem. This threat of material permanence undercuts the easy and nearly automatic transcendence involved with youthful love. When we are in love, when we revere another person, we often come to *assume* the primacy of spirit, that another person's identity is not defined by body or matter but by some other stuff which is necessarily immortal. We do not imagine, really, that this stuff can wither and die. Spirit *is* animation, personality or consciousness unconfined by the body and time, as shown too by the children of such poems 'We Are Seven' and 'Anecdote for Fathers.'

Lest this sound too romantic, let me cite Joseph Priestley, whom Wordsworth had read by the time he wrote this poem.

> It has generally been supposed that there are two distinct kinds of substance in human nature, and they have been distinguished by the terms matter and spirit, or mind. The former of these has been said to be possessed of the property of extension, viz of length, breadth and thickness, and also of solid-

ity or impenetrability, and consequently of a *vis inertiae*; but it is said to be naturally destitute of all other powers whatever. The latter has of late been defined to be a substance entirely destitute of all extension, or relation to space, so as to have no property in common with matter; and therefore to be properly immaterial, but to be possessed of the powers of perception, intelligence and self-motion. (xxxiii)

Priestley argues that the soul is produced by the body, and is not simply harboured there, and that, as in Locke, all ideas are produced by physical objects as taken in by the senses. His ultimate point is that matter must have motion and force, be capable of generating it, and that these characteristics are not to be attributed to some other entity. The poem does not attempt to prove or oppose this idea, and Priestley's argument must be considered heterodoxy to our traditional notion of Wordsworth's understanding of spirit. Indeed, Priestley scoffs at the idea presented as an accommodating metaphor in the 'Intimations Ode,' that 'this foreign principle [spirit] must have been united to [the body] either at the time of conception, or at birth, and must either have been created at the time of such union, or have existed in a separate state prior to that period' (41). Yet the poem does aim to confront the problem posed by Priestley, though in an abstract and open-ended way. Priestley too sees the fact of death as the main evidence for the primacy of matter. He argues repeatedly that if soul and body were actually different and separate, then we should see some evidence of their disconnection in death, or the process of dying: 'if the soul be immaterial, and the body material, neither the generation nor the destruction of the body can have any effect with respect to it' (41). Instead we see only evidence of the mind developing and deteriorating in tandem with the body. That we believe otherwise, Priestley insists, is the result of a comfortable illusion created in part because we believe that matter is inert, so that something else must be giving it motion and force. As in the first stanza of Wordsworth's poem, this identity, personality, or 'soul' becomes a thing in itself. Yet nature denies this belief in the starkest way when someone we love, and know deeply and intimately, dies. We must see then, and perhaps for the first time, that life is itself material. And so thingness, or identity, is suddenly and dramatically converted from spirit to matter. That the memorialized person of Wordsworth's poem comes to have neither 'motion' nor 'force' suggests initially that the speaker feels that she is now only matter according to the traditional illusion that Priestley argues against, that her spirit has simply departed. Yet 'she' continues to move, 'rolled round in earth's diurnal course.' This movement is of the material realm, not the spiritual, the spinning and orbiting of masses already perfectly explained by Newton and Kepler. Her 'being' is now utterly indefinable. Most of all, she is merely memory, a 'thing' capable of being discussed only in the past tense. She is now 'with rocks, and stones, and trees,' all *things* of stark materiality.[17]

It is as though what is most shocking about death is that it presents the incommensurate relation between life and the matter from which it seems to spring.[18] The most startling aspect of the poem is its denial of the need to make the meaning of her life and death *for the speaker* explicit and complete (which is what one expects to be the motivating desire of any elegiac poem). The change of perspective marked by the change in tense in the second stanza is the focus of the poem's lyricism; the gap between the stanzas is both a figure for the fact of the girl's death, and a figure for the absence of any narration which would make meaningful for the speaker her passage from absolute life to absolute death, from spirit to matter. What has occurred in this unnarratable gap is that the otherness of the poet's idealization of the girl or woman as a figure of Innocence – which in Wordsworth is a pure spirituality – is converted to the otherness of the material. The poem represents this transformation not as the result of a process, narrative or otherwise, but as a contrast that is inexplicable in any terms. There is no resolution or consolation offered. Transcendence, or an affirmation of immortality, or even a comprehensible connection between matter and spirit are all absent. The life of the dead girl is in no way reducible to matter even if in the end it literally *is* reduced to things of the earth.

The poem depicts how we as observers of death, and for whom death itself is 'other,' are forced to make leaps between evidence of spirit and matter. It presents too the difficulty of defining what forms a singular object. The loved person seemed singular, an identifiable 'being,' but now is not. In the second stanza 'she' still exists, though without motion or force, but the speaker does not, or cannot, say what 'thing' she now actually is, or is a part of. What afterlife there is is not recognizably a life. The rapid change in perspective of the last sentence suggests movement from the particular to the general, that matter is in some sense indivisible and extends beyond the merely earthbound. She may be of the soil, the landscape, the nation, or the earth. Once we have seen that life is profoundly connected to matter, we are presented with the problem of how to divide matter, classify it, identify where one thing ends and another begins.

The poem thus presents the fact of materiality to thought, which, in spite of our sense that refuting idealism involves only kicking a stone, as Samuel Johnson did in refuting Berkeley, is not actually a simple thing to do. Indeed, that we so easily succumb to the idea that there is no nature, that the material for sophisticated readers is always in some way ideological, an *idea*, suggests the degree of our own idealisms, born, like those of Shelley and Coleridge, by an intense bookishness. Wordsworth's poem imagines, and struggles to represent, a realm of nature which precedes categorization by social forces, of being political and economic. There is a nature, and it is inimical to matters of being and all that stems from it, a fact which from time to time we really do encounter. Part of the poem's uncanny dialectic is to connect the profound otherness of the dead girl to that of elemental nature. They are not the same thing, but, to the speaker's consciousness, they are equally remote. At the same time, consciousness is grounded in this otherness, this nature. It cannot exist without it, and is seemingly capable of spanning and encompassing it.

We might call this an existential environmentalism, or an occasion of the material sublime, and it seems to me to be the distinctive way in which Wordsworth 'grounds' his larger dependency on that 'Nature' to which 'the individual Mind' is 'fitted,' and which is 'exquisitely ... fitted to the Mind' (*Prospectus* to *The Recluse*, PW, 5:5, ll. 63–8), in its most fully sentimentalized version (he is capable of both extremes). The *Naturphilosophe* Hans Christian Oersted expressed this more orthodox romantic idea this way: 'The world and the human mind were created according to the same laws. If the laws of our reason did not exist in Nature, we should try in vain to force them upon her; if the laws of nature did not exist in our reason, we should not be able to comprehend them.'[19] This idea is familiar to us as Wordsworth's and Coleridge's faith in a Spirit or God whose mind invests the material world with life, form, and meaning, and of which human consciousness forms a small portion. But it is always only a faith, a belief, which Wordsworth expresses as an ideal (as in the *Prospectus* and the 'Intimations Ode' for instance) with a joy and enthusiasm that speak of the moment of conviction. This idea *is* ideological in exactly the way that Liu suggests; it is, among other things, anthropocentric and does not lead necessarily to the kind of environmentalism hoped for by Kroeber and Bate. (We cannot today breezily celebrate with Wordsworth 'the creation ... which [Nature and Mind] with blended might accomplish' [ll. 69–71]). In Wordsworth's elegiac poems, however, we see that this faith does not always exist, that it is tested in moments of despair. In its place is a kind of naked empiricism which seems an essential route to truth, even if it finds nothing, or leads to a pragmatic assumption of the commonality of consciousness or the productivity of the projections of consciousness, with which Wordsworth is normally quite pleased.

Lest it seem that I am hanging my argument on a very slender thread, I would like to survey a few other examples of Wordsworth's lyric openness to the material before a closer examination of just a few. My aim is to demonstrate that Wordsworth's meditations on the material sublime are not incidental, but are a crucial component of much of his most important poetry. In the *Lyrical Ballads*, significant poems include the unusual elegies 'The Thorn' and 'Simon Lee.' These poems pose questions about the origins of thought, and of how thought may spring from, and be connected to, physical objects. Indeed, as has often been noted, Wordsworth is here extraordinarily self-conscious about the creation of emblems out of material facts. 'The Thorn' is specifically about how a tree may stand by and for bodily remains, and of how a body may be translated to and from the earth. The speaker's problem in the poem (among the many that have already been argued for) is an exaggerated and seemingly more immediate version of the problem which faces the poem's readers – what to make of various forms of evidence that would explain the story of Martha Ray. He knows the rumours from others, the insistent accounts of what 'Some say,' with his own voice inevitably becoming the loudest amongst this murmuring. But what he insists on, even as he attempts to reveal apparently supernatural agency, is the primacy of the *physical* evidence, the particular details of the 'spot' which literally marks the tale. Much of the 'garrulous' speaker's narrative energy, in fact, is spent recording what we can now see, and what he has seen, in the setting where what for him is the crucial event of Martha Ray's life took place. Before he gets to the tale of her misery and isolation, her desertion by Stephen Hill, and the subsequent birth and death of her child, the speaker gives a nearly obsessive description of the spot, marked as it is by the thorn introduced in the first stanza.

> There is a Thorn – it looks so old,
> In truth, you'd find it hard to say
> How it could ever have been young,
> It looks so old and grey.
> Not higher than a two years' child
> It stands erect, this aged Thorn;
> No leaves it has, no prickly points;
> It is a mass of knotted joints,
> A wretched thing forlorn.

> It stands erect, and like a stone
> With lichens is it overgrown. (*PW*, 2:240–1)

The description continues for another six stanzas, and even when he begins the actual narration of Martha's story, he continues to add descriptions of the thorn, the mossy hill, the pond, and the crag on which they may be found. The intensity of his gaze is marked in part by the telescope he has trained on her. We might say that part of the poem's ironic undercutting of the speaker lies in his protesting too much; he would clearly like his audience to believe that the story he is telling, with Martha Ray and her child at its centre, is as real as the shrub he keeps directing our attention towards. His text is but a web of words and surmises, but the real trick is Wordsworth's, who makes us attempt to imagine how it might be that this battered tree could ever be imagined to stand for the life and consciousness of a dead child (and perhaps too his mother), even by the highly excitable speaker. Ultimately, we need to move beyond the satire aimed at the speaker, his yearning for sensational narratives which offer substantial and even marketable meaning, to the real world of things (including now the bodies of the woman and child) that has fuelled his imagination. For all his excess, the speaker does create sympathy for the two victims, and, moreover, the vitality of his own imagining is seemingly produced and sustained by his own return to the physical reality which is both the site and the emblem of Martha's story. What is most striking about his description is precisely his insistence on the thorn-tree as something physically palpable, and seemingly both permanent and fragile. It is 'old and grey,' and 'like a stone / With lichens ... overgrown,' he repeats. It is as weathered and resistant as stone, but weirdly, the 'melancholy crop' of lichens and mosses (from the child's purported grave?) which covers it seems 'bent / With plain and manifest intent / To drag it to the ground / ... To bury this poor Thorn for ever' (ll.13–22). The thorn is at once dead and alive, permanent and impermanent, organic and inorganic – an extraordinary mixing of categories that perhaps has as its primary tension the opposition of stasis and dissolution.[20] It is an example, as Marshall Brown has argued about the repeated image of the 'old grey stone' in Wordsworth's poetry, of those 'figures [which make] figurations possible. They are the mass of substance through whose chinks we glimpse spirit' (319). Yet even as the crop of life on the apparently dead tree does present us with a kind of predatory spirit of death or destruction that yearns to return life to the ground (which is in itself an echo of the geological understanding of the effect of wind and water gradually to flatten the earth), in this poem the human spirit of Martha is utterly absent. Though she is not actually dead, her inaccessibility makes her seem already with her child. Opposed to the speaker's ambitions for his narrative, the poem as a whole stands as an elegy for the child and the mother. We may wish to follow the narrator in ascribing supernatural spirit to the spot, but the Thorn's very status as an emblem and its utter materiality argue against it.[21] Indeed, the presence (or absence) of Martha and her child is in the end thoroughly mixed with the primal otherness of materiality which the Thorn much more immediately presents to consciousness. This is a form of heteroglossia not imagined in Bialostosky's influential reading of the *Lyrical Ballads*, and constitutes a profound sympathy for the irrecoverable otherness of both Martha and her child, mediated through the dramatic but more palpable otherness of a specific physical reality.

A simultaneous rooting and contrasting of consciousness in materiality occurs as well in 'Simon Lee.' Indeed, part of what most commentators have noted as the strangeness of these two poems is not just that they are generically mixed, but also that their examinations of what amount to the life-stories of other individuals are intensely mediated. The relation between consciousness and the physical is in 'Simon Lee' approached hesitantly and indirectly, which befits a poet in an experimental mode. But if 'The Thorn' is about absent bodies, 'Simon Lee,' like 'The Old Cumberland Beggar,' is in part about the frailty of bodies, and their physical otherness. It is easy to overstate this thematic element of the poem, but part of the surprising effectiveness of 'Simon Lee' is that it reveals Priestley's suggestion that the health of the mind depends on the health of the body, and that while the body may connect us to nature through its physicality, this version of materiality need not be particularly comforting either. Thus, just as the poem decomposes the structure of the ballad in its final stanzas, it also presents us images, and two stories, revealing Simon's bodily dissolution. This correlation is not as arbitrary as it perhaps seems. As in many of the *Lyrical Ballads*, the clear motive for the poem is an experiment in representing someone else's consciousness, and this poem too suggests that the apparent solidity and clarity of mind or character, like the apparent solidity and clarity of aspects of materiality (both of which, we might say, are assumptions of the ballad form), dissolve under a steady scrutiny. Death and aging are only the most obvious affronts to our illusions of permanence. Indeed, in all of the poems I have examined there is an epistemological obligation to uncover and to some degree undermine our own desire for this permanence, as well as our final ability to connect it to the physical world. The poem does not rely on geological images, as the previous two poems have, but the comically reductive images of Simon's body and the final image of the severed root suggest the quirkiness, the absurdity even, of some fully realized connection between consciousness and the physical world. By the end of the poem, the narrator mourns Simon's loss of vitality and dignity, which Simon may do as well, but the image of the severed root works symbolically to figure Simon's death, the final dis- and re-connection that is not long off. That he has been struggling to sever it himself introduces a vaguely suicidal note which is appropriate to a tale about the physical 'disease' of aging. Or Simon's struggle to cut the root can be read as an attempt to sever his connection with the determining material world, a desire that is probably as pervasive as the desire to find some genuine contiguity.

We have seen, in the examples I have traced so far, perceptions of the natural world that stand in stark contrast to the apparently readily accessible and fully formed faith expressed in 'Tintern Abbey' that we can, by observing our surroundings carefully enough, feel the 'spirit' that 'rolls through all things.' Hartman has argued as well that 'the strongly neutral or "it" aspect of much Wordsworthian landscape reveals an imagination in man or in nature which is strangely "unnatural," dehumanized.'[22] My account makes the same point, but I am trying to recuperate this aspect of Wordsworth's poetry as an end in itself, rather than as a cause for a momentarily (and apparently) triumphant and autonomous imagination. What can it mean to see the gulf between consciousness and nature not as a motivation for poetic progress, but as a genuine, repeated, and even primary, experience? My over-arching argument is that such moments are as close as we can get to an objective grounding for thinking about the natural world, whether strictly in Wordsworth's terms or in those of environmentalism. Wordsworth returns to these moments both because he wants to move to some more personally 'fructifying' philosophy that might come of them, and because he is drawn to authentic and fundamental problems of consciousness and its relation to the world. Such problems are produced for Wordsworth in the very act of writing poetry, of representing consciousness representing the world. In the *Essay Supplementary*, he complains that Ossian-Macpherson's imagery is especially 'insulated, dislocated, deadened, – yet nothing distinct' because 'it will always be so when words are substituted for things' (*Prose Works*, 3:77). The latter part of the criticism is either utterly banal (when, in the poetry about nature, are words not substituted for things?), or a frank admission of his own failures. It may well be both. That language does not bridge the gap between self and the otherness most fundamentally found in materiality is consistently admitted in Wordsworth's poetry.

We have seen this already in the silences of 'Slumber' and in the explicitly mediated structure and imagery of 'The Thorn' and 'Simon Lee.' All three poems imagine the limits of consciousness, and the borderlines of materiality, through direct or indirect meditation of death. Imagining the end of consciousness seems to take us directly towards the physical (an idea most succinctly expressed, perhaps, in Keats's plea to the nightingale that he might to its 'high requiem become a sod'). And this is an attempt to imagine as well a 'mode of being' that takes us out of the realm of language. 'Resolution and Independence' is a self-conscious fable for this dilemma, one which takes a poet explicitly committed to the productivity of poetry, and determined to ignore physical evidence of decay and mortality, into a realm of artificial disconnection – a 'self-confrontation,' as Hartman calls it (*Wordsworth's Poetry*, 272). In the poem, two dramatically opposite visions of nature are presented: an apparently immediate one, characterized by a sky that 'rejoices in the morning's birth' and a mirthful hare; and the seemingly abstract one of the poet's imagining, characterized in part by the departed storm, the primordial landscape of the moor, and the figures which the speaker begins to imagine on it. Moving from one to the other seems to hinge entirely on the mood of the speaker, and this change, though it is presented simply as part of an inevitable cycle ('from the might / Of joy in minds that can no further go'), is in part the result of an awareness of death, represented explicitly by Chatterton and indirectly through thoughts of the end of the poet's youth, gladness, and productivity. The landscape is throughout abstract and symbolic, rather than particular, and is in any case utterly responsive to the creative imagination of the speaker. It changes as he does. That the body of the leech-gatherer is capable of being transformed into 'an old stone,' a 'sea-beast,' and a 'cloud' suggests the mind's ultimate control, that this is a poem about internal states, using things for its own purpose. The materiality of nature is a backdrop against which the productivity of the mind allows it to forge its own permanence – first for the poet's projection of joy, and then for his feelings of blank desertion. As such, the poem is a kind of anti-elegy, a celebration of the mind's ability to divorce itself, even if only momentarily or in the language of poetry, from nature and death.

In the speaker's apparent victory over despair at the end of the poem, we have a glimpse of an autonomous and self-sustaining consciousness that is frequently the end point of the poet's poetic process. (For Hartman [*Wordsworth's Poetry*, 240–1] it climaxes in the Crossing of the Alps episode of *The Prelude*.) Yet it remains significant, I think, that the poet seems to manipulate his fall into despair, and his recovery, by configuring nature as ultimately inhospitable to being. The images of the leech-gatherer as an erratic boulder and as a sea-beast, and of the moor as a barren and lonely place, suggest a post-deluvian setting – the reference is both biblical and, as Bewell points out, geological, an entire landscape transformed by catastrophe (272). The old stone and the sea-beast are both analogues for things out of place and from another time. They are beyond comprehension, like the poet's own mortality. The body of the old man stands in for the speaker's own, as may be the case too in 'Simon Lee.' That it is dramatically morphed from 'primitive' rock to seemingly prehistoric animal flesh and to vapour before it is fully recognized as a 'decrepit Man' suggests the poet's deep awareness of a physical realm that exists before consciousness and identity. What matters is that the man, unlike the forms of nature, is finally revealed to the poet to have 'so firm a mind,' one that seems now to stand in stark contrast to the mutability even elemental nature reveals when viewed from the expanded time-scale of geological investigation.

The poem shows Wordsworth effecting a symbolic escape from the materiality of his own body, achieved by daring to imagine a barren wilderness that does not stifle a human vigour characterized by repetitious autobiography. (It is one of the poem's bleak ironies that the poet as audience for the old man's narrative is so unreceptive.) Wordsworth is always aware that the imagination is separate from nature, that, as in 'Tintern Abbey,' it may remain firm and creative after the poet has been nursed by apparently more benign landscapes. What is most interesting to me about his poetry is his reluctance to leave landscape and the glimmering awareness of materiality it offers. The imagination may easily create, as Keats documents in 'Sleep and Poetry' and Coleridge posits in his definition of 'fancy' in the *Biographia*, without direct reference to a physical realm. Wordsworth can convince himself that the mind can survive in a decaying body, and so may temporarily escape what is perhaps the most obvious kind of physical determinism. In book 5 of *The Prelude*, Wordsworth realizes a similar vision of deep time, of the fundamental permanence of the physical world even as it undergoes cataclysmic change:

Should earth by inward throes be wrenched throughout,
Or fire be sent from far to wither all
Her pleasant habitations, and dry up

> Old Ocean in his bed left singed and bare,
> Yet would the living presence still subsist
> Victorious; and composure would ensue,
> And kindlings like the morning – presage sure,
> Though slow perhaps, of a returning day.   (5.29–36)²³

This is an extraordinary passage, a keen anticipation of our contemporary sense of the ruggedness of life – that the planet as a whole (or Gaia, as Lovelock has envisioned it) can withstand massive change, and even extinction, and yet revive and continue through new species and ecosystems. The passage is also strikingly original in departing from geological sources. Rather than fires, Cuvier and Werner imagined floods, which nonetheless did not dramatically alter the organic order of things. Wordsworth moves beyond Revelation as well in imagining the end of the world without the end of life. This is a vision of nature as profoundly resilient, and yet also – and this is the crux of this famous episode – profoundly indifferent to and different from human life, which Wordsworth clearly imagines *not* surviving this apocalypse.

> But all the meditations of mankind,
> Yea, all the adamantine holds of truth
> By reason built, or passion (which itself
> Is highest reason in a soul sublime),
> The consecrated works of bard and sage,
> Sensuous or intellectual, wrought by men,
> Twin labourers and heirs of the same hopes –
> Where would they be?   (5.37–44)

Bewell argues that the episode shows that nature after an apocalypse would be but a 'barren desert' without human culture, thereby revealing that for Wordsworth 'nature [is] as much a product of human labor as art is. His consistent conflation of nature and culture ... does not indicate confusion, then, but instead a profound recognition that the things of nature and the things of mind are inseparably linked' (261). While it is clear that Wordsworth does frequently conflate nature and culture, this crucial passage, and others that I have examined so far, express precisely the opposite awareness – that nature and consciousness are fundamentally different. Thus the poet's complaint, his repeated despair over the impermanence not just of his own life and work but of humankind in general:

> Oh! why hath not the mind
> Some element to stamp her image on
> In nature somewhat nearer to her own?
> Why, gifted with such powers to send abroad
> Her spirit, must it lodge in shrines so frail? (5.44–8)

The 'shrines' are the physical monuments of culture of which his prime examples are books, but the passage suggests the human body as well. Crucial to the entire episode is an understanding that nature and consciousness consist of different 'elements.' What the poet despairs of saving is in the profoundest sense immaterial – it is meaning itself, which he here easily imagines as not his own, but that of the historic development of the entire culture, produced despite the ever-present threat of decay and mortality. The passage imagines culture as at the highest level separate from nature. The dream inspired by this despair (or vice versa) is as in 'Resolution and Independence' a kind of pragmatic resolution to hold the imagination and its products as ends in themselves in spite of their impermanence and nature's impermeability. The elegiac moment here is utterly abstract and is produced by imagining the death of the human species.

Implicit in this insistence on the duality of world, and on the inimicalness and profound otherness of the material, is still a reverence for its primacy. This is suggested by the consistency of the poet's return to a sense of nature's otherness, even as he continues to struggle to devise for himself an understanding of how the imagination may function independently to produce poetry and art. It is a struggle precisely because Wordsworth cannot dismiss the primacy of nature's reality. This reality remains a kind of touchstone for contrasting, even grounding, human creativity. The more imagination and perception are removed from the real, the more autonomous and perhaps productive they become, but also the further they are away from matter and something objective. There is repeatedly in Wordsworth the sense that words are immaterial, but also that culture is immaterial, that to the degree we lose even an oblique connection with materiality we become somehow captured by an illusion of our own devising, and thus unanchored – even if we cannot in any case trace the path of the anchor line.

We can see examples of this return to materiality's otherness in the sonnets 'Composed upon Westminster Bridge' and 'The World Is Too Much with Us' (*PW*, 3:38, 18), which present a strikingly ironic vision of the materiality of nature. Both may be seen as arguing that it is normal for us to take for granted our control of nature, both our ability to re-create the land to produce a cityscape and our 'getting and spending' the things of the 'world.' Yet the 'world' is most truly 'with us' when we can be awed by its physical power, as is the case for a hypothetical pagan creed. It is with us too if we can imagine, with the speaker on Westminster Bridge, that the sun may rise over a purely physical environment, one in which human being is utterly absent, and the cityscape thus instantly becomes a part of a whole, physical earth –

> silent, bare,
> Ships, towers, domes, theatres, and temples lie
> Open unto the fields, and to the sky;
> All bright and glittering in the smokeless air.
> Never did sun more beautifully steep
> In his first splendour, valley, rock, or hill;

That this vision results from (or is perhaps produced by) feeling that 'all that mighty heart is lying still' suggests again the extinguishing of culture and consciousness. These are bleak and reactive poems, but they show that Wordsworth appears to root what for him is a restorative turn not so much in an idea of consciousness within nature, or of consciousness liberated from it, as in an awareness of nature's fundamental physicality.

Many of the crucial episodes of *The Prelude*, though for the most part not explicitly elegiac, reveal an awareness of how consciousness springs from the material realm even though it is not reducible to, and remains fundamentally different from, that nature. A poem charting the growth of consciousness will, not surprisingly, question how consciousness arises, not just from education, social experience, and self-reflection, but more abstractly, from its physical environment. This occurs in several of the poem's most lyric passages, including the well-known episodes about the Boy of Winander, crossing Simplon Pass, the spots of time, and the boat stealing. In each of these passages 'visible scenery' is said to enter the mind, not as a coherent wholeness – either as the framed form of the picturesque or as the inspirited harmony of 'Tintern Abbey' – but as isolated, detailed, and often apparently lifeless things. For instance, in the 'pauses of deep silence' that follow when the owls fail to respond to the Boy of Winander's 'mimic hootings,'

> ... a gentle shock of mild surprise
> Has carried far into his heart the voice
> Of mountain torrents; or the visible scene

> Would enter unawares into his mind,
> With all its solemn imagery, its rocks,
> Its woods, and that uncertain heaven, received
> Into the bosom of the steady lake. (5.407–13)

What is imagined here is a pre-conscious, even accidental, connection to a materiality that the boy has not known or sought. The owls are a sign of real consciousness in nature that directly resembles that of the boy – an actual 'living presence.' This reality which enters and perhaps begins to form his mind is at once ephemeral, based in part on optical and aural illusion, and eternal and enveloping – the world's 'given.' The description is vague and generic; the 'solemn imagery' is undetailed, yet it points powerfully to real experience. Indeed, the unspecific nature of the account adds to a sense that the reality that is uncovered lies beyond the poet's own perception or immediate experience. Yet we do gain a sense of the complexity of the act of perception; it is modulated by inevitable recreation, producing an 'uncertain heaven' of the reflection of the sky in the temporarily 'steady' waters of the lake, an illusion of infinite depth (seeing beyond the surface of the water into the heavens) and permanent shallowness (noticing the lake as mirror). The heaven is uncertain because its image is temporary, perhaps wavering in small watery movement, and rare. It is uncertain too if we see the image as foreshadowing the death of the boy. His 'afterlife' is similarly undecidable, either materially now of the earth, as his downward gaze into the lake and the poet's at his grave might suggest, or spiritually now removed, as suggested by the reflected gaze upward into heaven. This final significance comes from the perspective of the poet or the reader, after the death of the boy. The experience we may surmise to be the boy's alone is an awareness of the unknowable reality of physical nature. This comes to the reader's awareness as an absence, something fundamentally different from the life of owls, the boy's own life, the process of his perception, and the text which represents them all. Probably we connect the boy's moment of contact to our own experience, deep memories of discrete landscapes which have, as Barry Lopez suggests, become part of an inner landscape (*Crossing Open Ground*, 61–72). In the larger context of the passage, our sense of the boy's experience is structured by an awareness of his death. As the poet stands 'A full half hour ... / Mute, looking at the grave in which he lies' (5.421–2), we repeat the poet's repetition of the boy's initial silence. The absence of consciousness, for the boy, the poet, and finally the reader produces or reproduces a powerful sense of what surrounds the void of consciousness, and a yearning to penetrate its silence, somehow to know what it is. This is also the yearning to know what comes after life, if finally consciousness does stand on its own or if and how it is truly nursed by nature. What the boy and the poet have seen are not simply objects of consciousness then, but its soil, the same stuff the body springs from and returns to, suggested here in part by the proximity of the boy's grave.

Similar primarily visual memories (of a looming hill, a naked pond, a mountain torrent) are at the centre of each of the passages of *The Prelude* mentioned above, and speak of 'huge and mighty forms that do not live / Like living men' (1.424–5). These episodes have been examined by other critics for how they represent the development of self-consciousness, but it has not been argued that they also suggest a kind of awe and mystery arising from the very fact that consciousness can exist in environments of 'visionary dreariness.' Each of these familiar episodes is characterized by the silence of the speaker, his inability to express an *immediate* understanding of things – as though all that consciousness can do with the confrontation of materiality is to retreat and allow memory to rework initial impressions, thereby demonstrating its own power in the face of things that do not speak to it. Indeed, they are crucial episodes for the poet precisely for what he has been able to do with the primary experience (the frustrated attempt to make sense of mysterious and elemental forms in nature) in retrospect. He can celebrate the 'unfathered vapour' of the imagination and the 'vivifying virtue' of memory because they define the ability and desire of consciousness to give meaning to nature. Even so, these passages also express an awareness of the importance of mere appearances, of the bare surface of things rather than some underlying and unifying idea or power. There is a reluctance to describe in any real detail the natural settings that inspire the poet's climactic turns. It is as though Wordsworth is determined only to account for his response to them, the growth of consciousness. Even the celebrated account of the Gondo Gorge tends towards generalization rather than a sense of the specific:

> The immeasurable height
> Of woods decaying, never to be decayed,
> The stationary blasts of waterfalls,
> And everywhere along the hollow rent
> Winds thwarting winds, bewildered and forlorn,
> The torrents shooting from the clear blue sky,

> The rocks that muttered close upon our ears,
> Black drizzling crags that spake by the wayside
> As if a voice were in them, the sick sight
> And giddy prospect of the raving stream,
> The unfettered clouds and region of the Heavens,
> Tumult and peace, the darkness and light – (6.556–67)

What is characterized is the very 'face' of nature, its inscrutable and inimical visage; the violence and chaos that the poet has seen in the ravine are 'characters of the great Apocalypse, / The types and symbols of Eternity' because they are already transformed or personified ('like workings of one mind') into a symbolic order. The characterization offered here is a kind of reward, in the narrative structure of the episode, for the poet's recognition of the independent power of his imagination, which comes immediately after his failure to have seen anything in particular in his crossing of the Alps. It is a direct assertion of his ability now to transcend nature's reality into one that is explicitly biblical and mystical. Yet it is possible to see nonetheless that the primary wildness of nature, its alienating power, reveals to Wordsworth the necessary creativity of human imagination, and that we thus continue to feel the presence of its essential materiality and otherness.

These references to primary nature exist within the poetry as monuments about which Wordsworth has nothing directly to say – types of things, rather than an actual attempt to name the things. These descriptions do not really amount to a Wordsworthian typology, for we feel their reality by the measure of experience Wordsworth has attached to them. We know it *is* a particular landscape that has affected him, just was we know this to be true of Clare and White, though the latter pair left much more specific evidence in their writing. Wordsworth's creation of an idea of his own consciousness, the creative power of his imagination, and its connection to a fully inspirited nature are not so much the result of a transference of a 'spirit of place' to an idealized 'nature' of which consciousness is fully a part (as Hartman has argued [*Wordsworth's Poetry*, 212–13]), as a necessary act of projection in the face of an inexplicable absence, of the failure of nature's reality to signify. But it is not even a projection, since consciousness indisputably exists. The great strength of Wordsworth's poetry, especially *The Prelude*, is that it repeatedly makes us see that consciousness is the most immediate object of consciousness, the only thing we can talk about. Before 'Rocks and stones and trees,' or even a 'churchyard' that 'hangs / Upon a slope' and the objects that mark and make a 'grave,' Wordsworth is in the first instance mute. The inability to speak is initially a recognition of the fact of materiality, and secondly an awareness of the inexplicability of its invisible effects.

In denying an explanation for the existence of consciousness in a material world, but recognizing the latter as omnipresent and foundational, these lyric moments in Wordsworth form a kind of refutation of associationism, even as they accept the existence of the fundamental problem that it attempts to solve – of how consciousness arises in a primarily physical world. Different as Wordsworth's lyric moments are from Hume's critique of Locke, one gets a similar sense of the absurdity of the attempt to account for the creation of consciousness.[24] It is as though because such an argument must rely on language and narrative, the very stuff on consciousness, the fundamental importance and immediacy – the very *presence* – of the material will be denied. Poetry is not going to escape this either, but a poetry of images of the material is at least more likely to point us in the right direction. One could argue that the best solution is just to *be* in nature, to perceive it directly; I take this to be one of the central didactic points of Wordsworth's nature poetry – that the act of perceiving the physical world in a 'wise passivity' is better than the poetry about such an act, the theme of Wordsworth's parable 'The Tables Turned.'

The problem of the actual relation between consciousness and the material is confronted more bluntly in Coleridge, for whom it is a central preoccupation. It is indeed the primary motivation for his interest in the physical sciences in general, and Hartley's speculation about neural vibrations specifically.[25] 'Frost at Midnight,' for instance, presents a similar silence before the inexplicable relation of mind and matter. Indeed, there is no better representation of the romantic awareness of this problem than the poem's twin emblems for consciousness in the pattern spontaneously generated by frost, and in the fluttering film of soot which is suspended by invisible forces above the coals of a dying fire. Both are 'companionable forms' because they are analogies for the mind which perceives them. They are apparently self-directing, free and lifeless, but also (as frost and soot) ultimately inert and material. The central problem which the poem's speaker is unable to resolve is how to understand the existence of consciousness given that it springs from, or is even buffeted helplessly by, the literally and figuratively 'dead' stuff of ice and ashes. The problem here too is one of language, of seeing in the physical world actual *signs* of co-substantiality and not mere analogies and projections of desire (as the 'stranger' must finally remain). How does one glean a sense of nature as a home or origin when it remains foreign? For Coleridge here and elsewhere the answer to this question is deferred to a future faith: in this case, to that of his child raised to 'see and hear / The lovely shapes and sounds intelligible / Of that eternal language.'[26]

For Wordsworth this faith in the connection between consciousness and the material is not so much of a leap as might seem necessary from the stark opposites in which Coleridge presents the problem. Both Bewell and Bate, as I said above, have argued for the relative pragmatism and empiricism of Wordsworth's notion that nature is both the foundation of consciousness and its nurse, and that these connections may or may not be benign. We see evidence for this idea in Wordsworth's vision of London as brutalizing to consciousness in book 7 of *The Prelude*, and of Michael's land as essentially ennobling, however tragic and destructive intervening forces may be. Yet for me, Wordsworth is more helpful in revealing how and why making a connection between consciousness and the material requires a leap of faith in the first place. Wordsworth frequently depicts a strong faith that nature is inspirited, that it contains and nurtures consciousness, or that consciousness may easily transcend it, and these moves are the usual focus of both praise and criticism by his readers. That the faith becomes automatic can make it rather insipid, but it begins, and periodically returns to, an awareness of the material that decentres consciousness, reminding us that human being is not at the heart of what is real.

My final example is from *The Ruined Cottage*, and I choose it not only because it offers a fine instance of the awareness of the material that has been my subject, but also because recent criticism of the poem exemplifies precisely the kind of solipsism that the poet seeks to redress in it – Kenneth Johnston, who gives it a sympathetic reading, calls it 'a *locus classicus* for a worst-case scenario of Romanticism's supposed elegiac evasions.'[27] My aim here is a thus a double one. Crucial to understanding how the perception of the material in this poem works is a concurrent awareness of the difficulty of talking about that which is fundamentally different from consciousness. For Wordsworth an attempt to represent an awareness of the material takes the form of lyric, because lyric is frequently a way of tracing multiple and ineluctable origins of thought and being. As in most of the examples I have mentioned above, lyric here offers the possibility of an openness before the world, and that there is greater plenitude in resisting the potential completeness of narrative. At the centre of the poem is a dilemma of how to represent what has been separated or removed from consciousness, which is both Margaret and the cottage and land she tended. As in many of Wordsworth's poems about others, *The Ruined Cottage* attempts to represent consciousness by closely associating it with forms of (or in) landscape. In contrast to *Michael* or 'Simon Lee,' though, in this poem the main object is already gone, and is presented in explicitly mediated terms through the memories of the Pedlar. Readers of the poem have the double problem of learning how Margaret existed in her tiny (nearly sealed) environment, and, as in 'A Slumber Did My Spirit Seal,' what it means to attempt to know her through what is in this poem an almost obsessive scrutiny of her remains.

For Liu the poem shows the dual artifice of lyric and nature in Wordsworth. He argues that the poem shows Wordsworth as a kind of Pedlar of the misfortunes of others, converting what ought to be a historical documentary of the social causes of Margaret's suffering into pure 'images' of nature which speak of a false humanism. This lyric turn denies the proper 'ownership' of the story, so that the value of historical truth is turned into the purely private value of a literary aesthetics. As Liu puts it: 'Instead of presenting [Margaret's] misfortune as a narrative or drama able to capitalize upon tragedy with traditional authority, Wordsworth peddles his tale as incipient lyric. The danger is that when we spot the hidden capitalization in lyric we will feel defrauded. Stripped of the full tragic grandeur by which "change in fortune" once opened out from private to public concerns and set within a history of literal economic crisis, poetic peddling seems unscrupulous and exploitative ... Lyric consciousness gained by converting ruin into 'rich' souvenirs (called 'images') is by definition selfish: dedicated to the increase of the lyric "I"' (*Wordsworth*, 348). Lyric for Liu functions according to a monopolistic or mercantile economy, transforming the public property of history into mystified icons, a kind of money that increases the value of the poet's stock on a literary exchange. On an epistemological level, lyric becomes the form that allows for the usurpation of meaning. The narrative of tragedy, presumably, markets itself for public gain, truly sharing the meaning of Margaret's misfortune. Lyric confiscates meaning by taking the facts of her misfortune out of history and narrative and presenting them as a kind of 'found art.'

I want to dispute this reading in part because of its already idealized understanding of the material, to show that there is an important awareness of the physical world that precedes imagining it as capital. Liu's valorization of narrative, his faith in the power of consciousness to account for what he feels to be the entire range of the material conditions of existence, is almost a defining feature of the kind of anthropocentrism that the poem seeks to undermine. We may counter his argument by noting in the first place that his reading of the poem ignores the overall mixture of forms in the poem, and reduces its notion of the riches of the imagination as an offering of an open-ended exchange of meaning – the Pedlar speaks to the poet who speaks to the reader – to a kind of theft. The poem is not a lyric as 'A Slumber' is; we know the *story* of Margaret's tragedy and its historical context from the poem itself. Yet the story is incidental. It barely matters within the poem how Margaret came to die alone and in misery; what counts in the poem is *that* she died and would be utterly forgotten except for the Pedlar's fragmented memories. The frame of the narrative itself, of a wandering Pedlar telling pieces of the story that he knows to a wandering poet, highlights the distance of the teller from the tale and the deferral of any kind of closure. The narrative cannot be complete; a full history of Margaret's misfortune is no more available to the reader than it is to its tellers. History is not being denied; rather a lack of access to the meaning of an other's suffering is being acknowledged. It is

>   a common tale,
> An ordinary sorrow of man's life,
> A tale of silent suffering, hardly clothed
> In bodily form.   (ll. 231–4)[28]

It is because the body is absent that we must turn to other matter. The Pedlar does this explicitly in noticing and rehearsing the specific details of the change in material conditions that are the overwhelming signs of Margaret's waning influence on her surroundings – the spreading tufts of weed, the yellow stone-crop, her loom and bench, the path created by her pacing, and the many other features of the changing 'aspect' of the cottage. The Pedlar's relentless description of these mere appearances becomes the centre of the poem (as well as where Wordsworth began [MS B ll. 152–243]) because they are all the information he has – indeed, as much as anyone who has not written autobiography can leave behind. These descriptions become merely images, as Liu says, because we cannot know what happens in between, just as we cannot know what exactly is being obliterated. The cottage itself – 'four naked walls / That stared upon each other' (ll. 31–2) – is the central marker of this silence, a monument which is at once permanent and without any explicit meaning. The physical remains, Margaret's material effects, cannot be made to speak, to reveal secrets or give up meaning. Confronting and representing the silence of these material effects is the central desire of the poem's two characters, and it is enacted by the careful descriptions. These descriptions are lyrical, therefore, because they point to meaning that cannot be delivered. These lyric moments do not attempt to suppress or mystify the meaning of the story as it stands, but to complicate it, to present precisely the troubling issue of how we are to take the meaning of another's suffering, and of how consciousness may survive and exist in elemental environment. As Kenneth Johnston has argued, the poem insists 'that the socio-economic and political explanations are not the only ones, and are insufficient or barren without their personal, psychological, and emotional complements' (38). And, prior at least to the reconciling conclusion added in MS B, the poem refuses a final reconstruction of Margaret's 'humanity'; its lyric moments oppose the hesitating narrative of her life by standing as objects (like the self-staring walls) that can speak only of the void left by her death, and the primacy of things. A passage notorious for being removed from later versions but at the centre of its first version (MS A) appears almost to revel in this fact.

> She is dead,
> The worm is on her cheek, and this poor hut,
> Stripp'd of its outward garb of household flowers,
> Of rose and sweet-briar, offers to the wind
> A cold bare wall whose earthy top is tricked
> With weeds and the rank spear-grass. She is dead,
> And nettles rot and adders sun themselves
> Where we have sate together while she nurs'd
> Her infant at her breast.   (ll. 103–11)

This description is startlingly specific. It forces us to visualize Margaret's bodily dissolution, and to be aware as well of the relative permanence, and what is literally the monumental indifference, of the surrounding environment. The spot she tended has certainly changed, but we feel most of all the permanence of this change. What is unsettling about the passage (presumably for Wordsworth as well) is what we might call its egalitarian spirit – though we are aware that the physical changes are in part the result of Margaret's death, the scene now before the speakers remains valuable precisely because of its immediacy and reality. We are not really encouraged to look through these things to some semblance or re-accretion of Margaret. They now *are*, while she is not. And so these things before the Pedlar and the poet are signs of her death which are yet utterly silent about it and indifferent towards it. The passage is an attempt to face or reveal that 'sympathy / With nature in her forms inanimate / With objects such as have no power to hold / Articulate language.'[29] But that sympathy for nature's forms need not reveal a reciprocating or primary sympathy in nature, and it is this fact that the poem struggles with. Indeed, the Pedlar is Wordsworth's imagined ideal for the kind of intense scrutiny of the physical world that Wordsworth explores in the poem:

> ... he had an eye which evermore
> Looked deep into the shades of difference
> As they lie hid in all exterior forms
> Near or remote, minute or vast, an eye
> Which from a stone, a tree, a withered leaf
> To the broad ocean and the azure heavens
> Spangled with kindred multitudes of stars
> Could find no surface where its power might sleep
> Which spake perpetual logic to his soul
> And by an unrelenting agency
> Did bind his feelings even as in a chain   (MS D, f. 67r)

Wordsworth's consistent desire for this scrutiny is to uncover some primary similitude between consciousness and nature, to make things speak their 'perpetual logic' to a receptive consciousness which knows its language. Wordsworth would, in book 3 of *The Prelude*, connect these lines with a period of idealism – a faith in his own ability to find a continuity between the physical realm and his imagination which he seems unproblematically to allow is a matter of deliberate projection.

> To every natural form, rock, fruit or flower,
> Even the loose stones that cover the highway,
> I gave a moral life: I saw them feel,
> Or linked them to some feeling: the great mass
> Lay bedded in a quickening soul, and all
> That I beheld respired with inward meaning.
> Thus much for the one Presence, and the Life
> Of the great whole.   (3.124–31)

The 'great mass' is made to seem enveloped within his own 'quickening soul,' just as the power of memory to rework external images reveals to the poet later that 'the mind / Is lord and master, and that outward sense / Is but the obedient servant of her will' (*Prelude*, 11.271–3). The dialogue in *The Ruined Cottage*, however, is between the poet and the Pedlar, not between consciousness and the material; they do not articulate 'the one Presence'; or rather, they reveal it as residing within materiality rather than consciousness.

MS B ends with a repetition of the fact of Margaret's death and that she remained rooted to 'this wretched spot' (l. 523). No explicit attempt is made to answer the question of why 'in the hour of deepest noon, / ... we thus with an untoward mind ... / And feeding on disquiet thus disturb / The calm of Nature with our restless thoughts' (ll. 187–98). The memory of Margaret is given one last repose, as it were, before it dies with the Pedlar. The poem is a substitute for the experience of the Pedlar, whose experience represents Margaret in fragments, and her experience is deeply rooted in the place that still remains. None of these can really be seen as an incarnation of the other – the contrast between what is gone and what remains does not allow us to see the poem as reproducing what is lost, or conferring on its language any real substantiality, as David Haney has argued (69ff). In much of the troubling addendum, however, the poet attempts to overcome the 'impotence of grief' by reconstructing living connections to the being of the dead Margaret in those signs which still survive ''mid the calm oblivious tendencies / Of nature,' as though these 'shews of being' and the poet's ability to reconstruct a sense of actual being from them were in some sense ameliorating. It is perhaps the same mistake Liu makes in arguing that Wordsworth's images ring false because they do not manage finally to revive the full meaning of Margaret's tragedy, finding a sufficiency only in the relations and affiliations between past and present beings.[30] He is, we might say, corrected by the Pedlar (and by Wordsworth's further cancellations). The Pedlar's advice is worth examining again because it points (however obliquely) towards what I have called above an 'existential environmentalism':

>   no longer read
> The forms of things with an unworthy eye.
> She sleeps in the calm earth, and peace is here.
> I well remember that those very plumes,
> Those weeds, and the high spear-grass on that wall,
> By mist and silent rain-drops silver'd o'er,
> As once I passed did to my heart convey
> So still an image of tranquillity,
> So calm and still, and looked so beautiful
> Amid the uneasy thoughts which filled my mind,

> That what we feel of sorrow and despair
> From ruin and from change, and all the grief
> The passing shews of being leave behind,
> Appeared an idle dream that could not live
> Where meditation was. I turned away
> And walked along my road in happiness.
>
> (ll. 510–25)[31]

In contrast to much of the deleted addendum, the Pedlar's advice returns the Poet and the reader to the stasis of the image – here not what can actually be perceived, but memories of a perception inaccessible to the Pedlar's audience. Yet it is a specific perception, of specific things at a precise moment. It is as though Wordsworth were unwilling to allow us even the illusion of some *thing* which the reader could hold as a token for the memory of Margaret. The tranquillity this offers is that of blankness, the ephemerality of thinking that hovers over the fact of actual phenomena. Meditation does not so much connect being to the physical world as lead to an awareness of the stark contrast between them. Nothing, then, is finally reconciled; rather, the narrative impulse is stopped, and this itself becomes a source of a happiness that is immediate but temporary because it is explicitly not an act of closure. That is, the Pedlar suggests what Shelley wrote in 'To a Skylark': 'We look before and after, / And pine for what is not.' We are not allowed to forget what actually *is*, in the present, though the poet would like to. The image of tranquillity does not attempt to resuscitate Margaret by dispersing her being into the visible vegetation, as Liu argues, for the vegetation is throughout the poem part of the hostility of her environment (like the adders and worms). Indeed, this is explicitly what the Pedlar refuses to do; rather, the peace the Pedlar preaches ends the desire to overcome death by finding traces of human being in materiality; and this awareness comes from a meditation that must find the immediate perception of things sufficient. Nature, which may include the temporary shows of being, *is* real and primary; it continues to evolve as consciousness and its signs are wiped out. Meditation here does not point to anything larger, to a 'secret spirit of humanity' or a 'quickening soul' in which we may still find some precise identity for Margaret, but simply to the ground from which being springs.

The message here is not even to preserve this ground, only to recognize it. The poem reveals that nature need not be a fertile ground for being, simply that it is the only ground. It is as though it were too easy, in grieving over someone's death, to suppose that being begins and ends elsewhere. This is especially true, of course, in elegy, which makes formal demands that a life be remembered and evaluated according to numerous conventions that define and determine a life's *meaning*. Grief produces its own peculiar fictions. *The Ruined Cottage* undermines elegiac conventions by refusing the completion of narrative, and by confronting the most brutal facts of absence in the physicality of remains.[32] It reminds us of the wonder that life and consciousness exist at all, but this wonder is tempered by an awareness that in nature we are only fellow travellers, that human consciousness is not primary, and, contrary to the inclinations of contemporary culture, that the material realm may not yield its crucial secrets to consciousness. It is a lesson which we are too ready to forget.

II

The Meanest Thing That Feels: Anthropomorphizing Animals in Romanticism

The previous chapter presented Wordsworth's occasional confrontations with nature as pure materiality as a way of de-idealizing the poet. Wordsworth's deep recognition of nature's 'otherness' is an important insight not just for romantic studies but also for ecologically oriented criticism, which itself too easily slips into versions of idealism. This chapter presents another complicating move consistent with my more general aim of surveying ways in which the otherness of nature is recognized within romanticism. If the physical world can be seen in the poetry of Wordsworth, for instance, as a realm at some level inimical to being rather than as a consistent mirror for his developing self-identity, then we can as well begin to see how the possibility of consciousness in nature might take forms other than purely self-referential or anthropocentric. While the purpose of the previous chapter was to show how Wordsworth can, in Paul Fry's apt phrase, be better seen as grey than green, as conscious of the inert, inorganic, and permanent in the physical world, the focus in this chapter will be how we can see in romanticism in general, and Wordsworth in particular, a recognition of animal life as a mode of consciousness and being distinctly other than the human kind. I am arguing that we can see in romanticism a pre-figuring of a contemporary phenomenon; extending consciousness and being to animal life is a first step not only in environmental philosophy but also in current scientific projects of understanding and grounding consciousness in neuroscience, and in the related disciplines of evolutionary biology, socio-biology, and ethology.[1] While these sciences are very far from equating consciousness, or individual subjective experience, to the material processes that they reveal to be important contributing factors, they share the anti-Platonic awareness that human consciousness is not itself a supremely transcendent force –

that while even as we experience it as a separate and different from the material realm, we can and must acknowledge its myriad connections to material processes. Thus, to cite but a few examples, ethological studies like those by Frans de Waal of specific primate societies reveal social and individual complexities in non-human animal behaviour (particularly in the realm of peacemaking and cooperation) which bear striking similarities to human experience.[2] Evolutionary biologists are attempting to explain consciousness in general as an entirely random product of evolution (arguing against the popular belief that evolution must necessarily have been progressing towards that end), and that human consciousness is but one version of a set of genetic adaptations that has been several million years in development and has been shared by many other species. Sociobiology has argued for the evolutionary origins of cultural behaviours (of which human culture is considered as only one example among many), and thinkers as diverse as Donna Haraway and Daniel Dennett have argued for the possibility that consciousness and being may be extended to, and derived from, entirely mechanistic processes. These investigations have the cumulative effect of decentring human consciousness, making it seem less a special gift from a benign creator (still the predominant belief in most cultures) than itself necessarily a product of nature.

An openness to the material, in both romanticism and contemporary science, includes an awareness of the contingency of consciousness. Wordsworth may recognize that nature and consciousness are separated by an intractable gulf, and may respond to this with silence, or by projecting consciousness onto the world. Another response, though, like that of some contemporary science, and most contemporary versions of environmentalism, is to examine specific and physical evidence of the existence of kinds of consciousness and being in the natural world. And this is precisely what we can see within the romantic period's burgeoning of interest not just in documenting and categorizing life (as I explore in chapter 4) but also in recognizing individual animal being. Animal consciousness is a specific species of otherness, worthy of attention in its own right, and a potential bridge to the deeper, categorical otherness of nature.

There is further reason for pursuing this line of investigation. That romanticism explored alterity in a profound and original way used to be an article of faith for scholars of the field. One way or another, it was felt, romantic poets and artists uncovered and made known forms of otherness within nature, society, and consciousness itself. For at least the past fifteen years, however, this easy generalization has been challenged by feminist and new historicist critics. Both argue that the alterity supposedly uncovered by writers of the period (Wordsworth's version of nature and Shelley's *Epipsychidion* being nearly paradigmatic examples) is in most cases an idealized projection of the writer's ego; worse yet, they argue, the apparent otherness of women, the working classes, ethnicity, and material social forces is only further obscured, driven deeper into alterity as it were, by foregrounding the all-knowing, visionary consciousness of its canonical authors. It has become very nearly a given of recent criticism that romanticism has feminized nature so that it may be characterized as both nurturing and infinitely malleable, a body or entity whose creative powers may be usurped even as it is literally inscribed by male desire. As a necessary feature of this move, it is argued, women are 'naturalized,' made a part of the landscape and so assumed to be part of an otherness which, finally, denies them the possibility of becoming self-possessing subjects. Feminist environmentalists like Carolyn Merchant have argued that this association is not so much a feature of romanticism as it is a characteristic of western male thought. Yet it is fair, I think, to say that romanticism represents a peculiar climax of these ideas, because it is a period in which the *idea* of nature comes under intense scrutiny.

While the revisionist view of romanticism's reification of self and its mystification of nature is not exactly in danger of becoming a new hegemony, it is clearly complicated by a recognition of the particular forms of attention romantic-period writers paid to the natural world, including its animal life. It seems to me that representations of animals in romantic art and poetry reveal a profound interest in a genuine otherness in nature (the sentience of animals) which potentially stands outside the nature/femininity equation as understood by feminist critics of romanticism. That is, femininity is far less different from masculine consciousness than the kinds of 'being' romantic writers and painters found in animals, which afforded them an explicit means of exploring nature, as well as their own being, in terms of species differences, rather than covertly through gender. A recognition of this exploration ought to make us careful when we look for large areas of overlap in the history of the alterities of gender, race, and animality, as much ecofeminism, for instance, has done. Certainly, entire classes of humans have been and continue to be symbolically connected to animality as a means of degrading them, of dehumanizing their perceived difference, often as a prelude to their actually being treated as animals typically are (including their brutalization and extermination). But focusing on this overlap tends to obscure the history of our actual understanding and treatment of animals, and our overwhelming tendency to ignore them as living, independent beings with some claim to natural rights. What I take to be a characteristic romantic interest in the specificity of animal being works instead to dissolve and refigure large-scale categories of difference, both between individuals and between species. Differences are not erased, but they are made less monumental, and they are less keyed into a hierarchy of anthropocentric values. This interest, furthermore, anticipates the efforts among some contemporary environmentalists to decentre our view of the world, to place human beings firmly within, rather than outside or on top of, the natural world.

My argument begins with the realization that the act of representing animal life is, like most acts of representation, a phenomenon whose complications we readily ignore. Most of us trained to even a high-school level of sophistication in the biological sciences know that in representing non-human sentience most scientists hold that we are too prone to anthropomorphize, to ascribe human characteristics of emotion or thought to animal appearance, behaviour, and consciousness (about which, elementary science teaches us, we can actually *know* almost nothing). Indeed, as a number of recent commentators on ethology have noted, the prohibition against anthropomorphism within biology is one of the most tortured and resilient of scientific constructions, a testament to the continued power of behaviourism within the sciences.[3] Yet twentieth-century ethology is not solely responsible for the prohibition against anthropomorphism. The *OED* reminds us that the term originally applied to investing images or ideas of god with human attributes. Contained in this historic notion is the sin of inverting hierarchies within the so-called 'chain of being,' which is a kind of hubris when projecting upwards, but is felt as a form of self- (or species-) debasement when projecting down. As Harriet Ritvo and other historians have observed, people interested in animal welfare were derided from the very beginning for even implying that non-human animals might have 'rights' (as evidenced by the response to Coleridge's 'To a Young Ass,' for instance), and today most of us feel that an individual human life is incalculably more valuable than any quantity of animal life, and so we feel no difficulty in destroying large numbers of them for food and medical research (Ritvo, 125ff). The prohibition against anthropomorphism is thus more than merely a scientific phenomenon.

Anthropomorphism at its most obvious, as in much children's literature, strikes us as naïve and quaint, a sign of a charming delusion; when it is relentlessly commodified, as it has been by Disney, it becomes grotesque, an exploitation of both animal life and childhood imagination. Yet it is difficult to imagine what a truly objective account of animal being would be, one which would forestall any kind of additive imagining. Perhaps only the most clinical kind of representation could succeed, a map of a specific animal's anatomy, for instance, but only by literally deconstructing the individual animal. Abstractly considered, the problem of how we are to view animals objectively, to see them as they are and not as they are like us, probably has no solution. We cannot, finally, distinguish those features of their subjective being (emotions, desires, intelligence, and so on) which are truly theirs from those we are familiar with because we experience them ourselves. From one perspective, the problem is just an exaggerated version of how we overcome individual human subjectivity, how we come to assume enormous similarity among our fellow humans. Here too we make assumptions about the experience of others based on our own, aided, of course, by the dynamics of a system of language which is at once individually and communally generated. But with animal life there is clearly much more supposition involved, since indeed we only have any kind of access to a shared language in extraordinary circumstances (such as when chimpanzees are taught human sign language).

Yet the prohibition against anthropomorphizing animal life might itself be seen an instrument of anthropocentrism, which turns all that is not human into an otherness subservient to human needs. The sheer volume of representations of animals in popular and high art attests to our historic and sustained interest in animal life; and so it is striking that the general prohibition against anthropomorphism has very nearly prevented serious analysis of this interest. Such representations are very often strikingly ideological. It is not difficult, for instance, to see in many depictions of horses and farm animals (in both high and popular art, and at least since the early eighteenth century) not simply the valorization of human domestication of nature but the association, even the co-opting, of this value by the aristocratic, landowning class, so that paintings or other representations of the hunt, the race, or simply the ride simultaneously display conspicuous leisure, wealth, and dominance (in all senses of the word). Similarly and equally obviously, the anatomy chart is ideological in that it turns the rat on the dissection table into a collection of parts, of mere objects, which we may manipulate at our will. The rat's life, or even the question of what that life is worth, is subsumed in the high gloss of scientific factuality.

What is striking about the romantic representations of animals that I wish to explore, however, is that they force readers or viewers to confront the problems raised by the issue of anthropomorphism (which existed in the eighteenth century, as I have suggested, as a matter of the accepted hierarchy of species rather than science education), as well as ideologies inherent in certain acts of representation. romantic depictions of animals force us to acknowledge that animals are a kind of life in nature that is at once much like our own and yet different from it, not capable of being reduced to merely human designs or desires. Animal life thus neatly suggests how nature can both seem fully invested with a kind of being which seems continuous with our own and yet possess an irreducible otherness which makes it seem wild. The romantic representation of animal life suggests, finally, how we might move beyond the notion that every such act of representation must be anthropomorphic, and that whenever we imagine animal life we are necessarily projecting onto them characteristics which are the sole province of humanity. Indeed, an examination of the representation of animals in the romantic period can enable us to see that the concept of anthropomorphism, and the consequent prohibition of it, are inherently features of anthropocentrism.

Animals appear in literature and art of all periods, but even a casual survey of the art and literature of the romantic movement reveals that there is increased attention given to animals and the 'animal.' In such a survey, we might think of the magnificent horses of Delacroix and Gericault, or Stubbs's widely imitated images of a lion attacking a horse (which have become visual clichés for the many vague ideas associated with romanticism). Although we do not stop to think about it much, the poetry of the romantic period is also rife with descriptions of, references to, and meditations on, animals, many of which have become, like Delacroix's horses, paradigmatic or exemplary moments of the literature of the period. The most famous animal of English romantic poetry is Coleridge's albatross, while Keats's 'Ode to a Nightingale,' Shelley's 'To a Skylark,' and Coleridge's 'The Nightingale' are among the best-known poems of the period. Coleridge was almost as well known to his contemporaries for his naïvely utopian 'To a Young Ass,' which addresses a donkey as a 'Poor little Foal of an oppressed race' and 'hails' it as a 'brother.' Shelley spent considerable energy in *Queen Mab* and in two pamphlets on 'the vegetable diet' explaining how humankind's abuse of animals (most of all through eating them) was a palpable 'root' of evil, and that its elimination would necessarily be a key to the establishment of a genuine utopia. Blake is probably most prolific of all the poets in his references to animals of almost all kinds, though we need look no further than *The Marriage of Heaven and Hell* – in which he asks 'How do you know but ev'ry Bird that cuts the airy way, / Is an immense world of delight, clos'd by your senses five?' – to get an immediate sense of the complexity of his interest; it includes both a striking awareness of animal sentience, and a sense that the variety and complexity of life is a profound metaphor for the disunity of nature after the Fall. John Clare's poetry displays the most consistent interest in translating the careful observation of individual animals in their habitats into the substance of poetry, though Joanna Baillie, in her portraits of country life, frequently presents a similar kind of attention. Wordsworth, as we shall see, also displays a consistent interest in animals and their relation to man; *The Excursion*'s Wanderer, for instance, is said in book 2 to have 'loved' all animals 'In his capacious mind,' and to 'acknowledge' that they have 'rights' (*PW*, 5:43, ll. 41–53).

The existence of animals in romantic-period art has been assumed simply to be part of the landscape, as it were, as obvious and relatively uninteresting, perhaps, as Wordsworth's love of trees and flowers. When they are noted at all, animals in poetry and art have been immediately converted to figures, as symbolic devices signifying the poets themselves (as in the many poems which emblematize birds as solitary singers) or as synecdoches of nature and the spirit that animates it. This is a step so automatic that we barely pause to reflect on how or why we do it, what it means to say that animals represent, or even *are*, nature. For instance, recognizing animals as a part of the landscape can distance humanity from nature in allowing us to regard the 'bestial' and instinctive as being other than culture; or it can bring us closer to nature, since countless similarities between animals and humans have been recognized, even above the protestations of religious thinkers like Descartes, who notoriously and influentially argued that animals were equivalent to machines because they could not have souls. Recognizing the complexity of seeing and representing animals can revitalize our understanding of what nature was for the romantic writers. Like Jonathan Bate in his book on the pragmatics of Wordsworth's 'environmental imagination,' I dispute the common critical dogma that concepts of nature are always used in romanticism in general and by Wordsworth in particular to validate the supremacy of individual (human) consciousness, and are always framed by and reducible to definitions of culture (Bate, *Romantic Ecology*, 56–7). What is centrally important about the animal to the romantic artists and poets I examine below is that it presents them with an otherness that stands at the boundaries of understandings of the human.

My first example of the representation of animals, a painting by George Stubbs titled *Freeman, the Earl of Clarendon's Gamekeeper, with a Dying Doe and a Hound* (1800), neatly highlights the historical complexities surrounding the representation of animals in the romantic period (see frontispiece). The painting depicts a gamekeeper who is lifting the head of a dying doe by the ear, and who holds in his other hand an only barely perceptible knife with which he is about to slit the doe's throat. Blood oozes from a bullet wound, and the gun which presumably produced the wound lies on top of the gamekeeper's hat just behind him. The doe stares pathetically and directly at the viewer; the gamekeeper also stares directly, but his look seems rather to be of defiance, or at least complete indifference towards the act he is about to finish. The superbly painted hound seems almost a mirror image of the doe, and stares up at the gamekeeper with its ears back. The dog may simply be excited by the kill, or it may appear to be looking pleadingly at its master, as if asking him to spare the doe.

To the modern viewer, I think, the painting seems unambiguously to suggest the cruelty of killing the doe. The painting's dark background, which suggests both the gloom and perhaps the furtiveness of the act, also helps to highlight the trio of living creatures in the foreground, at the very centre of which is the doe's apparently anguished face (they appear uncannily as though suddenly lit up by a spotlight). The painting frames the moment of taking an animal's life; the gamekeeper is poised as if to ask the viewer what he or she makes of the killing of an animal, utterly lacking the glory and thrill of the hunt (a frequent subject of Stubbs's painting, as it was of animal painting in general). The doe's eyes appear to plead directly with us to intervene, while the placid expression of the gamekeeper points to a tension typical in Stubbs between the apparent naturalism of the scene and its animal life, and the posed or artificial look of the humans in it (who, unlike the animals, presumably do actually pose for Stubbs). Moreover, simply by looking up at us the gamekeeper appears to want to remind us that what he is doing is simply and only a job – he is culling the herd for his master in order to maintain its health (so that, not incidentally, the master may continue to hunt it with his hounds). Inasmuch as the painting creates sympathy for the deer in its dying moment, it allows us to anthropomorphize the suffering of the deer, and at the same time to question the nature of that anthropomorphizing. Indeed, the gaze and pose of the deer are not at all unlike that of the dying warrior or woman in many classical paintings, lying not quite horizontally, eyes supplicatingly towards a higher power, who in this case is the human viewer. The painting's style invites grand emotion, while its topic seems to deny it.

In fact, the painting's extraordinary ambiguity neatly puts it at the centre of two different controversies of the era in such a way as to appeal to audiences on both sides of both debates. The most inflamed of the controversies had to do not with the cruelty of hunting (which I shall return to below), but with the control of hunting. The Game Laws, first written in 1671, prohibited all hunting of game except by landowners. The aim of these laws, beside the obvious one of preserving game so that the wealthiest would always have something to hunt, was also, according to Steven Deuchar, to keep guns out of the hands of the lower classes (79ff). Equally important, the laws were a way of strengthening the very act of 'owning' land. Not only did landholders own the soil and stones and trees, but they had rights to whatever animal happened to wander onto their property. The wild products of nature were effectively made property by these laws, which ran directly counter to the much older belief that the fruits of nature, particularly game, were made for everyone to exploit. Thus at the centre of opposition to the Game Laws was the common understanding that nature was in some way defined by wild animals. These animals were thus seen as a sort of 'public' property, to be hunted for food by anyone. By the time of Stubbs's painting, opposition to the Game Laws had reached a height. Poaching was considered a right by many of the working class, and wealthy Londoners considered that all forms of hunting ought to be a privilege open to them as well.[4] The controversy put the gamekeeper in a peculiar and uncomfortable position. He was a symbol of the country gentleman's right of ownership, and, moreover, was a mere labourer with rights that otherwise only these gentleman had. To all those whom the Game Laws had turned into poachers or poachers-in-waiting, the gamekeeper was the real poacher. This animosity was supported by the fact that the black market for game was largely supplied by gamekeepers. These tensions are neatly captured by the irony of the fact that the gamekeeper's name – foregrounded in the title – is 'Freeman.'

For the patron of Stubbs's painting, on the other hand, the work presents an image of the gamekeeper as efficient and boldly indifferent, and it emphasizes the duty of the responsible landowner, even when it is unpleasant, to maintain the health of the herd by culling it. The image also speaks of the generosity of the earl who allows himself and his interests to be represented by one of his servants. To the public who could buy the print of the composition, however, the painting suggests that the gamekeeper, who appears to be alone in the woods at night, is a poacher. His look of indifference becomes one of explicit insolence. He is only a servant, and yet he is able to hunt; the Game Laws have put him in a situation in which he is exceeding his station in life; his affectation is perhaps suggested by the way his gun is posed on his hat. To the non-landholding viewer, nature in the painting appears wild and free, as represented in the dark and foreboding background. There is, moreover, no sign of ownership here, and the animal's anguish in death, and the hound's apparent sympathy for it, suggest that the gamekeeper and his actions are somehow contrary to nature and to natural sympathy. The fact of culling itself would surely have been seen as a painfully obvious reason to liberalize game laws by those who opposed them; landowners have so many deer that they brutally eliminate excess. A legitimate source of food, and possibly excitement, is explicitly wasted.

The controversy over the ownership of game highlights for us the way that an animal painting can point to politically opposed ideas of nature. For those who commissioned paintings by Stubbs, for instance, the animals painted, whether highly bred horses or the animals of the hunt, represented the country gentleman's control over nature; he is revealed as being comfortably atop an apparently natural hierarchy. It is not hard to imagine that, like the actual animal itself, the painting conferred on its owner a sense of possessing the energy, grace, and power of the original.

What makes Stubbs's paintings distinctive, however, and what makes them noteworthy in a study of the representation of animals in romanticism, is that they also very often attempt to render the animal as strange, distant, and 'other' than its would-be owner. That is, they represent animals as having an energy and presence *not* possessed or even understood by the humans around them. Paradoxically, this is achieved by attempting to give the animals expression, by painting them as possessing and communicating emotion, which we might recognize as a form of anthropomorphizing. They are made to look different, that is, by making them look remotely human; they seem different from what we perhaps expect, because they suddenly seem somewhat like *us*, instantly blurring in the minds of their viewers hierarchies and distinctions as old as the Bible. This is especially remarkable because in eighteenth-century England most animal painting was stiff and two-dimensional. The opposition of animal naturalness to human woodenness occurs in nearly all of Stubbs's paintings that show humans and animals together. Without exception, the animals in these paintings have expressions which reveal real intensity, fear, courage, or sympathy, while the humans are stiff, placid, and relatively indifferent to those around them. (Notable examples include *The Grosvenor Hunt* [1762], *Lord Grosvenor's Arabian* [1765], *Gimcrack on Newmarket Heath* [1765], and *Warren Hastings* [1791].) To begin to allow animals expression in this way, even to raise the issue of anthropomorphizing, is also to begin to entertain the possibility that animals can be considered to exist as individuals, to possess some kind of consciousness and self-consciousness, or, more simply, to be subjects.

This apparent bias towards animals brings us to the second controversy which the *Freeman* painting highlights or exploits. That is, this painting too is clearly capable of arousing its viewers to feel sympathy for the animal suffering by the hand of man. By 1800 Stubbs could not have been unfamiliar with the debate concerning cruelty to animals, especially suffering caused by hunting. That it was possible to be cruel to animals was not in itself a new idea (Plutarch, Pythagoras, Montaigne, and St Francis, and, less famously, Margaret Newcastle had all written against cruelty to animals), but the late eighteenth century gave rise to the organized movement against cruelty, which attempted to define precisely what cruelty to animals would be, and introduced the more radical idea that non-human animals could have rights. The history of this movement has been the subject of considerable recent research by such historians as Harriet Ritvo, James Turner, and Keith Thomas, and there is not space to rehearse it here.[5] It will suffice for my purpose to note that the first laws against cruelty to animals were passed in England in 1822, and that the debate existed so visibly that, by the 1830s (when the RSPCA was formed), to advocate laws on the behalf of animals ceased to be considered the work of revolutionaries or madmen. For some the idea of eliminating cruelty to animals was a consuming passion, but for many others a concern for animal welfare was a self-evident extension of moral sympathy. To give just a few examples: William Hogarth's engravings *The Four Stages of Cruelty* (1751) depict the origins of a murderer in the tormenting of animals; Samuel Johnson wrote in the *Idler* against vivisection; James Thomson's *The Seasons* argues in favour of vegetarianism and against hunting, as does Cowper's *The Task*; in *Emile*, Rousseau preaches vegetarianism as a way of countering widespread cruelty to animals; in his *Dictionary*, Voltaire attacks Descartes's argument that animals were mere machines; and in a footnote made famous by animal liberationists, Bentham in his *Introduction to the Principles of Morals and Legislation* (1780) argues that animals must be accorded certain rights simply because they, like humans, can suffer pain.[6] Even Linnaeus, whose system of classification might be seen to buttress the idea of a hierarchy of species, defines the animal kingdom as those beings that 'have feelings.'[7] As Deuchar argues (45–62), the painting of hunting scenes enjoyed a kind of renaissance in the mid-eighteenth century, and one reason was that such paintings were designed to give hunting credibility and respect as a pastime for gentlemen, since in the (urban) public mind it was not associated primarily with nobility and vigour, but with drunkenness, rowdiness, and prodigality. By 1790, however, opposition to hunting had come to include the argument that it was cruel to the animal.

One would have expected, then, that in painting a picture commissioned by a landholder, Stubbs would have avoided scenes of animal suffering and possible cruelty. That Stubbs risked showing hunting (or the maintenance of a herd for hunting) in an unglamorous light suggests again that he had a fine sense for appealing to all possible audiences. Pro-hunting viewers could see in the painting simply the realism of the act, which confers upon them a sense of their understanding of and proximity to nature's inescapable violence. For these same viewers any sympathy for the animal which the painting seems to invite is to be overcome (Freeman's bold gaze seems almost to demand it) or simply ignored, just as such sympathy must be suppressed in the act of hunting itself, written off as the product of a new and artificial sentimentality which encouraged the belief that animals could feel. Moreover, pro-hunting viewers could easily take comfort in the still widely held and orthodox belief that animals could not feel fear or even pain, that hunting was simply and purely an act of exercising a god-given right to 'harvest' nature's diverse bounty. Hunting confirmed our place at the top of a carnivorous chain of being. Indeed, in general during this period, representations of hunting (including those by Stubbs) frequently capture the moment of the kill, presumably to display the prowess and power of the hunter, and to draw attention to precisely the moment of the hunt which was to be understood as important and natural. Nervousness on the part of hunters about killing, one would think, would lead to the suppression of representations of this act (which is generally true in most popular representations of hunting today), and celebration instead of the chase, or the preparation. As the end of the elaborate ritual that hunting often became, killing was glorified precisely because it seemed to stand for some moment or act well beyond ritual and cultural significance. It betokened contact with something primary and natural. Killing could thus become simply an end in itself. For instance, one Colonel T. Thornton, author of very expensively produced travelogue entitled *A Sporting Tour through the Northern Parts of England, and Great Parts of the Highlands of Scotland*, describes in extraordinary, tedious, and ultimately comic detail (and with elaborately reproduced prints) the sheer volume of animals of all kinds killed during each day of his hunting travels. Thornton and his companions seem to have shot, fished, and netted anything that moved; a typical day's outing of simultaneous hunting and fishing (a technique Thornton is clearly quite proud of developing, done from a boat, with dogs on shore) yielded six ducks, three sea-gulls, one scart (a cormorant), one raven, as well as fifty-seven trout and ninety-four perch, with 'a sea-eagle narrowly missed' (43).[8]

If the work of Stubbs raises the issue of anthropomorphizing without answering it, or by playing to both sides of it, we can find within romantic poetry a serious attempt to confront the issue directly. Poets like John Clare, Robert Burns, the early Coleridge, and Wordsworth raise the possibility that it is the concept of anthropomorphism itself that is at fault. In seeing signs of subjectivity in animals, we are not necessarily projecting human qualities onto them, but recognizing in them natural attributes which we share with them. Writing this sympathy off as merely the projection of human characteristics – which the very introduction of the concept of anthropomorphism has the effect of doing – errs not only in its underestimation of animal being but also in its extraordinary exaggeration and deification of human being. One of the effects of this anthropocentrism is to cut us off from animality, and perhaps nature as a whole, to turn it into a mechanical realm which we imagine ourselves fully capable of controlling and manipulating. The romantic poets provide us with early textual examples of what Margot Norris has called a 'biocentric' imagination, one which attempts to collapse the 'cardinal distinctions between animal and human.' More radically, such a biocentric vision aims not simply to justify feeling *for* animals, but to open up the potential for feeling *like* animals. Animal life is seen as possessing a purity of desire, a fullness and self-sufficiency, that humans lack. As Norris explains, there is a 'difference in natural and cultural ontology: the animal's desire is direct and appropriative while the human's is mediated and directed toward the recognition of the "other"; the animal's natural power is sufficient for its kind while the human's biological power is inadequate to capture recognition and achieve prestige and must be supplemented by signifiers and symbols; the animal is autotelic and lives for itself in the fullness of its being while the cultural man lives in imitation of the desire of the "other," driven by his *manque-à-être*; the animal surrenders to biological fate and evolutionary destiny while the human disregards the physicality of what is and reads his fate in the gaze of the "other."'[9]

To say that romanticism questions the prohibition against conceiving animal sentience will perhaps seem surprising to those critics who, with Geoffrey Hartman, have interpreted its 'return to nature' as enacting primarily the discovery of individual human consciousness, as well as those who, with Hartman's historicist critics, argue that this return effects only an escape from social and historical awareness. As Bate suggests (*Romantic Ecology*, 55–7) for both Hartman and his critics nature is a cultural fiction which allows for an artificial and remote space where the self may become, or appear to become, independent and self-actualized. To find, or perhaps rediscover, the biocentric strain in English romanticism, let us turn to some examples.

Robert Burns wrote a number of animal poems, including 'The Auld Farmer's New-year-morning Salutation,' the anti-hunting poem 'On Seeing a Wounded Hare,' and the more famous 'To a Mouse.' The stark contrast of man and the 'Wee, sleekit, cow'rin, tim'rous beastie' in this last poem will perhaps initially be read as the comic and naïve thinking of its narrator's peasant persona, the point of which is to disarm sophisticated criticism of the homey saw at the poem's conclusion that 'foresight may be vain: / The best laid schemes o' mice an' men / Gang aft a-gley' (ll. 38–40).[10] But we can also read the poem as an attempt abruptly to undermine our sophisticated and immediate sense that the travails of a mouse are not worthy poetic matter. Most of the poem's readers, then and now, think of mice as vermin, pathetically small scavengers. The poem bluntly invites the reader to put herself into the position of one who has spontaneous sympathy for the mouse, to imagine briefly the thoughts of the speaker, who is in turn capable of imagining the world of the mouse and so is able to be

>   truly sorry man's dominion
> Has broken Nature's social union,
> An' justifies that ill opinion
>   Which makes thee startle
> At me, thy poor earth-born companion,
>   An' fellow mortal.   (ll. 7–12)

Anthropomorphism here is either muted by, or made to seem identical to, the process of adopting the perspective of the peasant narrator. This has double implications, especially since, as Keith Thomas explains, part of the rhetoric of social domination by one class of humans over others has always included portraying the masses as animals that needed to be controlled or domesticated (45–6). The poem suggests an uncomfortable analogy between the narrator's compassion for the mouse and the reader's compassion for the narrator or for peasant-farmers in general. Readers perhaps initially recoil at the realization that they have in some way reduced peasants to mice (what we might call the trick of the poem), assuming them to live blindly in the present, buffeted by fate, just as the narrator describes the mouse in the final stanza of the poem. The way out of this bind is to do as the narrator does, which is momentarily to invert the hierarchy – to imagine and even celebrate the life of the animal as sharing a root identity with humans in nature (here simply the struggle to live). The final effect of this is to reforge 'nature's social union' to include animals, as well as all classes of humans, into the realm of what we might simply call life that is to be respected.

If Burns represents an early example of a romantic interest in animals, John Clare represents its culmination. It is impossible to read through even a sampling of the poetry of John Clare without being struck by how his concern for the rural poor (figured very often by the poet himself) parallels his concern for animal life. Both are classes of beings whose welfare is ignored by the oppressive classes that own and increasingly occupy the land they live on. Yet the sheer volume of poems on animal life, and the continuous harassment of that life by these same working poor, attests finally to the independence of Clare's interest in detailing the life of the animals around him. Recent critics have focused on both the ideological and ecological significance of Clare's particular attachment to Helpston and Northamptonshire, but only James McKusick and Johanne Clare have really emphasized Clare's exploration and representation of animal life. No poet in English has written such consistently fine poetry on such a wide range of creatures. Of course Clare, like Gilbert White, is a kind of naturalist who documents his affinity with the specific 'natural habitat' of his own life by transforming his observations of the natural world into both poetry and prose. The nature of this affinity is captured in the range of Clare's anthropomorphism, which displays a striking unselfconsciousness in speaking for features of landscape as well as animals. Johanne Clare (174ff.) suggests that Clare's descriptions of animals, particularly birds, are not so much about projecting human consciousness onto them as they are a deliberate borrowing of animal attributes (particularly solitariness and freedom) for the poet's sense of self. I am going to reserve a fuller discussion of some of Clare's anthropomorphic poems for a later chapter, in a slightly different context, but it needs to be pointed out here how Clare's near obsession with animal life is in many ways the climactic moment of this interest within romantic-period writing. Part of the myth of Clare as a peasant poet is of his isolation from literary culture, with his interest in animality more or less coinciding with the decade preceding the formation of the RSPCA. But the relative success of his poetry has no doubt much to do with the receptiveness of British readers at the time to accounts of nature and rural life in general, and of animal being in particular, that had in part been stoked by the earlier romantics, as well as by the burgeoning of a populist natural history (inspired by the likes of Gilbert White as much as Linnaeus) to which Clare saw himself contributing.

Be that as it may, Clare's poetry is important for its consistent interest in revealing animal subjectivity, making his readers aware of its myriad forms, and inculcating respect for its 'privacy,' as he stresses how hidden and remote this subjectivity generally is to human observers. Poems like 'The Marten,' 'The Fox,' 'The Badger,' and 'The Hedgehog,' for instance, coolly document how these animals are harassed, hunted, tortured, and killed by 'boys and men.' The cruelty is plain, but is not satirized or explicitly commented upon; it is accepted, it seems, as the natural behaviour of rural folk (as in 'The Fox') and of the urban poor as well, who bring the badger to the 'noisy streets' to be baited. Human cruelty is presented as merely characteristic behaviour, as is that of the animals, who feign death, attack when they can, and try above all to escape. The cruelty indeed serves in these poems (and almost all the animal and bird poems in which humans harass animals) to highlight the intelligence, courage, and inherent nobility of these animals, who cling to life, and their particular place in nature, as fiercely as any human could. They continue to struggle for their lives even in the face of non-stop brutality, as is the case for the badger, whose capture and successive baitings are described over some forty lines. Here is the final verse-paragraph of the description:

> The frighted women takes the boys away
> The blackguard laughs and hurrys on the fray
> He trys to reach the woods a awkward race
> But sticks and cudgels quickly stop the chace
> He turns agen and drives the noisey crowd
> And beats the many dogs in noises loud
> He drives away and beats them every one
> And then they loose them all and set them on
> He falls as dead and kicked by boys and men
> Then starts and grins and drives the crowd agen
> Till kicked and torn and beaten out he lies
> And leaves his hold and cackles groans and dies.   (246)[11]

The passage, and these poems, are more subtle than they perhaps appear.

One is repeatedly struck in reading them of the oddness of the topic *for* poetry. The descriptions seem nearly clinical in the repetitiveness of the struggle. What is celebrated though, honoured by being elaborated in poetry, is the grim determination of a single animal, whose only desire is to exist away from human interference. The narrative here is simply tragic. In the other poems I mention above, the climax is the escape of the animal, figured not just as fleeing from human pursuers but also as returning to the den (though in 'The Hedgehog' the hunting continues – 'And no one cares and still the strife goes on' [248]). These animals escape not just physical abuse but also the poet's gaze, and they return, in a sense, to themselves. The predominant trope in Clare's poetry of mammals and birds is of their desire to remain hidden. As Elizabeth K. Helsinger suggests, 'to be unseen, in these poems, is to remain "unknown to wrong" ("The Nightingales Nest") where "wrong" is equated with the reduction to a possession that seeing can symbolize' (251). What is celebrated in Clare – not so much in any one poem as in the accumulation of them – is the ability of living beings to preserve their individual connections to the natural world, which is the peace of genuine privacy.

In Clare's poetry about human life as well, peace is the ability to hold one's place, to be secure in a secluded spot. It is a profound ecological and ideological insight to see that this peace is an ideal not just of the rural poor whose place in the land is threatened by enclosure, but also of the animals whose homes are shown in Clare's poetry in danger of being usurped by hunters, farmers, and curious seekers. (One rarely encounters animal predation in the poetry, except that of dogs; in 'The Marten,' an owl defends the harassed marten, to be 'Left free from boys and dogs and noise and men.') This concern for the privacy of animals is an integral part of any understanding of their ability to have rights – not just to be legitimate objects of our sympathy, but to be thought capable of 'possessing' the 'homes,' they inhabit on the land (figured tirelessly by Clare in his descriptions of nests and dens). These 'hidden homes,' as he calls them (in 'The Woodlarks Nest'), are 'as safe as secresy,' signs of animals' deliberate intelligence and their desire to remain undisturbed. The homes suggest the sanctity of their ability to enjoy themselves in nature, just as Clare's far less numerous poems protesting the demise of a rural way of life are nostalgic for a time when rural lands provided stable environments for human domestic happiness. Moreover, the sense he develops of what is lost as Helpston's commons are enclosed – of the secluded places where he could be alone, watching and enjoying the life around him – is what he leaves relatively unexplored in the animal life he documents. That is, he presents animal life in a such a way that we feel that he is continually recognizing himself to be a potential interloper in their affairs. Rather than supposing what their actual happiness might consist of (all we know from his poems is that it is domestic, birds singing for mates and mothers taking care of their young), Clare typically reminds us instead of the threats even seemingly innocent passers-by can pose; thus the reed bird's nest is

> hid in thickest shade
> Where danger never finds a path to throw
> A fear on comforts nest securely made
> In woods of reeds round which the waters flow
> Save by a jelted stone that boys will throw,
> Or passing rustle of the fishers boat. (235)

Certainly, as McKusick argues, Clare's interest in animal lives comes in part from his vicarious enjoyment of (or longing for) qualities he ascribes to them, like the moorhens' ability to 'dive and dare and every gambol trie' from the safety of their nest in the 'bare roots' of an 'aged tree,' 'Till they themselves to other scenes can fly' (221), which speaks tellingly of Clare's simultaneous homelessness and confinement. Yet no matter how Clare implicitly or explicitly sets up animal life as a kind of counter-reality to his own, these poems document an extraordinary sensitivity to animal being which justifies our sense that in the romantic period animals were beginning to be seen as independent, conscious, and capable of possessing rights.

What Roderick Nash has described in *The Rights of Nature* as the progressive expansion of natural rights to include not only oppressed classes of humans but also animals specifically and nature in general was not an unknown strain of revolutionary thought as early as the late eighteenth century. The idea was that a truly reformed society would liberate not only unenfranchised people but also oppressed and exploited animals. There were several publications during this period which called attention to the plight of animals, and these are undoubtedly a source for Shelley's similar arguments in his vegetarian tracts published over a decade later. Both Thomas Paine and Mary Wollstonecraft reflect an occasional interest in animal welfare in their writings on societal change. As the radical vegetarian John Oswald wrote in 1791, since the 'barbarous governments of Europe' were 'giving way to a better system of things … the day is beginning to approach when the growing sentiment of peace and goodwill towards men will also embrace, in a wide circle of benevolence, the lower orders of life' (Thomas, 185).

It is in this spirit, certainly, that Coleridge wrote his poem 'To a Young Ass,' which presents the poet's encounter with a chained ass and her foal. The asses are described as being part of 'an oppressed race,' and the bulk of the poem is given to a description of the speaker's sympathy for the plight of animals who are made miserable by overwork and neglect. Like Robert Burns and John Clare, Coleridge connects the fate of animals to the fate of the working poor, and the poem ends with an explicit comparison of the animals' imagined owner with the asses themselves:

> Poor Ass! thy master should have learnt to show
> Pity – best taught by fellowship of Woe!
> For much I fear me that He lives like thee,
> Half famished in a land of Luxury!
> How askingly its footsteps hither bend,
> It seems to say, 'And have I then one Friend?'
> Innocent Foal! thou poor despised Forlorn!
> I hail thee Brother – spite of the fool's scorn!
> And fain would take thee with me, in the Dell
> Of Peace and mild Equality to dwell,
> Where Toil shall call the charmer Health his bride,
> And Laughter tickle Plenty's ribless side!
> How thou wouldst toss thy heels in gamesome play,
> And frisk about, as lamb or kitten gay!
> Yea! and more musically sweet to me
> Thy dissonant harsh bray of joy would be,
> Than warbled melodies that soothe to rest
> The aching of pale Fashion's vacant breast.   (ll. 19–36)[12]

The plight of animals in the poem can easily be read simply as an allegory for the situation of the working masses in England, a topic which it would have been dangerous for Coleridge to write about explicitly in 1794. Yet the plight of the poor is made relatively explicit; the speaker fears that the asses' master 'lives like thee, / Half famished in a land of Luxury!' (ll. 21–2). These lines suggest that the poem's sympathy for the foal is to be taken literally, as an example of the poet's (not unproblematic) spirit of compassion and egalitarianism that fired his early zeal for the Revolution and his utopian scheme for a Pantisocracy. As Richard Holmes has suggested, we can find in Coleridge's sympathy for animals an early source for his idea of the 'one life within us and abroad,' a sense that individual spirit is reflected or circumscribed by a spirit of and in nature (*Coleridge*, 81–2). We are always ready to think of this later idea Platonically, that the 'one life' is an abstraction sensed or understood only by the deepest inward reflection (an idea which is indeed encouraged by 'Eolian Harp' and much other writing by Coleridge on the topic), but the early poem encourages us to take seriously the possibility that the idea of a conscious spirit in nature is made literally present in signs of consciousness in animals. So in 'To a Young Ass' the speaker unabashedly imagines in detail the spirit of the foal, now diminished by a society increasingly cut off from nature, and as Harriet Ritvo demonstrates, notoriously abusive to animals and the poor alike.[13] The 'Dell of Peace' is Edenic, nature returned to an imagined pre-industrial state in which every spirit would, like the foal, take spontaneous pleasure in its natural setting.

The utopianism of the poem will still appear to most of us, no doubt, as embarrassingly naïve. Certainly Coleridge was ridiculed for the poem when it appeared, and became the obvious target of much satire. Yet the poem is a strong sign of how his thinking about nature and animals begins. Coleridge did write a few more poems that include significant references to animals. One of these is 'The Nightingale,' a poem about how to ascribe meaning to the apparent sentience of a bird. Of course, the poem is also a meditation on the process of interpreting external signs in general, of creating symbols, and of understanding the (im)possibility of spontaneity within the form of the lyric. Yet this meditation takes the form of a debate over the nature of anthropomorphizing; the speaker wants to know the song's meaning for what it is, and not project onto it the melancholy of literary tradition. The bird in the poem, and, indeed, in all of the great bird poems of the English romantic tradition, is itself part of the 'presence' of nature, a sign that consciousness can be something other than human. Nature in these poems is neither impenetrable nor entirely material, but contains 'a Life, a Presence like the Air,' as Wordsworth puts it in 'The Green Linnet.' While animals are never equivalent to the totality of the 'spirit' in nature which Wordsworth, Shelley, and Coleridge at their most idealistic strive to know, they are at least the most palpable sign of its existence.

Indeed, the romantic gesture of putting the self into nature, of sensing that individual consciousness is a part of a larger spirit, seems to have roots in, or is at least reflected by, the undermining of the hubris of anthropocentrism. In 'The Nightingale,' and even in such poems as Shelley's 'To a Skylark' and Keats's 'Ode to a Nightingale,' which are much more explicit in their desire to transform the bird into a symbol for something human or suprahuman, the song of the bird is the immediate evidence of other life that can take the poet beyond the confines of his life and his art, allowing him to understand an ideal process in which the poet would, as Coleridge writes in 'The Nightingale,'

> have stretched his limbs
> Beside a brook in mossy forest-dell,
> By sun or moon-light, to the influxes
> Of shapes and sounds and shifting elements
> Surrendering his whole spirit. (ll. 25–9)

Loving nature, or knowing it, has as a preliminary requirement the realization that there *is* life beyond human life that is worth considering.

In the light of such evidence for Coleridge's early thoughts on animal consciousness (noting that, as with most ideas in Coleridge, the complete evidence is far from consistent),[14] it is possible to offer new insight into the most famous 'animal poem' of the period, *The Rime of the Ancient Mariner*. The poem is revered because, like 'Kubla Khan,' it is so rich. Most contemporary readers have given up the search for a single and complete interpretation of the poem, arguing that it self-consciously confounds the very idea of singularity. The reading that most of us will find the least satisfactory is the one that is most obvious, the one that first-time readers of the poem will often turn to as a way of giving meaning to the poem's weird narrative. That is, the poem can be understood as an elaborate and ornamental account of the wanton killing of an innocent and noble creature and the rightful (if extreme) punishment of the Mariner for this act. The poem is to teach, as the prose gloss tells us, 'love and reverence to all things that God made and loveth,' a moral made equally explicit in the final stanzas:

> Farewell, farewell! but this I tell
> To thee, thou Wedding-Guest!
> He prayeth well, who loveth well
> Both man and bird and beast.
>
> He prayeth best, who loveth best
> All things both great and small;
> For the dear God who loveth us,
> He made and loveth all. (ll. 610–17)

The homily is dissatisfying because it seems incommensurate both with the punishment the Mariner endures for his crime of killing the bird, and with the self-consciousness of the poem's symbolism. Most of us, I think, either ignore these lines of the poem, or read them as a sign that the Mariner has not yet grasped the full significance (even the horrifying significance) of his story. The poem provokes us because of the ease with which we can convert the bird, and the apparently unmotivated act of killing it, into symbols for far larger and more profound themes, so that, for instance, the albatross becomes a symbol for Christ, or the act of killing it an act of defiant (and romantic) heroism; or the poem as a whole becomes a deliberately uninterpretable object, the careful reading of which brings us vividly before unresolvable questions about the nature of sin and guilt and knowledge. In short, none of us would accept that the poem is really about hunting.

And yet I would like to propose that it is possible to read the poem as an 'animal' or anti-cruelty poem, one which allows us to take its proffered moral seriously. Indeed, it seems to me that the strangeness of the poem, its deliberate supernaturalness, can in part be taken as a strategy for making unfamiliar – and thereby allowing us to reconsider – a moral that would be found merely childish by the majority of its readers. Moreover, the supernatural aspects of the tale – the details of the voyage, the spirits which direct the ship and the punishments of the narrator – have the effect of blurring the boundaries between human and non-human in both directions of the traditional hierarchy. The reversal we saw in Stubbs's painting is apparent in this poem too; the imagery throughout appears bent on making humans appear beastlike, strange in appearance, and driven to behaviour by instinct and compulsion, while aspects of the natural world appear to possess human or godlike consciousness. The Mariner's drive to tell his tale seems almost reflexive, and he is often described as appearing beastlike and strange; he is called a 'loon' (l. 11) (meaning both bird and madman) and is described as being 'long, and lank and brown' (l. 226) by the Wedding-Guest (who himself 'beat[s] his breast,' attempting to break free of the hold of the tale). Likewise, his strange appearance frightens the Pilot and the Hermit.

The most dramatically strange and consistent feature of the poem is the degree to which nature is personified. *Every* aspect of nature – from the sun and moon and wind to the ice and the currents – is inspirited, described as a conscious entity who appears to choose to behave as it does. Examples abound: 'The sun came up upon the left, / Out of the sea came he' (ll. 25–6); 'And now the storm-blast came, and he / Was tyrannous and strong; / He struck with his o'er-taking wings, / And chased us south along' (ll. 41–4). The poem is a *tour de force* indulgence of the so-called pathetic fallacy. That nature is imbued with spirit is made to seem an increasingly literal truth in the poem, the overwhelming effect of which is to make humanity appear frail and small. Another effect is to make less strange the idea of the spirited albatross, and its apparent connection to the rest of nature (the sailors think it is responsible for the weather, a superstition which the poem makes terrifyingly real). Because the poem can make us believe that spirit is everywhere, we accept too that the Mariner's blessing of the water-snakes is a significant moment, even if it does not end his punishment. The poem encourages us to suspend disbelief so that we may engage in the speculation that nature is spirit as humans are. We may then bless and find beauty in all living things as the Mariner does. The poem boldly asserts that human spirit is animal spirit, as implied too in the stunning moment when the spirits of the sailors seem to be transformed into birds:

> For when it dawned – they dropped their arms,
> And clustered round the mast;
> Sweet sounds rose slowly through their mouths,
> And from their bodies passed.
>
> Around, around, flew each sweet sound,
> Then darted to the Sun;
> Slowly the sounds came back again,
> Now mixed, now one by one.
>
> Sometimes a-dropping from the sky
> I heard the sky-lark sing;
> Sometimes all little birds that are,
> How they seemed to fill the sea and air
> With their sweet jargoning! (ll. 350–62)

By the end of the poem we are to believe, if only momentarily, that to kill an albatross is to kill a spirit, to offend all of nature. Even if this is an idea that will not survive the cold light of reason, the poem has perhaps made us unsure of the traditional distinctions between human and beast and angel, which may help us to understand nature not as culminating in human consciousness, but as filled with other kinds of being.

Coleridge conceived of his greatest contribution to *Lyrical Ballads* as pursuing the same ends as those of his collaborator, which include conveying the 'truth of nature,' and 'the loveliness and the wonders of the world before us' (*Biographia Literana*, 2:5, 7). In the poetry of Wordsworth, like that of Clare, we can find animals consistently represented as sympathetic beings, to be considered both as a means to an awareness of spirit in nature and as sentient beings that are ends in themselves. As I have already noted, in book 2 of *The Excursion* Wordsworth matter-of-factly praises the Wanderer's recognition of the 'rights' of animals. Although the possibility that animals had rights seems to extend naturally from the pre-Revolutionary rhetoric of the rights of man and woman, it was a step taken by relatively few (including, most notably, Bentham).[15] Indeed, most who wrote in favour of humane treatment of animals did so with the explicit premise that humans are far superior to animals, and that cruelty to animals needs to be avoided primarily because it reflects poorly on our moral supremacy. As far as I know, Wordsworth does not explicitly refer to 'rights' of animals anywhere else in his prose or poetry. Yet the fact that he mentions it at all ought to alert us to the possibility that his love of nature includes a specific concern for animals, and is not immediately or primarily an abstraction – a figure for a deity, or an antidote to (and thus an idea circumscribed by) culture.

Much of Wordsworth's poetry about animals is not often read, probably because it appears sentimental. Such is the case, for instance, with 'The Pet Lamb: A Pastoral,' composed in 1800 and published in the edition of the *Lyrical Ballads* of that year. It records the poet's encounter with a young girl and her tethered pet lamb, whom she has just fed. The girl begins to leave the lamb, but is stopped by its plaintive cries. She turns back to the lamb with an expression so filled with beauty and compassion that the narrator imagines what she might say 'If Nature to her tongue could measured numbers bring' (l. 19). The device is awkward and unusually artificial for a poet keen on representing the authenticity of others' voices. Yet the poem foregrounds the act of the poet imagining the love of the child for her lamb, which is very like the child's imagined speculation on what ails the lamb.

> Poor creature, can it be
> That 'tis thy mother's heart which is working so in thee?
> Things that I know not of belike to thee are dear,
> And dreams of things which thou canst neither see nor hear.
> (*PW*, 1:246, ll. 49–52)

The acts of both the poet and the child are a kind of anthropomorphism, the projection of spirit and feeling. But the child's love for the lamb is spontaneous and sincere, and in the context of Wordsworth's understanding of the holiness of childhood is a sign of her spiritual ascendancy. She demonstrates a primal sympathy with nature that adults have lost, but which the poet regains through her. (In this sense, the poem is very like 'Anecdote for Fathers' and 'We Are Seven,' which attempt a similar recovery of childhood imagination.)

Indeed, the child here serves to negate the possibility of mere projection. That children love and sense the 'humanness' of animals is for Wordsworth the discovery of something that is real and fundamental, rather than a delusion of anthropomorphism (which is nonetheless how most adults react to children's feelings towards animals). That the child's sympathy is expressed through a love for a lamb will perhaps seem accidental, or will resonate as being primarily symbolic – the lamb represents Christian innocence and purity that the child shares. But to leap into the interpretive habits of adult consciousness is to miss the point in Wordsworth's poems about children. We have first to recognize the unselfconsciousness of the child's behaviour (even as we do so through the self-consciousness of the adult narrator), which is evidence for the existence of a primal sympathy with the spirit of nature that grows dim with the development of self-consciousness.

Such poems as 'To a Butterfly' or 'The Kitten and the Falling Leaves' represent a similar relation between children and animals. The most profound of these is 'There Was a Boy,' which poignantly juxtaposes an account of the boy, who 'Blew mimic hootings to the silent owls, / That they might answer him' (*PW*, 2:206), and the description of the adult speaker standing mute over the boy's grave. Hartman's classic reading of the poem as I argued in the previous chapter, emphasizes its figurativeness, how its two episodes display Wordsworth's memory of 'the shock of self-consciousness.' Such a reading perhaps leaps to the second verse-paragraph too quickly, ignoring the uncanniness of the owls' 'responsive' hooting. Their mimicry of the boy, and the silence which follows, have the effect of suddenly expanding the boy's awareness to the entire scene around him, and are palpable but haunting signs of a consciousness in nature that is both like and unlike human being, what Hartman calls a recognition of 'nature's ... separate life' (*Woodsworth's Poetry*, 20). The voices of the owls join the 'jocund din' of the boy's 'mimic hootings' and the 'redoubled' echoes, but they are not the same as the boy's voice – not mere mimicry or echoing. The nature the boy perceives here is not a benign projection, infinitely yielding or comforting to human consciousness. While the silence that follows the hooting may well suggest the utter indifference of a purely material reality – an awareness which I argued in the previous chapter is also one Wordsworth entertains about the natural world – the voices of the owls are a palpable sign of something intermediary, a realm of consciousness in nature which is both starkly different from the poet's own and yet alive and partially responsive in a way that rocks and stones and trees cannot be.

More often, though, Wordsworth's poems about animals depict the narrator engaged directly in the activity of imagining the mind of an animal. The best of these is probably 'The Green Linnet,' though 'To the Cuckoo' and 'To a Skylark' are similar. Also notable are 'Fidelity,' 'Incident Characteristic of a Favourite Dog,' and 'Tribute to the Memory of the Same Dog,' which unabashedly celebrate the apparent humanity of specific dogs. The effect of these poems is to show that the act of sympathy to animal being is not a projection, but a natural and easy perception. A more substantial poem which makes a similar case for the moral importance of a sympathy for animal being is 'Hart-Leap Well,' composed and published in 1800 (*PW*, 2:249–34). As with *Rime of the Ancient Mariner*, criticism of this poem has converted its concern for the death of an animal almost instantly into a relatively abstract sympathy for nature. That is, it is read immediately as primarily figurative, representing what Hartman calls 'Wordsworth's animism, his consciousness of a consciousness in nature, [which] is the last novel superstition of a demythologized mind. All nature-spirits are dissolved by him except the spirit of Nature.'[16] This is no doubt true, but readings of the poem which convert its content to Wordsworth's general theory of nature ignore the fact that the poem is so aware of its figurativeness that we need to be wary of turning the poem into allegory or symbol. The poem is in part about the danger of creating symbols, of how art can be against nature. Indeed, 'Hart-Leap Well' seems to me to be much like 'Simon Lee' in the degree to which it aims to make the reader uncomfortable with the act of figuration. Although the earlier poem is also about a huntsman, 'Hart-Leap Well' aims to inspire a profound sympathy for the hart.

Like 'Simon Lee,' 'Hart-Leap Well' begins confidently and jauntily in the ballad mode, so that the reader expects a celebration of the apparent heroism of Sir Walter's gallant hunt. He rides 'with the slow motion of a summer's cloud,' and mounts another horse, 'the third / Which he had mounted on that glorious day' (ll. 2, 7–8). The hunt is a neat allegory for the narrative thrust of the ballad that Wordsworth exploits in order to frustrate in many of his *Lyrical Ballads*. That is, the end of the hunt is like the expected fulfilment of narrative, the climax that bestows a sense of completeness to the chase itself. The reader is drawn by the thrill of the hunt, and the 'purpose' or moral of the tale, common to ballads. Yet by the fourth stanza the thrill and riotous excitement of the mass hunt have turned already into a solitary, and slightly ominous, pursuit.

> A rout this morning left Sir Walter's Hall,
> That as they galloped made the echoes roar;
> But horse and man are vanished, one and all;
> Such race, I think, was never seen before
>
> ...
>
> Where is the throng, the tumult of the race?
> The bugles that so joyfully were blown?
> This chase it looks not like an earthly chase;
> Sir Walter and the Hart are left alone. (ll. 13–16; 25–8)

The end of the hunt fails to deliver, both for the reader and Sir Walter. What began in joy has come down to the elemental final moments in which the hart must die. Oddly, and again like the narrator of 'Simon Lee,' the narrator here breaks in to announce that he will not describe how the hart dies, but says simply that 'now the Knight beholds him lying dead' (l. 30). Part of the reason for the omission is no doubt to allow Sir Walter to describe in his own words how the hart leapt to his death, so that his celebration of that fact will seem even more isolated, more his responsibility alone; there is also an increasing reluctance on the part of the narrator to share the game of the hunt, or its narrative, which breaks off completely in the second part.

By the ninth stanza, Sir Walter alone searches for the proper and necessary conclusion to the hunt, which in an actual hunt was to be the killing of the stag by the dogs as the riders stood by (as in Stubbs's painting *The Grosvenor Hunt*), an act which was to bestow upon the whole process a meaning that went far beyond the single death of the hart. That Sir Walter is alone is one of his problems. By the mid-eighteenth-century, stag and fox hunting had become 'conspicuous' (to borrow Thorsten Veblen's sense of the word), and explicitly were not regarded as a mere means of putting meat on the table. Hunting (as opposed to 'shooting') amounted to chasing dogs who were chasing game, and so was defined in terms of seeing the kill, and even more, by the hunter being seen as watching the kill. Hunting was in part a public gesture, made explicitly so in painting. As Deuchar explains, the country gentlemen who almost solely formed the hunting class sought to represent hunting as a sport that lent nobility to its participants, one that not only was connected to the historic recreation of kings, but also was virtuous because it was manly and vaguely martial (43–50). Moreover, it represented a kind of return to nature and so could be evidence of a vigorous relationship with the wilderness – much as Isaak Walton's *Compleat Angler* had argued for fishing in the previous century. Hunting was an act of leisure which revealed the physical and spiritual health of the hunter, a man at the top of society who could yet easily descend to and return from an apparently primal activity. This descent also involves an enactment of the supremacy of man over beast, and by extension, nature. There is an uneasiness here between the emphasis on the nobility of the sport and its primal aspects, which is reflected by the very fact that, as we saw with Stubbs, paintings were commissioned by hunters in order to lend to their activity the prestige and gloss of art.

Hunting can easily be seen not as a return to nature but as an abuse of it, yet another way in which man attempts to assert his domination over the natural world. Unlike the Stubbs painting of 'Freeman,' which is deliberately ambiguous about hunting, 'Hart-Leap Well' is clearly a critique – the first part is a parody of hunting and the art which celebrates it. Sir Walter understands the hunt, and particularly the final great leap of the hart, as a sign of his own power and supremacy. That the hart's final act was a great leap is not a sign of *its* vitality or desire to live, nor a sign of a power or spirit in nature that exists independently of humankind, but is for the hunter a spectacle that might be used to signify the hunter's uniqueness: "'Till now / Such sight was never seen by human eyes'" (ll. 55–6). Thus Sir Walter celebrates having seen the kill by building an elaborately artificial 'pleasure-house' and a 'small arbour, made for rural joy,' which are clearly to be monuments to himself and his pursuit of pleasure (and which may remind us of Kubla Khan's more abstract sins against nature). We see in retrospect too that Sir Walter's treatment of his horses (the last of which is initially filled with joy, but is by the end a 'dumb partner') and his dogs (who appear to die of exhaustion) foreshadows his exploitation of the natural world. Hunting as represented here is defined by the absence of sympathy for the being of animals in particular, and nature in general. It is a failure of sympathy and understanding, signified as well by the fact that Sir Walter thinks his monuments will last 'Till the foundations of the mountains fail' (l. 73). Unlike the shepherd and the narrator-poet of the naturalistic second part of the poem, Sir Walter does not feel a connection through the animal to nature as a whole.

The poet and shepherd can easily connect the lifelessness of the site to the sympathy of a Being

> that is in the clouds and air,
> That is in the green leaves among the groves,
> Maintains a deep and reverential care
> For the unoffending creatures whom he loves.   (ll. 165–8)

These are the words of the shepherd, the idealized example of one who lives within nature and understands himself to be a part of it, in contrast to Sir Walter, who defines himself and his art against it. Put simply, the shepherd's relationship with nature is reciprocal, while that of the knight is purely self-interested and exploitative. Unlike the hunter, the shepherd can imagine specifically what might have driven the hart to return to the well, to make the great leap.

> Here on the grass perhaps asleep he sank,
> Lulled by the fountain in the summer-tide;
> This water was perhaps the first he drank
> When he had wandered from his mother's side.
>
> In April here beneath the flowering thorn
> He heard the birds their morning carols sing;
> And he, perhaps, for aught we know, was born
> Not half a furlong from that self-same spring.   (ll. 149–56)

This projecting of human consciousness onto the animal is a version of anthropomorphism. Indeed, as John Hodgson argues, the 'humanity' of the hart is underscored by the resemblance of its death to that of Herbert in *The Borderers* (77). But the force of the poem, the switch from parodied ballad to the more familiar and naturalistic mode of what Frederick Garber has aptly called the 'poetry of encounter,' and the contrast between the egotistical knight and the self-effacing shepherd, work to blur the distinction between projection and what we might call seeing naturally, and, finally, make the act of recognizing the being of an animal a profoundly moral act.

Wordsworth's critique is not a sentimental cry against cruelty to animals, but an assessment of hunting as an act of violence against nature, a failure of the imagination. A neat corollary of this is also a critique of the ballad as encouraging that 'degrading thirst after outrageous stimulation,' which Wordsworth objects to in his *Preface* to *Lyrical Ballads*. As Andrew Griffin has argued for 'Simon Lee,' Wordsworth parodies the ballad form as a kind of narrative that appeals only to the immediate gratification of the reader's desire for sensory delight and explicitly delivered meaning (much like Sir Walter in the hunt). Wordsworth's aim in both poems is to turn narrative into something less predetermined, a process of active sympathy which engages the complexity of another's consciousness. With its moral – 'Never to blend our pleasure or our pride / With sorrow of the meanest thing that feels' (ll. 170–80) – 'Hart-Leap Well' is perhaps more explicit than 'Simon Lee,' because the call in the former poem to recognize the feeling of animals is in itself a challenge to conventional anthropocentrism; it is also a challenge to enact a sympathy as complex and as self-effacing as that which the poet demonstrates for Simon Lee.

Another ballad which can concern us here is *Peter Bell*, which tells of the moral reform of a (socially) humble and thoughtless man through his abuse of an animal. Summarized this way, the poem reminds us of Coleridge's *Rime*. That this specific similarity has received little critical attention is surprising, since the unusual prologue and mawkishly 'humble' story of *Peter Bell*, together with the introductory letter to Southey in which Wordsworth explains that the poem was composed to show that 'the Imagination ... does not require for its exercise the intervention of supernatural agency' (*PW*, 2:331), clearly make the poem a kind of reply to Coleridge. *Peter Bell* has never been popular with critics, in part because it is too faithful to the ballad-form as Wordsworth understood it, and in part because it is too self-consciously a poem that aims for a naturalism opposed to Coleridge's supernaturalism. But while the poem is not particularly subtle or complex, it is surely noteworthy that Peter Bell's villainy is exemplified by his repeated and explicit cruelty to an animal, and that his salvation is brought about by the example of sympathy and virtue provided by the faithful ass. As in 'Hart-Leap Well,' a natural sympathy is demonstrated as developing through a sympathy for animal being, and this sympathy does not simply reflect well on human character, but is part of an enlarged conception of the proper arena of one's affections. Both poems depict a process of recognizing that the individual self is not supreme and isolated and that human consciousness in general is only one species of consciousness among many.

I hope that by now what I have been rather blandly calling Wordsworth's 'concern' for animals will be taken as more than merely a kind of pity. It is a complex sympathy that at once recognizes a deep-rooted commonality between humans and animals, and a respect for the individuality and even incomprehensibility of non-human consciousness. That his idea about animality is not a casual by-product of his reverence for nature but an integral part of it is further suggested by his long poem *The White Doe of Rylstone*. A full-length study of the poem is not warranted here, but it is worth trying to understand both why Wordsworth thought the poem was 'in conception, the highest work he had ever produced,' and how at the same time it demonstrates what he called the 'Apotheosis of the Animal' (*PW*, 3:548, 547). The poem tells the story of the destruction of the Norton clan in an ill-fated rebellion against Elizabeth and the new Anglican church. As John Danby has noted (132–3), the story of the rebellion is subtly handled, capturing both the piety of Norton and its incongruity with his aim of starting a civil war to achieve this end. The story focuses on the passive resistance to his plan by two of his children, Emily and Francis, whose friendship and mutual support is the central bond of the poem. Indeed, it is Francis who, in a scene rife with Freudian implications, explains to Emily where her duty lies now that the rebellion is begun and the death of the entire family certain. Her task is simply to endure and to survive, to continue to live devoutly after Rylstone is destroyed.

> 'If thou art beautiful, and youth
> And thought endue thee with all truth –
> Be strong; – be worthy of the grace
> Of God, and fill thy destined place:
> A Soul, by force of sorrows high,
> Uplifted to the purest sky
> Of undisturbed humanity!'   (ll. 581–7)

Through Emily, the poem celebrates the consolation of a wise indifference to fate, of a consciousness that finds its home in an immanent divinity that reveals the transitory nature of human history (particularly that of sectarian conflict). Like many of the animal poems I have examined, however, this one also flirts with mere sentimentality; the vehicle for the representation of Emily's awareness of what we might call the sympathy of nature is the doe, a pet of her brother's which does not finally return to the forest after the destruction of Rylstone as he had predicted (ll. 560–6), but which comes to Emily, and continues to visit the ruins after she dies.

The appearance of the doe at the beginning and end of the poem suggests the pervading and enduring spirit of the animal, in contrast to the whirlwind events that destroy the male Nortons. The end of the poem insists on the naturalism of the encounter between Emily and the doe, even as it risks preciousness. The doe is not immediately to be taken as figurative; rather, Emily is the one who must interpret its presence, even as it becomes emblematic of her docile stoicism. Wordsworth spends several hundred lines describing the new relationship between the doe and Emily, in which the doe replaces human companionship. Although an 'inferior Creature' (l. 1831), the doe becomes almost human:

> she hath ventured now to read
> Of time, and place, and thought, and deed –
> Endless history that lies
> In her silent Follower's eyes;
> Who with a power like human reason
> Discerns the favourable season,
> Skilled to approach or to retire, –
> From looks conceiving her desire;
> From look, deportment, voice, or mien,
> That vary to the heart within.
> If she too passionately wreathed
> Her arms, or over-deeply breathed,
> Walked quick or slowly, every mood
> In its degree was understood;
> Then well may their accord be true,
> And kindliest intercourse ensue.   (ll. 1714–29)

In one sense, the consolation provided by the animal is simply that of a companion – Emily is, after all, utterly alone. But the doe also brings Emily to an Edenic consciousness in which she is attuned to the being of god everywhere, and takes satisfaction in the immediate fullness of her 'communication' (l. 1829) with the doe. The doe is literally a 'Presence' (l. 1744) that speaks of the larger presence of god.

The apotheosis of the animal in the poem culminates in the alignment of Emily and the doe; both are raised from their ordinary state to one where they are attuned to an apparent unity of being, and which separates them from their own species. Everything is idealized at the end of this poem, which tries hardest of any of Wordsworth's works to find consolation in thoughts of 'undisturbed mortality' (l. 1858), and its naturalism will seem very forced to most readers. Nonetheless, like the other poems I have examined, the awareness of animal being here has the effect of countering the myopic view that humanity is alone among creatures important and sentient. Indeed, true sentience, for Wordsworth, includes first and foremost the ability to sense life beyond merely our own. Emily is consoled because this awareness at once makes her feel part of an apparently natural community, and diminishes the importance of merely human affairs. As Danby writes, 'the Doe points to a super-harmony also into which the human must ultimately incorporate itself. Being is unitary' (142).

While *The White Doe of Rylstone* is Wordsworth's most significant attempt to include a representation of the animal in a poem whose purpose is explicitly to counter a kind of anthropocentrism, it is probably not his most successful. Part of the problem is generic; few readers are likely to see the end of the poem as naturalistic because so much of the rest of the poem insists on being conventional historical tragedy. In contrast to the story of the Nortons, the end will no doubt seem saccharine. It may even seem escapist – we avoid human suffering, it suggests, by turning to a celebration of a more innocent life. This does not mean, however, that the strain of biocentrism I see here, or in romanticism generally, is a version of willed blindness or misanthropy. Such biocentrism is based on enlarging one's sympathy, not undermining it with charges of anthropomorphism. The stark contrast between *The White Doe*'s historic content and its nearly utopian ending is perhaps better seen as a deliberate strategy, not unlike that of 'Simon Lee' and 'Hart-Leap Well,' which also attempt to startle the reader into thought through the uneasy conflation of genres. Tragedy is relentlessly anthropocentric; fate and nature are hostile, and our only consolation lies in recognizing individual nobility, the supremacy of human achievement. The achievement of Wordsworth and the other poets and artists I have examined is to wrench us from this too familiar mode and make us recognize the wider boundaries of life. What the representation of animals in romanticism suggests too is that the conception of nature by individual poets and artists is not entirely a cultural or intellectual construction, but can be seen to begin, and even end, in an awareness for palpably living beings that are not human. By undermining easy distinctions between nature and culture, being and non-being, these artists suggest that it is not so much the cultural construction of nature but rather the construction of a concept of culture that has reified human being to the exclusion of all other life.

III

Shelley's Ideal Body: Vegetarianism, Revolution, and Nature

We have seen in the previous two chapters how investigating nature, developing an openness to its physical presence and complexity, has included an awareness of diversity as a deep property of the natural world which is difficult for us to recognize. This diversity has been approached, in the romantic period, by recognizing the contiguous otherness of animal being, and by recognizing the metaphysical and epistemological difficulties involved in trying to construct an order of things from the data of the physical world. Indeed, the ability of individual writers of the period to think through, to defamiliarize and deconstruct, the established cultural, linguistic, and personal categories of the natural world is my topic throughout the book. In this chapter I wish to pursue a materialism which is in its clearest articulations startlingly holistic; it is evidenced in the romantic period primarily by Shelley, and is characterized primarily by the poet's desire to understand the connections of the self to the world through the body, and not, as in Wordsworth, through imagined and relatively abstract confrontations with death. This version of materialism is developed, by Shelley, through his lifelong interest in diet.

Though the fact that Shelley was a vegetarian for most of his adult life is well known, it has received little serious attention until recent work by Timothy Morton, and an earlier version of this chapter which I wrote before Morton's book was published.[1] This absence of attention is somewhat surprising, since his vegetarianism was for him neither a passing fad, as Neville Rogers has speculated (Shelley, *Complete Poetical Works*, 1:398), nor what we might today call simply a 'lifestyle choice' with little bearing on his intellectual life. Though many scholars continue to find it odd, Shelley understood diet to have important consequences on moral and physical health, and to be a defining feature of our relation to the natural world. Indeed, Shelley took the rationale for the 'vegetable diet,' as it was then called, seriously enough to write two different pamphlets on the subject: *A Vindication of Natural Diet*, which was revised as one of the notes to *Queen Mab*; and the unpublished and slightly more temperate essay *On the Vegetable System of Diet*, written probably a year later, in 1813. Both essays make moral, nutritional, and even what would be recognized today as environmental claims for vegetarianism. *A Vindication*, moreover, became a classic within the loosely related anti-vivisection and vegetarian movements of Victorian England. Nearly all commentators dismiss both essays, however, by citing what they take to be the most astonishing and ridiculous claim of the first essay, that a widespread change of diet 'strikes at the root of all evil,' that vegetarianism would be not simply an incidental part of utopian change but an initial and necessary step to positive and radical reform.

Of those biographers and critics who have not ignored these ideas, most have dismissed Shelley's vegetarianism as a sign of his youthful inclination to be led astray by enthusiastic but quixotic reformers like the Newtons and the Boinvilles, crusaders for a Monboddian primitivism which included a commitment to the vegetable diet, and with whom he formed a brief but enthusiastic attachment during 1812 and 1813. Richard Holmes, for instance, calls Shelley's writing on vegetarianism 'peculiar' and 'crotchety' and belittles it as only one of many bizarre outgrowths of Shelley's perennial instability and anxiety. Kenneth Neill Cameron is the only modern biographer to present Shelley's vegetarianism in any detail, trying hard to take it seriously even though he finds Shelley's thinking on the matter filled with absurdities, and thus deserving the ridicule Peacock, among others, gave it. Cameron concludes that, although he knows that 'vegetarianism is scientifically unsound,' it 'was not out of line with the scientific knowledge of [Shelley's] time,' and, since the first pamphlet was printed by an established scientific publisher, was probably not received as being as odd as it has seemed to modern audiences.[2] Prior to Morton's substantial book on the topic, only Henry Salt, a relatively little known Shelley and Thoreau enthusiast and late nineteenth-century animal rights advocate, had made a serious defence of Shelley's vegetarianism, arguing that Shelley 'boldly and consistently arraigned the prime cause of animal suffering, the removal of which must precede the establishment of a genuine human sympathy' for other animal species, and that 'Shelley's dietetic tastes must have had *some* influence on that spirituality of tone which makes him unique.'[3]

Timothy Morton's book makes a sustained and detailed case for how

Shelley's vegetarianism 'refashioned taste, in revolt against what he conceived to be the hierarchical powers which controlled consumption, production and culture. The revolt in taste delineated new relationships between bodies and their environments' (1). Like Morton, I will be concerned here with showing how Shelley is 'committed to the body in its material relationship with its environment, both social and natural' (12), but my argument differs substantially in emphasis. For Morton, Shelley's writings reveal primarily a symbolic intervention, one whose importance lies in the realm of discourse alone, rather than of both discourse and practice. The 'themes' of his book, as he says, are the 'representation of food and consumption ... [and] the political significance of figurative language as it constructs the discourses of diet' (10). Vegetarianism is, he argues, 'a discourse in its own right, with its own sets of authorities, images, rhetorical devices and repertoires of data' (82), but one gets the feeling, reading his far-ranging book, that eating is a matter of consuming words alone. It is a productive metaphor, but misses part of the materiality of Shelley's commitment to vegetarianism – that it could affect one physically, as well as morally, and that it could change one's relation to, and awareness of, the natural world. Though in these quotations Morton appears concerned with the physicality of Shelley's dietetic vision, his argument, sustained by a Bookchin-esque vision of social ecology, finally presents Shelley as 'always-already' idealistic; meat, animals, and the body's connection to the natural world for Morton are potent symbols which he sees Shelley as manipulating for the sake of utopian social change.[4] There is no doubt that Shelley *does* see diet and animal rights in symbolic terms, but I wish to suggest here that Shelley's understanding of diet, the body, and physical and social change is connected to a recuperation of the physicality of human existence in nature. It is not just a means for speaking about a connection with nature; it helps to define such a connection. For Morton, as for Shelley's contemporaneous critics, Shelley's vegetarianism is interesting because it is radical, but not because Shelley's claims for it might in some sense be empirically significant. My difference with Morton is thus quite simple; his argument claims the objectivity of a Foucauldian analysis which is capable of imagining a utopian evolution of political discourse. Mine aims to uncover an argument rooted in Enlightenment rationality about the merits of vegetarianism itself, and how the relation with nature which such a view reveals may be seen in some of Shelley's poetry. In my view, vegetarianism is for Shelley not just a matter of poetic intervention or rhetoric, but also a logical commitment to health and an attempt to ground symbolic utopianism in what appeared to him to be discernible *physical* laws.

Shelley's Ideal Body: Vegetarianism 101

Among other reasons, Shelley's vegetarianism is worth examining because current nutritional science, as most vaguely health-conscious readers will no doubt be aware, has found vegetarianism not only to be sound, but even to be more healthy than the so-called balanced diet advocated for years by the US Department of Agriculture, with its self-interested emphasis on animal sources for nutrition.[5] However, although we now have peculiarly contemporary reasons for seeing Shelley as a visionary in matters of diet too, Shelley's vegetarianism needs to be examined in the light of its historical context and his own understanding of it, and for the light it sheds on the nature of his thinking in general. Shelley's vegetarianism, far from being mere crankiness, or even dietary acuity, is a sign of the complexity of his thinking on matters of body, mind, and society, and offers evidence of his understanding of a kind of materialism in which a revolution of thought and of society might be influenced by the substances ingested by our body. Shelley's vegetarianism is an early moment in the development of his ecological sense of our place in the natural world. Like the later visions of nature of *Prometheus Unbound* and 'Mont Blanc,' Shelley's arguments about diet suggest the need to recognize that human consciousness is necessarily alienated from the material forces which largely determine it; and while Shelley feels, contrary to Wordsworth, that this alienation can never be completely overcome, his utopian hopes for the effects of diet propose that we can successfully recreate ourselves only by coming to know, and working within, nature's laws.

The direct sources of Shelley's vegetarianism, as Cameron and Clark noted several decades ago, are Plutarch's essays on vegetarianism, J.F. Newton's *A Return to Nature* (1811), and Joseph Ritson's *An Essay on the Abstinence from Animal Food, As a Moral Duty* (1802). What an exclusive examination of the immediate sources for Shelley's writing on vegetarianism misses, however, is a genealogy of ideas that might fully reveal how Shelley's argument for vegetarianism is not a sign of the peculiarity or idiosyncrasy of his thought, but rather a logical outgrowth of broader scientific discussions of the day. Such a genealogy would reveal that his defence of vegetarianism is part of a serious philosophical debate about the relation of the human body to nature, as well as the more abstract realm of political reform in the context of apparently natural laws. For instance, there was a great deal of debate in the eighteenth and early nineteenth centuries, spurred by a growing interest in comparative anatomy, as to whether humans were fundamentally omnivorous or vegetarian (then commonly termed 'frugivorous'). Almost every treatise on comparative anatomy or human health from this period makes a point of weighing in on one side or the other of this debate. Part of the problem is that the evidence was (and seems still to be) ambiguous. Animals physically most like us (the orangutan, thanks to Monboddo, being the most notorious example) were not, as far as anyone could tell, carnivores; humans have long intestines like them, suitable for slowly digesting vegetable matter, and lack claws or other obvious appendages for hunting and killing. Yet the fact remained that we seem to have been eating meat as far back as anyone could remember, and that we possess residual canine teeth. Many doctors, most notably George Cheyne and John Arbuthnot in the eighteenth century, and Abernethy, Wallis, and Beddoes in the early nineteenth, had argued that diet was profoundly connected to disease and well-being. Cheyne in particular suggested that the 'coolness' of the vegetable diet could cure most ills, since most sickness was accompanied by fever, and the only other treatment was the letting of 'excess' blood. He argued too that longevity had decreased, and disease increased, since humankind began eating meat in larger quantities.[6] It was assumed by many others that meat was simply the most nutritious food, since it seemed obvious that the body had to do very little to convert meat to flesh. Arguments about nutrition frequently drew on ideas of what we might call symbolic osmosis – that characteristics associated with a type of food would, in one way or another, be passed on to those who consumed that food. Thus many writers assumed that eating meat made one sanguinary, usually thought to be good (it was rarely explained more precisely); even more vaguely, the eating of meat was thought to give strength, energy, and courage, since these were characteristics associated with carnivorous, as opposed to herbivorous, animals. For instance, Thomas Graham, author of *Sure Methods of Improving Health and Prolonging Life* (1831), says that since 'animal food consists of parts which have been already digested by the proper organs of an animal, and applied to the same uses, it consequently requires only solution and mixture, whereas vegetable food must be converted into a substance of animal nature, by the proper action of our own viscera and therefore, requires more labour of the stomach and other digestive organs' (4–5). Drawing on cultural comparisons was also popular, and Graham argued that proof that we need both animal and vegetable food lay in the fact that 'Tartars,' known to eat only meat, were too fierce, while the Brahmin, known to be vegetarian, had a 'gentleness, softness, and mildness, directly the reverse of the Tartar, but with little elevation of mind; whereas, a proper mixture of both these kinds of aliment, forms individuals whose functions, both personal and mental, attain their highest state of perfection' (9–10). William Buchan, author of one of the most popular health guidebooks of the late eighteenth century, argued that it was not a good idea to eat the meat of animals that had been over-driven, since 'their humors, not being properly prepared or assimilated, remain crude, and occasion indigestions, gross humors, and oppression of the spirits, in those who fed upon them.' (He also blamed the general poor health of the English on their over-consumption of meat.)[7]

What is odd about this debate is that there seem to have been very few committed vegetarians around while it was taking place. In the eighteenth century, Cheyne argued for the vegetable diet on health grounds; Pope, Goldsmith, Thomson, and, most famously, Rousseau in *Emile* wrote briefly about the moral necessity of not killing animals for food, and many thousands of the poor simply could not afford a regular diet of meat. However, there was no concerted movement afoot as there is today, for instance, trying to steer people away from animal food. Even the Newton-Boinville set of Shelley's London could hardly be said to constitute a movement. Not unlike the equally prolific writing against atheism, writing about, and normally against, vegetarianism was not responding to an actual threat of change.

What the debate about diet seems partially to reflect is the much larger and more obvious concern in much of the self-consciously scientific writing of the day about the place of humankind in nature. It concerns, that is, a pre-Darwinian examination of how and where we are rooted to the natural world, an effort explicitly represented in the 'physico-theological' writing of such figures as Thomas Burnet, John Ray, William Smellie, and, of more direct influence on Shelley, William Paley, most of whom discuss diet in their work.[8] Each writer presents more or less totalizing arguments about the relation of humankind and nature, how evidence from the natural world argues for a particular thesis about the relation of human being to God. Specifically, Burnet argued (rather extraordinarily) for the ill-adaptation of nature to our needs because we are post-lapsarian and post-deluvian. The earth, he thought, had been grotesquely deformed by the Flood, and God's influence now was largely absent from nature. His central evidence was the apparent chaos of the earth as he found it, particularly in the appalling roughness and ugliness of mountains, and the irregularity of sea and land, as opposed to his conjectured paradisal world, which would have been 'smooth, regular, and uniform; without Mountains, and without a Sea' (53). The others argued, more influentially, for how the essential adaptedness of humankind and nature revealed the intelligence, benevolence, and active design of God in the present world. In some sense their arguments aimed to present what was obvious – that, as Ray had argued first, when we discover something of intricate complexity we assume it has been designed and constructed that way.⁹ This argument tended to go in two directions; first, what we might call the strictly utilitarian design idea, explicit already in Genesis and an important component of orthodox Christianity (and which reaches a kind of climax in Bacon's vision of a New Atlantis), that everything in nature is designed for the use of humankind; and, second, the more awed argument that though nature revealed much evidence of design, the design was an end in itself, and not simply for *human* benefit; there was far more life, beauty, complexity, and redundancy in nature than could ever have been created solely for the use of humans.¹⁰ In either case, theoreticians of nature had to make room in their conception of nature for precisely the apparent violence and chaos which Burnet had seen in the topographical evidence but others saw most obviously in the carnage of what we now call the food chain. As John Bruckner put it in his *Philosophical Survey of the Animal Creation*, though 'study of nature relieves us of fear,' of supposing an 'incensed Deity,' an important fact that is always threatening to recreate this fear is that 'animals thirst to destroy each other' (viii, xiv).

Diet, then, became a minor crux in the understanding of nature. Myths of the Golden Age (biblical or otherwise), as Shelley notes at the beginning of his *Vindication*, had generally envisioned a world without the obvious violence of carnivorism. Most post-Newtonian theoreticians of nature, however, had to account for the existence of animal 'rapaciousness' in a world that was to reflect the infinite wisdom of God in the present. Indeed, as William Smellie argued, in a passage quoted by Ritson (and thus read by Shelley), the violence of the natural world was most obviously seen in humankind: 'Of all rapacious animals, man is the most universal destroyer. The destruction of carnivorous quadrupeds, birds and insects is, in general, limited to particular kinds: the rapacity of man has hardly any limitation. His empire over the other animals which inhabit this globe is almost universal. He accordingly employs his power, and subdues or devours every species. Of some of the quadruped tribes, as the horse, the dog, the cat, he makes domestic slaves' (Smellie, 375–6). Yet for Smellie, as for Bruckner and most others, rapaciousness was not a sign of the degeneration of a post-Edenic nature, but rather evidence of the remarkable 'oeconomy' of nature. Indeed, the very notion of an economy of nature, of an intricately interconnected set of relations, necessary for either positive evolutionary change or the maintaining of an equilibrium, hinged on an attempt to account for the violence of the food chain. Both Bruckner and Smellie spend a good deal of time explaining the wisdom of widespread carnage, hoping to explain the mystery of God's ways to the otherwise appalled observer of nature. Bruckner is by far the most ingenious here, arguing that carnivorism allows God to create more kinds of species, and that diversity is necessary if every part of the globe is to be inhabited by life. He thought too that the intense competitiveness of the food chain might keep a check on populations of individual species, ensuring that no one species gains dominance, and so increasing overall diversity. Anticipating Malthus, Bruckner applies this logic to humankind as well. In a rather perversely circular argument, he states that because the unchecked growth of human population leads to 'violence, rapine, and murder' (81–4), population-depleting forces such as disease, carnivorous animals, and war are an essential part of the economy of nature. Smellie more brazenly argues that the extraordinary rapaciousness of humans – that there is no animal or landscape we cannot conquer – is evidence of our prowess as a species. This suggests another vision of the chain of being, in which carnivores are above herbivores; since humankind could be seen as the supreme carnivore, we could be seen in this way too as lord of all the natural world. For Smellie eating is the most powerful and immediate form of consumption in a very competitive economy. It is a sign of efficiency in a well-ordered system; thus Smellie demonizes wolves because they were thought to kill for pleasure.[11]

In writing about diet, Shelley also directly confronts ideas about innate violence and our relation to an economy of nature. Literally, examining diet is a way of talking about how we are connected to the world, of how we survive by taking it in. Eating is a product of natural and cultural appetites. It remains obvious, though, that eating involves an elemental conversion of matter; eating is the first version of self-fashioning. In the act of eating, we see how nature sustains us, and how we may control ('harvest') its bounties; and yet we are reminded too of our fragility and mortality, that we are indeed a part of the mutable and corruptible physical world. The extraordinary degree to which eating becomes fetishized in both high and low culture, the centre of persistent, elaborate, and sacred rituals, suggests that we both recognize this fact about eating and attempt to repress it. By celebrating our carnivorism, Bruckner and others were intent on revealing our apparent 'naturalness' and how we might recognize our pre-eminent position in the world by noting that we are at the top of the food chain, revealing both God's wisdom and that we are his favourites. As Smellie notes, we can (and do) eat almost anything.

Diet is interesting too because it can highlight the metaphysical problem of the relation of body to soul, the material and the spiritual. As I noted above, discussion of diet very often includes some notion of how food affects character. Milton presents this idea in Raphael's discussion of diet in book 5 of *Paradise Lost*. The passage is Milton's clearest presentation of his philosophical monism; since 'of Elements / The grosser feeds the purer' (110),[12] we are only slightly better than what we eat; and eating, as an account of physical and intellectual nourishment (the two are not ultimately distinct here) explains our pre-lapsarian potential:

> flours and thir fruit
> Mans nourishment, by gradual scale sublim'd
> To vital spirits aspire, to animal,
> To intellectual, give both life and sense,
> Fansie and understanding.

The Edenic diet is vegetarian but 'corporal'; the 'time may come,' Raphael further explains, 'when men / With Angels may participate, and find / No inconvenient Diet, nor too light Fare' (112). An error in diet is the central event of the poem (and of Genesis) too, a fact important to Shelley's first essay. The key point is that if diet determines who and what we are, then, barring the discovery of an ethereal food that actually sustains us (knowledge alone does not accomplish this even in Milton), we are inextricably bound to the natural world. In both Milton's version and the more common one in the eighteenth century which assumed that characteristics of food were transferred to the eater, spiritual being is tied to what we digest. We are animals, necessarily part of a material, even mechanistic world, even if 'one first matter all.' The tendency during and following the eighteenth century, though, would be to see this first matter as physical and mechanical rather than godly, coming directly from the natural world rather than only mediated by it.

So Shelley was on safe ground in arguing, as he does in both essays on the vegetable diet, that our choice of food is not a trivial matter, that it indeed says much about how we think we are connected to the natural world. And yet Shelley's vegetarianism makes an important move beyond the materialist position of those who would have led him to take diet seriously in the first place, if only because a large majority of those writing about diet and our place in the natural world were content with our potent position as omnivorous predator. Explicit materialists, like Priestley and Holbach, or implicit materialists, like Smellie, tended to argue that nature had produced the status quo – our natural physical position in the world was the way we had naturally and gradually come to be, even if certain excesses of civilization had led us astray.[13] This is true even of Erasmus Darwin, who, while making explicit the possibility of a presiding, immanent spirit in nature (not unlike that of John Ray), argued nonetheless for the primacy of the present moment; change in nature was for the best, and so our omnivorousness was (as in Smellie) a sign of the gift of our natural adaptability. In Holbach, another important direct source for Shelley's ideas of nature, he would have encountered not only a thoroughgoing materialism but a conservative sense of the inevitability of the momentum of evolutionary change moulded by nature. In *The System of Nature*, Holbach argues that 'Man always deceives himself when he abandons experience to follow imaginary systems. Man is the work of nature – he exists in nature – he is submitted to her laws – he cannot step beyond them, even in thought – it is in vain that his mind would spring forward beyond the bounds of the visible world – he is always necessitated to return. For a being formed by nature, and circumscribed by her, there exists nothing beyond the great whole of which he forms a part, and of which he experiences the influence' (17–18). Even the rather holistic versions of materialism presented by Darwin and Holbach should have suggested to Shelley the naturalness of a meat-based diet which was both historic and common. That Shelley resists this line of thought suggests that he felt that humankind's relation to nature could be recreated. By investigating the very idea of what is natural, he reifies neither the status quo nor a primitive state, but imagines how we might discover the conditions within which we can harmoniously live and develop. Shelley's case for vegetarianism thus attempts to reconcile the deterministic materialism which allows diet a physical (even metaphysical) importance with the utopianism, so evident in *Queen Mab*, which sees humans refashioning their material relation to the natural world in order to create a new spirituality.[14]

The tone and aim of Shelley's vegetarianism is evident from a brief mention of diet in his *Refutation of Deism*, written in late 1813, roughly the same time he is thought to have written *On the Vegetable System of Diet*. Indeed, the former essay succinctly presents the young Shelley's complex interest in materialism, and so a quick summary of the essay will be useful. The essay is written as a dialogue between Eusebes, a nominal Christian but thorough materialist, and the deist Theosophus. Eusebes uses Holbach, Priestley, and Hume to refute the view of nature popularized by Paley (but evident too in much of the physico-theological writing I outlined above) that nature's intricacy reveals the careful design of a

Creator, and that, moreover, the final 'end' of this creation is human wellbeing. Eusebes both questions our ability to deduce causes from perceived effects, of things in nature perceived *as* effects of a First Cause, and asserts that 'The greatest, equally with the smallest motions of the Universe, are subjected to the rigid necessity of inevitable laws' (*Shelley's Prose*, 132), which echoes Holbach. He argues too (from Priestley and Holbach) that 'Matter ... is not inert. It is infinitely active and subtle. Light, electricity and magnetism are fluids not surpassed by thought itself in tenuity and activity: like thought they are sometimes the cause and sometimes the effect of motion' (133).

Yet the argument rises above its immediate sources and, by focusing on what might be seen as the central contradiction or paradox of a Holbachian materialism, reveals Shelley's own desire to ground action for change in an otherwise deterministic world. This occurs in one sense because Hume and Holbach, though both empiricists, do not finally make an easy fit. Holbach's necessitarianism depends on precisely the reification of cause and effect that Hume throws into question. Furthermore, as Basil Willey puts it, Holbach 'cannot help thinking in terms of an unspoilt nature which he worships, and an erring humanity which he condemns. Our errors cannot be "nature" ... yet there is nothing which nature has not produced' (157). While Shelley is hardly consistent in this matter either – he argues in the note on necessity in *Queen Mab* that liberty and chance are both illusions, and further along in the *Refutation* that the mind is only an effect – Eusebes suggests that the appearance of an absolute material determinism can be undermined by imagining our own physical nature as other than it is: 'It is manifest that if the eye could not see, nor the stomach digest, the human frame could not preserve its present mode of existence. It is equally certain, however, that the elements of its composition, if they did not exist in one form, must exist in another; and that the combinations which they would form, must so long as they endured, derive support for their peculiar mode of being from their fitness to the circumstances of their situation' (*Shelley's Prose*, 132–3). Anticipating Darwin, Eusebes suggests the possibility of multiple adaptiveness, that individual beings (or species) can adapt to given circumstances in different ways (hence, for Darwin, the diversity of species). While Holbach explicitly rules out the possibility that nature may be other than as we find it, as indeed do Pope and many other Enlightenment thinkers, Shelley allows for the possibility that our physical adaptedness is not 'fixed.' Change can come both from an alteration of external circumstances like climate or from inner motivations like appetite. Both here and in the essays on vegetarianism, Shelley argues that nature appears to demand of animals the 'consentaneity of their frames to the circumstances of their situation'; but this is not the case for humans because our highly developed consciousness allows us to see nature as alien and other. The separation we feel from nature allows us (falsely) to assert our superiority over it, or to imagine the possibility of reforging our connections to the material that Shelley presents here. For better or worse, our consciousness – the ability to inquire and reason brilliantly presented by the essay as a whole – finally allows us some freedom to choose our evolutionary path. The argument suggests that nature only gains the appearance of being determined and determining in retrospect and from a rigidly teleological perspective; for Shelley, our future within nature is in some sense open.

Thus it is that Shelley can imagine change within what was for him an explicitly scientific and materialist realm which still holds in its sight the possibility of radical spiritual change. In the *Refutation* and in the two essays on vegetarianism, choice about diet is the most conspicuous means we have of adapting harmoniously within nature's laws, or of contravening them. In the *Refutation* Eusebes argues that 'Unnatural diet, and the habits consequent upon its use are the means, and every complication of frightful disease is the end, but to assert that these means were adapted to this end by the Creator of the world, or that human caprice can avail to traverse the precautions of Omnipotence, is absurd. These are the consequences of the properties of organized matter; and it is a strange perversion of the understanding to argue that a certain sheep was created to be butchered and devoured by a certain individual of the human species, when the conformation of the latter, as is manifest to the most superficial student of comparative anatomy, classes him with those animals who feed on fruits and vegetables' (*Shelley's Prose*, 133). The argument suggests that we have the freedom to depart from old or to create new adaptations, but those adaptations are necessarily constrained by physical conditions. We may eat so that we conform to natural laws or otherwise. Moreover, these laws are not clearly discernible, and so we can make the wrong decision even as we think we are making the right one. Like Holbach and many other philosophers of nature, though, Shelley argues that we can make attempts to learn these laws; they make themselves evident, for instance, in the study of disease and comparative anatomy. The emphasis is not only on curing individual disease and social ills, but more generally on reimagining our existence in nature by recognizing our complex connection to it. Far from being its lord or pre-eminent predator, as previous discussions of human diet conclude, or mere automata blindly adhering to nature's laws, humans are able to discover (and in some sense create) an ideal natural evolution by adapting to natural laws. As Shelley says in many of his prose pieces of this period, these laws are both ultimately mysterious and partially recoverable through observation, rational inquiry, and even, as is evident from Shelley's own trials with vegetarianism, experimentation.

Shelley's vegetarian argument aims to include and reconcile what is taken to be hard 'scientific' fact – things we can observe and document – and an ethical argument for how and why our connections to the natural world could be made better. While Shelley's interest in science has been well documented, his essays on diet are the only texts he produced which explicitly enter a debate which would have been recognized as belonging to the science of his day.[15] Indeed, the holism of his argument would not have struck contemporaries as out of place either, since arguments about our place within nature that led to more or less ethical conclusions were common not only to physico-theological writing but also to writers like Holbach and Erasmus Darwin. The interconnectedness of physical and moral action is one of the key tenets of Holbach, who argues that, in spite of the fact that 'all the errors of men are physical errors,' moral and social problems can be solved by the proper advancement of science (19). Priestley switched between experiments on the nature of air to his disquisitions on matter and spirit. For Shelley, as for many scientists of his day, truth was not discrete and specialized, capable of being marked clearly into kinds and fields, but was all part of the study of nature, whose truth could be pursued in multiple ways.

Nevertheless, the essays on diet present what is recognizably empirical evidence for the merits of vegetarianism. The primary scientific argument of both essays, like that of earlier writing on diet, is that humans, like cows and primates, are evidently physically adapted to eat vegetable rather than animal matter, and that a departure from this naturally prescribed state has led inevitably to disease. That we *are* naturally vegetarian is what was (and is) most factually contentious, on which the entire case rests, and *Vindication* begins trying to establish this. Its argument is largely borrowed from J.F. Newton, however, and is not, in rhetoric or aim, as scientific as the essay of a year later. (Although the two essays differ in tone – the earlier of the two is more prone to zealous overstatement – they make essentially the same case.) In the former, Shelley takes as evidence the myth of the Golden Age, Milton's account of Eden, and the story of Prometheus, all of which are allegories, he says, for the fact that humans have evolved into a perpetually diseased condition by turning from a vegetable diet to a meat-based one. His more convincing argument, taken up in both essays, is from comparative anatomy. Shelley's initial evidence in this matter was presented first by Plutarch, that we do not seem naturally inclined or able to kill animals for food; we instinctively shrink from both the act of killing, which we must invent tools and stratagems to accomplish, and the bloody flesh, which must be cooked or otherwise prepared to be made edible. More explicitly materialist still, Shelley draws evidence from the debate of his contemporaries about diet in making 'internal' comparisons about teeth, stomachs, and intestines, in all of which he finds humans to resemble known 'frugivorous' animals like the 'orang-outang.'

Equally important for Shelley as scientific evidence is that our error in diet has observably led to physical disease. In both essays Shelley argues that animal food is the cause of most physical disease, since truly 'wild' and thus naturally adapted animals appeared to him to suffer very little disease compared to man. The overwhelming presence of disease is the primary evidence that we continue to ignore nature's precepts. 'But no hour of the life of man is exempt from the dreaded invasion of a mortal malady ... Hospitals are filled with a thousand screaming victims; the palaces of luxury and the hovels of indigence resound alike with the bitter wailings of disease' (*Shelley's Prose*, 93). That 'half of every generation perished' before old age is no doubt true, and Shelley could not have known of bacterial and viral causes of disease. Yet the connection between diet and disease was more than just a wild hypothesis. William Lambe published several books in the first decade of the nineteenth century on cancer and diet which made the case that most diseases were caused by drinking polluted water and putrefied flesh, and thus could be cured (see note 6); he presented experiments with diet that clearly suggested that a vegetarian diet helped slow down and reverse cancerous growths. And, as I suggested above, it had been largely accepted since Cheyne that diet in general was important to health. That animal food in particular is a cause of disease is supported by Lambe and Cheyne and the relatively hard evidence from comparative anatomy that we are most like herbivorous animals. Shelley cites too the statistical evidence (however primitive and anecdotal) that none of the family of Newton or Lambe had died after switching to the vegetable diet, as well as his *own* experimentation with diet, since at the time of writing the first essay he had been vegetarian for eight months and 'the improvements of health and temper here stated is [sic] the result of his own experience' (*Shelley's Prose*, 90).

To answer the thorny problem of how it is that humans have turned to an unnatural diet in the first place, so that they now feel that meat is a necessary and desirable food, Shelley suggests, rather lamely, that similar wholesale changes of diet have been forced upon domestic animals, who then also display unnatural cravings for food. Implicit here, though, is the recognition of the unavoidable alienation of consciousness in nature suggested in the *Refutation* and most clearly in 'Mont Blanc.' Because we must think of ourselves as either above or outside the material world, we are capable of creating various 'appetites' for ourselves which we will nonetheless think of as being 'natural.' For Shelley these appetites are based on decisions of the past and present and determine different evolutionary paths. We may misunderstand the cause of our alienation, assuming it is owing to our perhaps God-given superiority, and deliberately place ourselves against and on top of the natural world. Or we may attempt to see how we are a part of nature, determined by it, and work to live as best we can within those conditions we can perceive.

Thus it is that both essays are explicitly speculative rather than overwhelmingly conclusive; they are a call to experimentation, to see if diet *can* reduce the prevalence of disease and create a people and a nation of a different character. Shelley speaks throughout the two essays of giving 'the vegetable system a fair trial,' of the 'experiment of change,' and that vegetarianism is 'an experiment which may be tried with success, not alone by nations, but by small societies, families, and even individuals' (*Shelley's Prose*, 85, 89, 95). The essays aim to convince not so much by the presentation of fact as by suggesting that the possibility of radical change is reasonable, accessible, and relatively simple. Both essays make the central case that an awareness of diet leads to an awareness of the interconnectedness of nature and consciousness, which, while not overcoming our alienation, will at least create in us an ecological imagination.

The beginning of the second essay emphasizes just this interconnectedness. Shelley states that because 'the influence of body on mind' has already been admitted by most philosophers, it needs now to be recognized how far this influence might go and in what way change might be effected: 'It belongs to philosophy alone to trace the remote effects of mistakes consecrated by habit, to mark their influence on individual character, to estimate the sum of a thousand unregarded events as affecting the welfare of society, and to trace to the influence of unnatural habits of life hatred, murder and rapine, wars, massacres, and revolutions' (*Shelley's Prose*, 92). Even as he counsels against expecting too much from a change in diet and warns that there will be 'no Utopian advantages' (he allows that some disease is hereditary, and that in any case disease has such a firm grip on humanity that widespread relief will not come immediately [*Shelley's Prose*, 84–5]) he argues that a change in diet will have effects far beyond those merely of physical health. In the *Vindication*, for instance, he wonders whether, 'had the populace of Paris drunk at the pure source of the Seine and satisfied their hunger at the ever-furnished table of vegetable nature, that they would have lent their brutal suffrage to the proscription list of Robespierre? ... Is it to be believed that a being of gentle feelings, rising from his meal of roots, would take delight in sports of blood? ... It is impossible that had Bonaparte descended from a race of vegetable feeders that he could have had either the inclination or the power to ascend the throne of the Bourbons. The desire of tyranny could scarcely be excited in the individual; the power to tyrannize would certainly not be delegated by a society, neither frenzied by inebriation, nor rendered impotent and irrational by disease' (*Shelley's Prose*, 85–6). It is passages like these that most readers have found hilarious or absurd. Certainly as examples of the effects of diet they are too specific to appear probable. Yet they are in one sense the crux of Shelley's argument. For his real point here is to suggest not simply that a change in diet involves the beneficial effects of freedom from the disease that prevents the mind from thinking rationally (and thus ethically), but also that the recognition of the prevalence of violence in a system of diet that requires the continual slaughter of animals would necessarily alert us to the general infection of violence in human being and culture. Shelley's thinking here is much like that of Gandhi, on whom he had a direct influence.[16] To conquer our predilection towards violence, our ability to accept its apparent necessity, violence must be resisted at all levels. The provision and consumption of food are not minor instances of this violence, but, as Derrida has recently suggested, are part of an instantiation of moral consciousness, an aspect of experience that forces the development of core ideas of self and other, life and death.[17]

We can also find Shelley's radical resistance to violence in such poems as *The Mask of Anarchy* and *Prometheus Unbound*. In both poems, hate is a pathological state that produces violence, and which can yet be overcome by massive will-power. In the former poem, the people return to the scene of the Peterloo massacre to convert the violence of the government's army to shame by conspicuously offering themselves to it. And in *Prometheus Unbound*, Prometheus must overcome what Morton rightly points to as 'a carnivorous torture' by recognizing the error of his own hatred before the inevitable movement towards peace may begin.[18]

Moreover, in one of the poem's most stunning passages, Prometheus recognizes that Christ's message of love is undermined by the iconography produced by organized religion, which is infected by violence. Prometheus's words to the spectre of Christ that appears before him represent Shelley's attempt to intervene in the reproduction of that iconography.

> Remit the anguish of that lighted stare –
> Close those wan lips – let that thorn-wounded brow
> Stream not with blood – it mingles with thy tears!
> Fix, fix those tortured orbs in peace and death
> So thy sick throes shake not that crucifix,
> So those pale fingers play not with thy gore. –
> O horrible! Thy name I will not speak,
> It hath become a curse. (1.597–604)[19]

The 'pale fingers' are Christ's own, figurative of a Church that dallies with violence, and those of his supplicants, catching the disease, as it were, of the hatred and violence done against him and in his name. This violence is preserved in the desire for revenge, and the production of various heathen (Roman, Philistine, Jewish) scapegoats, that the image of Christ's crucifixion enshrines. The passage reminds us in a startling way how the body matters, how it is the object and site of corruption, hate, and disorder. More subtly, the image of crucifixion reminds us that the body matters in the Christian church as well, but only as it is sacrificed, an act that is remembered in the ritual of communion, in which the body and blood of Christ are figuratively eaten. It is a potent image of consumption, in which violence and fear are intermingled with sacrifice and love. The passage reminds us that what we eat, both as actual food, and what we are fed by culture, determines who we are. As the Fury replies to Prometheus, 'In each human heart terror survives / The ravin it has gorged' (1.618–19).

Shelley's essays on the vegetable diet argue that the violence that we most casually accept and ignore is that which we inflict upon the animals we eat. It is not simply that this violence is all around us, that evidence of it exists from our food tables to the clothes we wear; it is also that this violence literally sustains us. Borrowing the idea that we are imbued with the characteristics of the food we eat, Shelley suggests too that we take on the characteristics of the manner in which we obtain our food. As we feed upon violence, our appetite for it is whetted. Moreover, our ability to rationalize or ignore the violence that is at the 'root' of our society makes us more likely to rationalize or ignore other kinds of violence. (Thomas More makes a similar argument in *Utopia,* and so has slaves do the butchering of animals outside the cities.) As Shelley argues at the close of the second essay:

> How can he be expected to preserve a vivid sensibility to the benevolent sympathies of our nature, who is familiar with carnage, agony, and groans? The very sight of animals in the fields who are destined to the axe must encourage obduracy if it fails to awaken compassion. The butchering of harmless animals cannot fail to produce much of that spirit of insane and hideous exultation in which news of a victory is related although purchased by the massacre of a hundred thousand men. If the use of animal food be in consequence subversive to the peace of human society, how unwarrantable is the injustice and barbarity which is exercised toward these miserable victims. They are called into existence by human artifice that they may drag out a short and miserable existence of slavery and disease, that their bodies may be mutilated, their social feelings outraged. It were much better that a sentient being should never have existed than that it should have existed only to endure unmitigated misery. (*Shelley's Prose,* 96)

By choosing to sustain ourselves on animal food we have chosen to wage a kind of war on nature, to 'torture' and exploit animal life, and to introduce physically and spiritually corrupting influences into our lives. We may choose to do otherwise, to exist in such a way as to minimize the harm we do both to ourselves and to other living things. And, it must be stressed, Shelley's enthusiasm for the reform is in large part due to the simplicity of it – a change of diet is easily in reach of every individual. A 'return to nature,' as both Newton and Shelley called it, does not mean a regression to a primitive past, but a move to a system that would quickly bring real benefits. That is, part of the relevance of the reform of diet is that it would bring about real social change. As well as necessarily changing the moral and physical health of the individual, it would have concrete political and economic rewards. Probably borrowing from a similar argument in Paley's *Moral and Political Philosophy* (599–601), Shelley argues that because the land and feed-grain needed to produce livestock could produce ten times the quantity of vegetable food, a wholesale change of diet could immediately produce enough food for everyone. Such a change would affect the political economy because 'it is only the wealthy that can to any great degree, even now, indulge the unnatural craving for dead flesh' (*Shelley's Prose*, 87). As well as increasing the food supply, the change in diet would ease competition for land, a primary force in the creation of class division. If land was freed from the inefficiency and inequality enforced by a system which demands that so much land be used for pasturage, there would be more land for more farmers, and respect for the land and its workers would necessarily increase. Vegetarianism is for Shelley a primary step towards the kind of agricultural society valued as well by Wordsworth. Thus, 'the spirit of the nation that should take lead in this great reform would insensibly become agricultural; commerce, with all its vices, selfishness, and corruption would gradually decline' (*Shelley's Prose*, 87). Readers of Shelley are familiar with his utopian politics from *Queen Mab* and *Prometheus Unbound*, but the two essays on vegetarianism present a practical and material, albeit prosaic, vision for how this change could occur. Shelley's agricultural spirit anticipates the similar vision of William Morris in *News from Nowhere*, in which the cooperative spirit of farming, and a respect for the intrinsic beauty and life of the land, create (for us at least) a particularly appealing utopia.

It is thus that Shelley says, most notoriously, that his proposed reform 'strikes at the root of all evil' (*Shelley's Prose*, 85). The claim is amusing because we do not generally take any of the proposed reasons for vegetarianism seriously – diet typically seems a matter too trivial to have consequences of the global reach that Shelley argues – and because we tend reductively to read the statement to mean that animal food *is* the cause of all evil. Yet Shelley's claim is worth taking seriously. In the first place, none of Shelley's arguments for vegetarianism is unreasonable, and, indeed, modern inquiry is proving them more reasonable all the time.[20] Secondly, Shelley means by the statement not that diet *is* the root cause of evil, but that a change to a vegetable diet goes to the core of our spiritual and physical being; it would force us to recognize the violence we blithely participate in, make us more aware of our connections to the physical realm, and improve our physical health. Indeed, what is most striking about the passage is that Shelley insists that we can consciously change the material 'roots' of our being, that we can dramatically readapt to our natural world.

Shelley's argument presents a fundamental ecological reform. In contemporary terms, his vegetarianism reveals an early instance of his resistance to an anthropocentric universe. In the sympathy and respect he here displays towards non-human animal life, his insistence on placing human life within nature so that we are in some sense ruled by it rather than vice versa, and in his utopian desire to imagine and create a new and harmonious relation to nature, Shelley undermines the traditional hierarchy of the 'great chain of being.' While Spinoza and Hume develop critiques of Christianity for its relentlessly instrumentalist and anthropomorphic view of nature, neither goes as far as Shelley in developing what I take to be a specific praxis for a relatively biocentric view of the natural world.[21] His environmental ethic is more thoroughly developed than that of Wordsworth, in part because Shelley is less sanguine about the existing 'fitness' of the human mind and nature. Shelley is more consistent in representing human consciousness as alienated from nature, and demonstrating that we need nevertheless to acknowledge how we are dependent upon and determined by its myriad presence. The ethic this defines involves a recognition that humans are neither the centre nor the end of nature, and more significantly that nature itself is an 'other' that must at once be held in awe and recognized as being different from, and only marginally available to, human consciousness. Moreover, Shelley argues in his essays on vegetarianism that individual, social, and political consequences resonate from a recognition of this fact.

I have tried to present Shelley's argument for vegetarianism as sympathetically as possible because the essays contain much of what is generally considered to be visionary in Shelley, and because his vegetarianism is an important impetus for an ecological aspect of this thought that is present in much of his later work. Shelley wrote no poetry about vegetarianism (though he occasionally refers to it in poetry written throughout his life), but the spirit which it both represents and helps to create is clearly present in *Queen Mab*, not only because one of its notes is a revised version of his first essay, but also because it presents an understanding of nature as all-encompassing in power, and yet capable of yielding a utopia:

>   Look on yonder earth:
> The golden harvest spring; the unfailing sun
> Sheds light and life; the fruits, the flowers, the trees,
> Arise in due succession; all things speak
> Peace, harmony, and love. ...
>
>   Spirit of Nature! thou
> Life of interminable multitudes;
>   Soul of those mighty spheres
> Whose changeless paths through Heaven's deep silence lie;
>   Soul of that smallest being
>   The dwelling of whose life

>   Is one faint April sun-gleam; –
>   Man, like these passive things,
> Thy will unconsciously fulfilleth:
>   Like theirs, his age of endless peace,
>   Which time is fast maturing,
>   Will swiftly, surely come.   (3.192–6, 226–37)

Utopianism here is sustained by an oxymoronic vision of a 'golden harvest spring,' a myth of perpetual and natural abundance which allows for our relation to nature to be defined by saturation rather than consumption. Consistent with the necessitarianism that Shelley was reading in Godwin and Holbach, the poem suggests the inevitable and unseen progress towards such a state of harmony, which neatly encompasses both our alienation from and our connection to the larger forces of nature. The later poetry to which I shall now turn exposes more fully the tension between a utopian natural world and the human desire to perceive and move towards that ideal, but continues the imagery of nature as all-powerful and as potentially both inimical and accommodating towards human desire.

Shelley's resistance to an idealism that would construe nature merely as a mask or an illusion, and thus deny the importance of confronting the determinism of the material that is an essential part of his ecological ethic, is suggested too by 'Mont Blanc.' In the next chapter I make a fuller case for how the poem suggests an open and indeterminate relation between consciousness and the natural world. It is worth noting here that nature in the poem is envisioned starkly as the inorganic base from which 'life' springs. From the poem's splendid opening metaphor likening the individual mind to a mere tributary of 'the everlasting universe of things' to its descriptions of the remoteness and inaccessibility of the Power that resides in and beyond the mountain, the poem works to depict the speaker's disorientation at recognizing the indifference of the material to the life it yet brings into being.

>   The glaciers creep
> Like snakes that watch their prey, from their far fountains,
> Slow rolling on; there, many a precipice,
> Frost and the Sun in scorn of mortal power
> Have piled: dome, pyramid, and pinnacle,
> A city of death, distinct with many a tower
> And wall impregnable of beaming ice.

> Yet not a city, but a flood of ruin
> Is there, that from the boundaries of the sky
> Rolls its perpetual stream (ll. 100–9)

The vision of Mont Blanc (vaguely reminiscent of the world view of Thomas Burnet) is the *ne plus ultra* of the natural world, which undermines utterly any sense of an anthropocentric nature. The arguments of instrumentalists that nature is created for humanity, or of some contemporary cultural critics that the concept of nature is created *by* us, cannot, I think, withstand the view (literally) of nature as the ultimate 'ground' that Shelley presents. We may recognize that we interpret and define nature differently as individuals and cultures, but we cannot get beyond the vision of nature presented here, that the material world is infinitely larger and more complex than we are, and is indifferent towards our existence. Consciousness itself, the poem argues, is ultimately determined by and grounded in the materialism of the universe, and yet the two are remote and inaccessible to each other. The poem depicts an incommensurateness which must baffle us into humility. This 'awful doubt or faith so mild' that can 'repeal / Large codes of fraud and woe' and allow us finally to be 'with nature reconciled' (ll. 77–81) is surely like the humility before nature represented as well in the essays on vegetarianism. There too, doubt about our mastery of nature reveals to us our dependence upon it and the need for a new temperance. It is with this recognition that we may begin to overcome the violence we do against nature, and in its name.

The 'Ode to the West Wind' suggests how human life is connected to the larger cycles of nature, which are both destructive and indifferent to the aspirations of humankind, and potentially restorative and benign. The poem shows that the ability to be in sympathy with these much larger movements is genuinely revolutionary. Ronald Tetreault has argued that the faith in change that the poem seeks to instil in the speaker and the reader is not 'a faith in Providence nor even in some immanent teleology at work in nature, but rather a variety of poetic faith in which the reader will accept the parallel between natural regeneration and social renewal through the convention of tropic substitution. What happens in nature, we are asked to believe, will happen in politics' (212). Shelley's vegetarianism reminds us, however, that natural forces, and our relation to them, are never merely tropes for the poet. Though a full awareness of our connections to nature eludes us, we can be certain of their existence, as Shelley felt a change in diet dramatically revealed. Certainly by attempting to represent physical and historical forces the poem seeks to produce a hope for revolution which, as always in Shelley, would be self-fulfilling. But the poem is very much about discovering that hope in the materiality of nature, recognizing that it is not merely born from or sustained by tropic substitution, but is fundamentally connected to physical forces. As in 'Mont Blanc' the speaker does not finally know the pathways of connection between nature and the self, but this poem expresses desire for certainty rather than revealing the thrill of profound doubt. Consciousness stands apart here too, isolated, and gazing at a spectacle in nature, but it seeks a sign of its own place in the physical order of things. The poem's most appealing image for this insulated connection within the natural world is of 'The sea-blooms and the oozy woods which wear / The sapless foliage of the ocean,' who 'know' the voice of the west wind, 'and suddenly grow grey with fear, / And tremble and despoil themselves' (ll. 39–42). The ability of marine plant-life to detect and react to the changing of the seasons is as mysterious, but certain, as the destruction of ancient Roman villas by nature's (and history's) slower-moving cycles of geologic and historical revolution. And it suggests the ability of the conscious self to respond to forces which seem to exert their influence in a different realm – of sky, earth, ocean, and deep time. In the immediacy of the present moment, the power of such long-term physical change can only be represented with deliberate (and startlingly lovely) imagery, seen here in reflections of 'old palaces and towers / Quivering within the wave's intenser day,' which are destroyed instantaneously as wind causes 'the Atlantic's level powers / [to] Cleave themselves into chasms.' There is an equivalency between consciousness and the watery reflections, suggesting at once the poet's ability to reveal the large cycles of nature and history in his poem, and the insubstantiality of his own existence within them.

Shelley represents the determining force of nature most dramatically, though, through the 'situatedness' of the lyric moment of the poem. As in the best moments of Wordsworth's nature poetry, we know here that the speaker is in a specific place at a specific moment, that he has seen something real. The description the poem offers is immediately symbolic of cyclic forces, as it generally is not for Wordsworth, but we know nonetheless that the speaker is witnessing the approach of a real storm, with winds that scatter leaves in front of it, and presaged as well by the high cirrus clouds which always travel in advance of major storms:

> Loose clouds like Earth's decaying leaves are shed
> Shook from the tangled boughs of Heaven and Ocean,
> Angels of rain and lightening. (ll. 16–18)

This is a poem, in other words, as Jonathan Bate has argued for Keats's great 'Ode to Autumn,' about real weather. Recognizing patterns in weather is a part of understanding the simultaneously chaotic and cyclic behaviour of nature, and noting the effects of those changes on one's immediate environment. Indeed, the west wind is both the specific wind that the speaker feels and the monolithic representation of all of nature's cyclic forces, seen here in the sweep of changes the speaker sees in the sky, on the ground and the water, and beneath the water. The wind is the force 'on whose stream' all these changes are carried, and these changes are imagined as occurring through several time scales at once – the immediate one of the approaching storm, the seasonal one of the approach of winter, and the eonic one of wholesale changes in climate and civilization. (Bate reminds us that 1819, the year both this poem and Keats's were written, was the first real summer in three years after the great eruption of the Tambora volcano in Indonesia in 1815, which put so much ash into the sky that average temperatures were reduced by several degrees for at least two years afterwards.)[22] The effect of recognizing these layered changes, and that one is powerless before them, is a moment of unique sublimity. The speaker's reaction is a strengthened desire to submit to these only partially knowable forces. Indeed, the poet's appeal to be transformed into a thing which is literally blown before this wind ('If I were a dead leaf though mightest bear; / If I were a swift cloud to fly with thee; / A wave to pant beneath thy power') is a desire to overcome the gap between consciousness and nature, to become one with the transforming powers of nature which must bring with them the new life of spring. Shelley wants to respond directly to the west wind rather than indirectly, as the 'sapless foliage of the ocean' does. The poet hopes as well that his own writings can have material effect, and foresees this by imagining the words as texts and spoken words, with physical form and presence, rather than as ideas or ideals:

> Drive my dead thoughts over the universe
> Like withered leaves to quicken a new birth!
> And, by the incantation of this verse,
>
> Scatter, as from an unextinguished hearth
> Ashes and sparks, my words among mankind! (ll. 63–7)

The effect Shelley hopes for his poetry is like that of the economy of plant life, which dies and is consumed without violence (without predation), even when it is burned. The leaves of autumn and of his poetry thus become the 'winged seeds' of the poem's opening stanza, which

>   lie cold and low,
> Each like a corpse within its grave, until
> Thine azure sister of the Spring shall blow
>
> Her clarion o'er the dreaming earth, and fill
> (Driving sweet buds like flocks to feed in air)
> With living hues and odours plain and hill: (ll. 7–12)

The physical processes which the speaker of the poem longs to be a part of are ambiguous, since neither weather nor its effects are really predictable; the speaker is clearly also awed by and fearful of these forces. Within the poem, they produce destruction, 'Black rain and fire and hail,' as well as 'moss and flowers / So sweet, the sense faints picturing them.' Three years of miserable weather after Tambora probably made the question 'If Winter comes, can Spring be far behind?' somewhat less than rhetorical for Shelley and his readers, as indeed fears of nuclear winter in the 1970s and 1980s did for us (current fears about global warming have reversed the question). But Shelley harbours no notion here that humankind can itself affect forces so much larger than we are. Indeed, the chaos that Shelley responds to also characterized European culture in the years immediately preceding the poem (and for which the long stretch of bad weather no doubt seemed ominously symbolic) – the repression of progressive movements by violence in England, and the apparent failure of these movements elsewhere in Europe. This is a cultural chaos perhaps analogous to the condition of corrupted individuals Shelley examined in the vegetarian tracts, of disease that stems in part from humanity's failure to heed an obvious natural order. ('I hold that the depravity of the physical and moral nature of man originated in his unnatural habits of life,' begins the *Vindication*.) As Morton suggests, the aim of Shelley's vegetarian revolution is to naturalize culture (*Shelley*, 135), and we can see this impetus in the ode in its attempt to see through culture to a natural order which would restore health and beauty to that culture. The beauty the poem offers is its own production as it depicts hope in the midst of despair, and a deeply perceived natural order in its brilliant *terza rima* sonnet structure, a cycle within a cycle, which echoes the world the poet feels he has seen.

IV

Romanticism and the Metaphysics of Classification

In 1991 a report in the science journal *Nature* presented genetic evidence that the red wolf is a hybrid of the grey wolf and the coyote. As reported in the *New York Times Magazine*,[1] the red wolf seemed thus to be a 'mutt' rather than a genuine species, a population with a distinct and long-lived genotype. This mattered because the red wolf was just being reintroduced in the Great Smoky Mountains of Tennessee, part of a program supported by the US Endangered Species Act. The Act does not allow for intervention on behalf of hybrids; only the preservation of 'true species' warrants the spending of tax dollars. Soon after the report was published, ranchers petitioned the US Wildlife Service to remove the red wolf from the list of endangered species on the grounds that it was not, after all, a species. Similar doubts about the genetic purity of other endangered animals (such as Canadian grey wolves, the spotted owl, and the Florida panther) have threatened attempts to protect existing populations. In each case, biologists have debated not just the genetic history of the specific population, but the very means by which a species should be defined. The preservation of individual animals, and even genetic subtypes, matters less to many scientists and environmentalists than does the preservation of a genetic type that is assumed to be both real and ideal. And yet how to define what constitutes a real species has clearly become a contentious issue.[2]

That there is disagreement over species definition probably surprises most non-biologists. Species seem natural and real enough; those of us who think of ourselves as amateur naturalists delight in our ability to recognize those features of birds, insects, mammals, trees, and flowers that distinguish them from other populations of similar organisms. Scientists and environmentalists commonly measure biotic diversity and value at the level of species. As one philosopher argues, 'Species are quite real; that there really is a bear-bear-bear sequence is about as certain as anything we believe about the empirical world. Species are ... processes, they are wholes, they have a kind of unity and integrity. The species line ... is more real, more value-able than the individual' (Rolston, 21). That species may be real, that organisms may be classed by degrees of apparent similarity and difference (that birds are different from reptiles, or beavers from monkeys), and that there is a final degree of these degrees of similarity among populations to which are given the fundamental names of species do indeed seem obvious. And yet determining what constitutes a species is a complex cognitive act that has seemed problematic since Aristotle began classifying animals. Contemporary biology does not seem close to resolving what is in fact an ancient debate. To what degree are any taxonomic classes real? That is, to what degree are they actual biological entities as opposed to arbitrary and artificial acts of classification; what relationships exist between those beings classed together? How do we decide what set of similarities and differences constitute a kingdom, phylum, class, order, family, genus, and species? What amount of incidental difference must accumulate before we recognize the 'essential' difference that appears to constitute a new species (since for all biologists species constitute the fundamental unit of taxonomy – it of all classes has at least to be right)? Indeed, how do we decide what a fundamental unit within nature is? There is radical disagreement here too. Richard Dawkins has suggested that the gene, a unit of genetic material, ought to be considered the fundamental unit of life, and that the organisms which are produced by and harbour these units are only a kind of by-product of the primary struggle of such genetic material to reproduce itself. (There are debates as well about whether natural selection operates at the level of individual organisms or populations.) At the other end of the scale, James Lovelock has proposed that the earth itself ought to be considered a kind of single, self-regulating organism. Moreover, proponents of so-called postmodern science, such as Jim Tarter, have suggested that the very process of recognizing singular objects in nature is flawed, and that we need to recognize the subjectivity, even the intersubjectivity, of whatever units of life we appear to behold; they argue, in other words, that there are no actual *units* of life.

Some contemporary biologists and philosophers of science who have examined this problem note that each of the many proposed definitions includes a large class of exceptions, and have thus given up looking for an objective definition. They allow that species, along with the rest of the taxonomic order, are merely heuristic tools for framing an essentially infinitely complex set of data.³ On the other hand, most contemporary biologists, Ernst Mayr most famous among them, insist that of all taxa, species at least are real entities, and can be defined by specific biological phenomena, such as the reproductive isolation of specific populations of organisms. Scientists following Mayr's lead have over the past thirty years increasingly seen the species concept in particular, and taxonomy in general, as necessarily revealing phylogeny, the evolutionary history of particular groups of organisms. For Mayr, the species is the essential unit of evolutionary change, and large numbers of biologists see it as their job to arrange taxonomic description so as to reveal evolutionary (as opposed to merely morphological) relationships. (Thus, for instance, because crocodiles share more recent ancestors with birds than do snakes or lizards, their placement in the taxonomic order of things ought to reflect this proximity; and this proximity can be determined by statistical analysis of genetic and morphological characteristics.) It was Charles Darwin who first observed that species are the level at which evolutionary change occurs and can be recognized; individual organisms within populations of their 'kind' express mutations, and the change is preserved if the mutation leads to the development of a new isolated population – and so, a new species is born. And yet, although Darwin aimed to explain the 'origin of species,' his insights paradoxically also throw the concept of species into doubt, since they reveal populations of organisms to be unstable, consisting of some members whose minor beneficial variations threaten the continued existence of the ancestral genotype. One of the startling features of *The Origin of Species* is that Darwin expresses such explicit doubts about the existence of the very phenomenon whose origins the book claims to reveal.[4]

Darwin's insight into the constant flux of populations revealed, among other things, the inadequacy of human perception and language to capture and represent the full complexity of the natural world.[5] Of course, Darwin was not the first to see this, either about science in general, or about the species concept in particular. He was just far more precise about the imprecision of our knowledge on this issue than writers before him, and many since. As I hope to demonstrate in this chapter, a large array of writers and naturalists examined the complexity of taxonomic issues before Darwin, and it forms an interesting and unexplored topic within the field of romantic studies. Though Linnaeus essentially began the fervour for taxonomy and classification in modern science in mid-eighteenth-century Europe (Allen, 36–40), the relation of taxonomy to the real world is a central topic of romantic-period science and touches on conceptions of the natural world held by such writers as Coleridge, White, Clare, and Shelley.

Arthur O. Lovejoy and Michel Foucault have most influentially argued that the ability to recognize and categorize species and other taxa has been a powerful example of an extraordinary and enduring faith in our ability to organize the world around us, and to determine our place in the order of things. For Lovejoy, the concept of the fixity of species underpins the whole notion of a great chain of being – 'an immense, or ... an infinite, number of links ranging in hierarchical order from the meagerest kind of existents, which barely escape non-existence, through "every possible" grade up to the *ens perfectissimum* – or, in a somewhat more orthodox version, to the highest possible kind of creature' (59), with humanity, of course, occupying the highest of the *visible* creatures. And yet, though the great classifiers of early modern Europe would use Aristotle's first attempts to classify animals to support their own ordering of species, Lovejoy finds in Aristotle an open acknowledgment of the indeterminacy that Charles Darwin makes relatively explicit. That is, though Aristotle begins classifying animals according to a functional morphology, he is aware too that there are no actual discrete 'kinds' in nature. He recognizes instead, as Lovejoy puts it, a fundamental 'shading-off of the properties of one class into those of the next. Nature refuses to conform to our craving for clear lines of demarcation; she loves twilight zones, where forms abide which, if they are to be classified at all, must be assigned to two classes at once' (56). Lovejoy argues that the concept of the great chain of being contained its own contradiction, since the demand for continuity and plenitude in the perfection of nature could not ultimately be reconciled with the empirical observation of an apparently finite number of species. Plenitude requires that all imaginable gaps be filled; but with no gaps, there are no discrete units. To Lovejoy, then, the overarching and more or less transhistorical idea of the great chain contains 'two diametrically opposed sorts of conscious or unconscious logic ... the habit of thinking in discrete, well-defined class-concepts and that of thinking in terms of continuity, of infinitely delicate shadings-off of everything into something else, of the overlapping of essences, so that the whole notion of species comes to seem an artifice of thought not truly applicable to the fluency, the, so to say, universal overlappingness of the real world' (57). Lovejoy traces the endurance of the inherently unstable idea throughout early modern Europe, where it receives triumphal expression in Pope's *Essay on Man*. Lovejoy finally sees a grand shift beyond the rigid hierarchy of the idea in German Romanticism, which he sees as celebrating the excellence of diversity, of shadings, rather than the excellence of a discrete ladder towards perfection.

While Lovejoy reveals the centrality of species concepts within the grand scheme of the history of ideas, Foucault argues in *The Order of Things* what is in a sense much more obvious – that the classification of the physical is fundamentally a matter of representation. Thus a history of taxonomy reveals a history of the changing nature of what language is believed to be and what it can do: 'Order is, at one and the same time, that which is given in things as their inner law, the hidden network that determines the way they confront one another, and also that which has no existence except in the grid created by a glance, an examination, a language; and it is only in the blank spaces of this grid that order manifests itself in depth as though already there, waiting in silence for the moment of its expression' (xx). Just as Lovejoy's history of the great chain of being reveals an abiding paradox between plenitude and continuity, Foucault's account of systems of order also reveals a permanent contradiction. Taxonomy appears to reveal coherence in the nature of the things themselves, and appears to depend, as Foucault says, on an utterly empirical process that produces tables of similarity and difference. That is, we have to see organisms with the utmost clarity to determine those features that give them a unique identity. Linnaeus devised a system of naming animals that apparently depended solely upon such a strict determining of species difference, so that identity and taxonomy could be united. A truly scientific language appears revealed through nature itself. Foucault argues not just that classification is at some point fundamentally creative and arbitrary, but also that the progress of taxonomy (and there is a great deal of progress for Foucault) is not the progress of empiricism. Rather than an increasing accuracy in our map of the living world, science produces the increasing power of discourse over the simpler reality of things. The key transformation in taxonomy, Foucault argues (somewhat reductively), is what we might call the internalization of difference. Prior to the work of Georges Cuvier, the early nineteenth-century French taxonomist, classification is purely a matter of visible characteristics – most notably in Linnaeus's scheme of arranging plant classification around their very visible reproductive organs. Cuvier's development of Aristotle's notion that all distinguishing characters of living beings must be determined by their comparative function meant the simultaneous added depth of animal innards – where the functions of individual parts can be determined – and of the added reasoning, guesswork, and narrative associated with determining what those functions were. Foucault associates this change with the virtual creation, in the era of Cuvier, of a complex idea of 'life' as that which seems to involve self-organization, separate from the merely physical world. Nature is finally divided into the organic and the inorganic, with the former representing a deeply embedded structure that needs ever more precise scrutiny to pinpoint and outline. The newly created science of biology, one feels in reading Foucault's account of its beginnings, is one of several discourses (economics and grammar provide other examples) which offer evidence of the ever-increasing power of discourse itself, in which referents are ever more invisible, more complex. Because Cuvier dramatically presents the power of the language of classification to order nature, Foucault sees Cuvier (who nonetheless believed in the fixity and permanence of species) as the most important precursor to Darwin, rather than Lamarck, who developed more or less at the same time as Erasmus Darwin an idea of environmentally conditioned evolution.

One could say in response to Foucault that the advance of taxonomy, of describing life, reveals an increased understanding of actual complexity, rather than just the increasing complexity and power of the domain of discourse. But Foucault reminds us that science works in the medium of language, which is as real as the physical world scientists investigate. That language moulds the phenomena to be studied is no especially profound insight. What I have been suggesting is that the species concept is a particularly striking instance of the language effect, and in exploring it, we come to see what is at stake in the act of classifying and naming. We name in order to distinguish, to contrast, and to remember, and yet naming fixes and generalizes our knowledge of the world we see. It is both an aid and an impediment to perception.[6] What Foucault shows most clearly is the manner in which language hides its own reality, and bestows a kind of 'ur-reality' to nominalist ideas. His history of taxonomy reveals the slide from an explicit nominalism to an incipient realism crowned by Cuvier and not upset by Darwin. His central exhibits are Linnaeus and Buffon, both of whom begin their taxonomic projects unsure of the fixity of species, content to produce explicitly 'artificial' systems for producing some convenient order among the animals and plants, but end their life's work convinced of the essential reality of the systems they have produced (Foucault, 128–44). These conclusions about the culturally constructed power of science are impressively confirmed by Londa Schiebinger's more recent analysis of the development of taxonomy in the eighteenth and early nineteenth centuries. Though not explicitly concerned with the species debate, Schiebinger gives numerous examples of how cultural biases about gender were incorporated into, and thus given a seeming objectivity by, the process of taxonomic description begun by Linnaeus.

These three writers all suggest that the Romantic period was an interesting and important time for the development of ideas about classification and the nature of species. Linnaeus caused a kind of revolution in natural history, and his ability to create a detailed and seemingly interlocking puzzle from the vast diversity of the natural world gave natural historians a sense that they possessed a method to order and understand it. Linnaean societies sprang up throughout Europe, as amateur and professional natural historians embraced the sheer scope of his system (which encompassed both the organic and inorganic realms) and enthusiastically adopted his method for *naming* species, which held the promise of revealing a stable and interconnected 'system' of nature. This all forms an extraordinarily fertile background for an examination of how writers in the period reflected upon the natural world. My concern for the rest of this chapter is to reveal the implications of varying species concepts for acts of perception, and the representations of those acts. In the romantic period there are writers who are fully aware of what is at stake in the act of classifying, in attempting to divine essence or type, from multiple instances. While taxonomy involves a desire to discover unity and pattern in the natural world, there are several writers of this period who resist taxonomy as potentially obscuring and devaluing specific acts of perception, seeing in such system a loss of detail rather than a gain of knowledge. Observing nature in order to fit organisms into their proper 'types,' many romantic writers realize, aids our abstract sense of how the natural world looks and works, but substantially mediates and prejudices specific observation. In the desire to know the world, classification presents a kind of bind. It imposes structure onto nature, and yet also reveals structure we might not otherwise see. Without naming kinds of trees, birds, or insects, for instance, we cannot be truly aware of the extraordinary variety of these and other kinds of life in nature. We need to keep a tally of what we see in order to know it. And yet, looking for kinds necessarily obscures individual difference. In looking for essential populations we see, dramatically, the many instead of the one, group identity instead of individuality.

In his *Essay Concerning Human Understanding*, John Locke reveals a formative awareness of the artifice of taxonomy, the inadequacy of language to reveal the essences of nature. In several chapters on the naming of 'mixed modes' and 'substances,' Locke sees the idea of species as the primary example of how we confuse essential and nominal realities.

Locke is puzzling over precisely the question of how we come to group an assemblage of individuals into a larger group, and what reality this group may be said to have. 'Why do we say, this is a horse, and that a mule; this is an animal, that an herb? How comes any particular thing to be of this or that sort, but because it has that nominal essence, or, which is all one, agrees to that abstract idea that name is annexed to?' (III, vi, 7).[7] Locke is describing the mind's dexterity in forming categories, and pointing out that this is a phenomenon crucially enabled by language. Yet there is, Locke observes, an empirical reality elided by these acts of categorization:

> That the species of things to us are nothing but the ranking of them under distinct names, according to the complex ideas in us, and not according to precise, distinct, real essences in them, is plain from hence, that we find many of the individuals that are ranked into one sort, called by one common name, and so received as being of one species, have yet qualities depending on their real constitutions, as far different one from another, as from others, from which they are accounted to differ specifically ... If things were distinguished into species, according to their real essences, it would be as impossible to find different properties in any two individual substances of the same species, as it is to find different properties in two circles, or two equilateral triangles ... Nor indeed can we rank and sort things, and consequently (which is the end of sorting) denominate them by their real essences, because we know them not. (III, vi, 8)

Like Foucault, Locke argues that our manner of grouping according to perceived differences and similarities is necessarily arbitrary at some level. And yet Locke allows that there is some real essence not just of the individual but also of some more inclusive category that any individual object must belong to. He argues both that we cannot accurately perceive the definitive essence of things in the world, and that the abstraction of sorting depends on levels of blindness – on the willingness to count some differences while ignoring others, and to assume some similarities where they appear to be hidden. Each level of generality is achieved only by a corresponding loss of detail of the real, of the individual specimens. The purpose of these abstractions is the 'true end of speech, which is to be the easiest and shortest way of communicating our notions' rather than 'the true and precise nature of things as they exist' (III, vi, 33, 32). This is an argument about how language is an inevitable distortion even of what we actually perceive. Implicitly, Locke is reminding his readers of an empiricism that resists the apparent reality of species groupings so that we may continue to perceive the precise detail of individual difference, to be alert to a more particular reality.

In spite of this apparent radical uncertainty over our ability to perceive species, Locke has a profound, and Platonic, belief in their actual existence. Indeed, as Lovejoy points out, Locke gives an extraordinary account of the belief in the fullness of the great chain of being – that every imaginable being ought to exist even if we cannot perceive it: 'That there should be more species of intelligent creatures above us, than there are of sensible and material below us, is probable to me from hence; that in all the visible corporeal world, we see no chasms or gaps. All quite down from us the descent is by easy steps, and a continued series of things, that in each remove differ very little one from the other. There are fishes that have wings, and are not strangers to the airy region; and there are some birds that are inhabitants of the water, whose blood is cold as fishes, and their flesh so like in taste, that the scrupulous are allowed them on fish-days' (III, vi, 12). Locke goes on here to argue for the existence of zoophytes, hypothetical organisms perfectly filling the gap between plants and animals. The argument here is not entirely contradictory, as Dr Johnson would later argue it was.[8] Our desire to categorize creates gaps in our understanding of the actual world; because of the limitations imposed on our perception by language, we see steps where, Locke believes, there should be a smooth continuum of marginally different individuals. Certainly Locke's belief in such a continuum is fantastic, since it would require an infinite number of individuals. This is particularly a problem for Locke because he does not allow for any notion of evolution – all types, all differences, must exist fully in the present, as in the past and future. But Locke's argument is important because it draws attention to the minute particularity and infinite complexity of the physical world, which the language of taxonomy in general, and a species concept in particular, allows us to gloss over.

Locke's account gets to the heart of the species debate in the eighteenth century. Buffon, in his early works, would reiterate the artifice of species, as would Goldsmith, who argued that all categories drawn from nature 'are perfectly arbitrary. The gradation from one order of beings to another, is so imperceptible, that it is impossible to lay the line that shall distinctly mark the boundaries of each. All such divisions as are made among the inhabitants of this globe, like the circles drawn by astronomers on its surface, are the work, not of nature, but of ourselves.'[9] The gradual acceptance of the possibility of change into the order of living things –

that kinds of animals could disappear, and even, apparently, new ones be created – brought an end to the belief in the completeness of nature's living beings. If fossils presented evidence of beings with no apparent counterpart in the present, then clearly there could not be a continuum of all possible beings in the present moment. But, as Erasmus Darwin imagined, the possibility of change also allowed for the possibility of perfection. Prior understandings of reproduction, the manner by which species or individuals maintained their fixed presence in nature, emphasized the perfection and stability of the process – that offspring were essentially the same type as the parents. The elder Darwin's understanding of animal generation, outlined in his long prose work *Zoonomia*, sees the reproduction of living beings as a more or less complete mixing of the features of the individual parents, allowing for the productive chaos of continuous variation much more fully theorized by his grandson. That is, the mixing of individual traits in offspring allows Darwin to envisage species and even specific mating families as inherently unfixed.

> In all these vegetable and animal modes of reproduction, I suppose the new embryon to begin in many points, and in complicated animals in many more points probably than in the more simple ones; and finally, that as these new organized parts, or rudiments of the embryon, acquire new appetencies, and produce or find molecules with new propensities, many secondary parts are afterwards fabricated.
>
> Thus it would appear, that all nature exists in a state of perpetual improvement by laws impressed on the atoms of matter by the great CAUSE OF CAUSES; and that the world may still be in its infancy, and continue to improve FOR EVER AND EVER. (1:437)

Erasmus Darwin, like his contemporary J.B. de Lamarck, argues that organisms actively respond to their environments by subtly changing certain features (typically imagined and illustrated through the example of the giraffe's long neck). Both argue that an organism senses changing opportunities in an environment, and responds by adding parts or making existing parts more complex, which changes are passed on to subsequent generations. Lamarck understands these changes to be ontogenetic, directing evolution towards a Platonic ideal, with each species finally reaching its preordained evolutionary destination. The idea of the fixity of species is thus maintained as a kind of abstraction by Lamarck (who nonetheless expresses doubt about the reality of all higher orders of taxa). Erasmus Darwin, on the other hand, is far less teleological, allowing for continual improvement, but suggesting no final ideal for each species. Indeed, many of Darwin's examples for the complexity of reproduction have to do with the vitality of apparent hybrids, that they become, in effect, new species.

I have been suggesting that the idea of species, and the nature of taxonomy in general, have formed an important background to writing about nature in the Romantic period. Specific literary examples include one that affirms the category of species and taxonomy in general as essentially Platonic. Coleridge is the only romantic-period author who explicitly and extensively concerns himself with the debate in natural history over the reality of species. In both his essay *Theory of Life* (written between 1816 and 1818) and his *Contributions to a Course of Lectures Given by J.H. Green* (written in 1828), he attempts to distil a theory of the order of life which has at its centre a belief in the reality of species.[10] Coleridge's aims in these writings are multiple, and I am interested here only in their relation to the concerns I have been discussing. Like Poe's cosmology *Eureka*, which it resembles in tone and ambition, *Theory of Life* has produced a wide range of critical opinion, though it is nonetheless not frequently examined. Owen Barfield, for instance, sees it as crucial to a thorough understanding of Coleridge, revealing his general understanding of nature as well as his specific scientific genius, whereas Norman Fruman, echoing René Wellek, dismisses it as plagiarized and self-aggrandizing mysticism.[11] To my mind, the truth is somewhere in the middle. Its tendency towards a bombastic tone and a rhetoric of wilful obscurity (about its presumed content, as well as its sources) certainly suggests an author who is as conscious here of creating textual *effect* as he is in his poetry. Indeed, in the passage I quote below, he explicitly revels in massaging what he calls the 'physiognomy' of language. And yet, also as in Poe's *Eureka*, there is a seriousness of intent that cannot be ignored. As Barfield and Thomas McFarland have argued, Coleridge attempts to present a theory of the natural world that would overcome Cartesian dualism as well as the thoroughgoing materialism of scientists like Holbach, and this aim is consistent with much of Coleridge's writing. Repeating a theme common in his criticism, he sets out in *Theory of Life* to find the key to all diversity in the natural world, a single underlying order, which is God as a first cause and a power of producing ever-increasing distinctness and complexity.

As Barfield notes, Coleridge begins his *Theory of Life* by resisting the trend in natural history to identify 'life' only with the organic realm. Like the *naturphilosophie* of Steffens and Schelling that Coleridge borrows from and works through, *Theory* aims to reveal an order behind all 'that really *is*' (506). The definition he comes to,

> the most comprehensive formula to which the notion of life is reducible, would be that of the internal copula of bodies, or (if we may venture to borrow a phrase from the Platonic school) the *power* which discloses itself from within as a principle of *unity* in the *many*. But that there is a physiognomy in words, which, without reference to their fitness or necessity, makes unfavorable as well as favorable impressions, and that every unusual term in an abstruse research incurs the risk of being denominated jargon, I should at the same time have borrowed a scholastic *term*, and defined *absolutely*, as the principle of unity in *multeity*, as far as the former, the unity to wit, is produced *ab intra*; but eminently (*sensu eminenti*), I define life as *the principle of individuation*, or the power which unites a given *all* into a *whole* that is presupposed by all its parts. (510; Coleridge's italics)

Coleridge here presents an apotheosis of the principle of the reality of species. The hierarchy of all living beings he finds to be determined by the ability of any given category of beings to seem distinct, both as a class among other classes and as individual specimens making up the class. His vision of the organization of organisms may be thought of as a more Platonic version of Lamarck's notion of environmentally conditioned evolution: species 'evolve' towards a predetermined ideal conditioned not by the environment a species finds itself in (as Lamarck has it), but by a prior law of distinctness. A species must become what a deeper, internal law (of individuation) has always meant that it should.[12] The proof of this thesis lies precisely in its ability, Coleridge claims, to serve as a taxonomic tool, to explain the reality of the patterns named by taxonomy, so that the logic of classification is itself a Platonic repetition of the logic of nature. 'The tendency to individuation,' he argues, 'more or less obscure, more or less obvious, constitutes the common character of all classes ... while the degrees, both of intensity and extension, to which this tendency is realized, form the species, and their rank in the great scale of ascent and expansion' (516). His actual evidence (and that of Steffens) is limited – more time is spent on trying to enlarge the domain of the proposition to include inorganic matter, as well as the fundamental 'forces' of the universe, than in developing an actual taxonomy. Nonetheless, Coleridge notes that at the bottom of the scale of organic life are such virtually amorphous creatures as jellyfish or coral, which show 'individuality is in its first dawn; there is the same shape in them all, and a multitude of animals form, as it were, a common animal. And as the individuals run into each other, so do the different genera' (539). Above these beings are molluscs, where 'we find the individuals separate, a more determinate form'; and above these are insects, fish, and birds. Coleridge presents only a very incomplete sketch of how each order appears to have more variety and be more visibly distinct, though each is still characterized by uniformity among any individual class of species.

The apotheosis of the distinctness of species is of course 'man': 'He has the whole world in counterpoint to him, but he contains an entire world within himself. Now, for the first time at the apex of the living pyramid it is Man and Nature, but Man himself is a syllepsis, a compendium of Nature – The Microcosm ... In Man the centripetal and individualizing tendency of all Nature is itself concentred and individualized' (550–1). Man unites all the opposite forces of nature. More to the point, man is the purest species and so is most clearly distinct from all others, evidenced most visibly by the large variety amongst its individual members and the supposed unique ability of each person to recognize his uniqueness. This belief is underpinned by what 'revelation,' 'the consenting authority of all countries, and of all ages,' and 'the imperative voice of my own conscience' tell Coleridge of the 'wide chasm between man and the noblest animals of the brute creation' (501). This theme is taken up in the notes for his *Lectures* as well, where he argues that 'The difference between Man and the larger number of the other mammalia consists in the absence of different species. The species is here the genus' (1397). In this text, though, we see more clearly the consequences of Coleridge's attempt to identify the essence of nature as the essence of humanity's apparent perfection as a species. While Coleridge can note the difficulty in clearly demarcating individual species ('who is to be judge what difference in the degree is equivalent to a difference of kind' [1389]), he quickly judges that this is not a problem when examining humanity as a species, *because* humanity is so clearly separated from the rest of the animal kingdom (here resisting the trend in natural history to recognize the proximity of human and certain primate species).[13] Coleridge wants to separate humanity from the rest of the animal kingdom while at the same time coming to an equivalent theory about essentialized differences of race. When in another fragment of these lecture notes he gets to the matter of race, he begins again by playing down essential differences, arguing that races are not in fact distinct species.[14] Yet much of the rest of the lecture also attempts to prove that humanity is a kind of microcosm of nature, so that within our separate and distinct species lies a miniature hierarchy of the races, which, by the end of the text, nonetheless come to resemble species. Explicitly borrowing from Blumenbach's *Ueber die natürlichen Verschiedenheiten im Menschengeschlechte*, Coleridge argues that the races form a distinct pattern, produced by different rates of degeneration from a pre-lapsarian ideal: 'the caucasian the center, on each side at each pole of the line the Negro & the Mongolian, & intermediate between the Negro & Caucasian Malay; & in like manner intermediate between the caucasian & mongolian the american' (1398). The centre race, Coleridge argues, is the 'historic' one, closest to the undegenerated original. Repeating another common pattern in these writings, the theory attempts to reconcile opposites by pasting them together like so many tattered bits of paper. His desire for an implicit 'unity in multeity' is maintained with the notion of *devolution* from a singular race; so too is his desire for a clear hierarchy with his own 'race' distinctly on top. Indeed, a fragmentary heading in the notes suggests that only 'the central Race saves man from Degeneracy' (1409), an example of which Coleridge suggests a little earlier: 'Of nations that have fallen by internal corruption, no possible force from without concurring, fallen from strength into impotence, from Civility into Barbarism, and from Knowlege [sic] into savage Ignorance, History supplies us with only too many instances; but of a tribe or nation at all approaching to the savagery of the native Brasilian, or even to the barbarism of the Negro or Caffer that wholly unaided from what [sic] by Merchants, Conquerors or Missionaries had ever made a single progressive step toward Civilization, the whole History of Man does not furnish even a solitary Example' (1407). It is not a big step from here to notions of pure and impure blood, hypostasized notions of absolute difference that confer absolute power and value, reproducing a virulent and literal Eurocentrism (though not, as Schiebinger makes clear [115–34], an unusual one). The ideological purpose of arguing for the existence of discrete 'natural' classes is here too an insistence on facets of difference that allow for the creation of a rigid hierarchy. Coleridge's science is informed by an idealism which prefers the high gloss of purely imagined and neatly arranged categories to the particular and tangled evidence the material world provides. This abstraction is characteristic of the *naturphilosophie*, and of Coleridge's desire to reveal a grand unified theory of organic and inorganic nature. It offers too a worst instance of the desire to use an idea of species in a totalizing theory of nature. The very notion of particularity, of individuation, is ultimately turned on itself and made the cornerstone of a theory that allows Coleridge, as Raimonda Modiana notes, to turn away from an 'early devotion to a close observation of the external appearances of nature' (138) to a Platonic scheme of absolute types.

The romantic period fortunately provides us with many examples of writing that questions, rather than reifies, systems of taxonomy and ideas about species difference and discreteness. There is, for instance, that writing in which specific attention is brought to the act of observing the complexity of the natural world. Here we may see the kind of empiricism outlined by Locke as an attention to the particularity of the material in which there is a resistance to categorization. And, as we shall see in Shelley, there is also a more abstract reflection on systematizing, in which notions of 'natural' hierarchy that are dependent upon ideas of fixed taxonomic boundaries (natural kinds) are undermined.

Gilbert White and John Clare provide the most obvious examples of the former mode. They are famously close observers of fauna, particularly birds. What typifies their observations is a steady resistance to the kind of abstract categorization that one finds in systematists like Cuvier and Linnaeus. Anticipating the kind of casual and relatively undirected scrutiny of nature that characterizes William Bartram, Henry Thoreau, and Aldo Leopold, White and Clare observe and record what they happen upon within a specific locale. There is no attempt to build towards a system, even within the particular environmental niche they have staked out. In White's *Natural History of Selborne* there is virtually no sense of method, or a theory of organizing data; his observations are recorded as he makes them, written in letters to like-minded observers, rather than as a treatise with formal organization. What is striking about individual letters is their utter lack of focus: White appears frequently to be simply listing his observations. Like systematists such as Linnaeus and Cuvier, however, White gathers specimens and records his observations as data to be used in what he sees as a collective process of determining species characteristics. He frequently debates the status of particular Linnaean species classifications, seeking to make them incrementally truer to the level of variation he expects exists within specific locations. It is as though White expects species to deviate as much from the apparent 'ideal' set out by Ray and Linnaeus as the topography of Selborne (also particularly described) does from any other location. He recognizes that the production of a taxonomic order is keenly dependent upon the observer. 'It is in zoology as it is in botany,' White argues: 'all nature is so full, that that district produces the greatest variety which is the most examined' (55). The truth that matters, White suggests, are not abstractions or universal similitudes, but facts that vary according to place and time. This is why White, like Clare, spends so much time observing the behaviour of specific animals rather than merely specific morphology, which provides the primary data for classification to systematists.[15] White's interest in behaviour is especially reflected in his fascination with patterns of migration. He wants to know why certain birds appear in Selborne on a cyclic basis; if they hibernate or leave; why, how, and where they go if they do indeed migrate. He is fascinated too by bird song, and its variety among and between species. He seems often to identify species just so that he can then go on to record the variety of individual behaviour within that species, as he does throughout the book for goat-suckers, sparrows, and swallows. 'System' he argues, 'should be subservient to, not the main object of, pursuit.'[16]

White's interest in animal behaviour leads inevitably to a willingness to characterize that behaviour in necessarily subjective, even anthropomorphic, terms. This is for him a relatively unselfconscious matter. That animals experience emotions (that, as he repeatedly observes, they love and hate, desire company, have fear) is demonstrated to him by their 'songs,' and their behaviour towards their offspring; animal emotion is as obvious for White as it is for Stubbs, Wordsworth, and the young Coleridge in their poems on birds and other animals, as I discussed in chapter 3. Like John Clare's willingness to see animals (and even landscapes) in similarly humanizing terms (as in 'The Badger' and 'Swordy Well'), this anthropomorphism is a vivid sign of a willingness to allow that consciousness, intelligence, and emotion are not features that define only human existence. Whereas one sees in attempts to categorize nature and delimit species the desire to impose modalities of difference, overcoming the scientific prohibition against anthropomorphism is a way of blurring boundaries between apparent classes of being and, as White shows, allows one to begin to observe animal being as other than merely a dead specimen. One sees more of the animal, and sees it more as an individual, when one does not see animals abstractly and morphologically as defining a species. Moreover, in seeing signs of subjectivity in animals, we are not necessarily projecting human qualities onto them, but can potentially be recognizing in them shared attributes. Writing this sympathy off as merely the projection of human characteristics – which the very introduction of the concept of anthropomorphism has the effect of doing – errs not only in its underestimation of animal being but in its extraordinary exaggeration and deification of human being (which we see in the later Coleridge). One of the effects of this anthropocentrism is to cut us off from the animal world, to turn it into a purely material and phenomenal realm, set in contrast to the spiritual one of human being.[17]

Seeing animals as so many different machines, as Descartes notoriously did, is a consequence of a rigid and imperial assertion of mental categories over the natural world. The alternative de-essentializing view is a willingness to accept the hybrid, in matters of both representation and reality. What I noted earlier as one of the radical implications of both Charles and Erasmus Darwin's insights into the nature of species was that all species are in some sense hybrids, a product of pre-existing species or types. Charles Darwin notes at the end of *Origin of Species* that 'hereafter we shall be compelled to acknowledge that the only distinction between species and well-marked varieties is that the latter are known, or believed, to be connected at the present day by intermediate gradations, whereas species were formerly thus connected.' His own insights mean that 'we shall at least be free from the vain search for the undiscovered and undiscoverable essence of the term species' (371). There are no pure types or natural kinds in nature. There is not a definitive bald eagle, or sugar maple, anymore than there is a definitive poodle. Every organism is a mutt. Indeed, it is not difficult to see how the breeding of domestic animals represents a paradoxical attempt artificially to produce what nature has failed to deliver – a pure essence of specific human-desired characteristics, a new realm of aesthetically and functionally efficient species.

The empiricism of White and Clare emphasizes the individual over the species, and is a way of seeing particularity and complexity in the natural world. This empiricism has a double effect. On the one hand, as the anthropomorphic language suggests, we can begin to sense the proximity of other animal life to our own existence. On the other hand, anthropomorphic language is itself clearly a kind of hybrid. If it is sufficiently self-conscious, aware that describing animal being inevitably involves an act of accommodation, as well as an awareness that there is an irreducible component of projection in speaking of and for animal being, then a sense of the otherness and difference of each animal is also preserved. 'Life' is not reduced to an amorphous sense of sameness. Clare's bird poems are wonderful examples of the double potential of anthropomorphizing. We realize in reading these poems that, like White, Clare is hoping to add to general knowledge about the animals he sees. Like White too, he seems content merely to list observed particulars, without any connecting narrative, as in 'Emmonsails Heath in Winter.'

> I love to see the old heaths withered brake
> Mingle its crimpled leaves with furze and ling
> While the old Heron from the lonely lake

> Starts slow and flaps his melancholy wing
> And oddling crow in idle motions swing
> On the half rotten ash trees topmost twig
> Beside whose trunk the gipsey makes his bed
> Up flies the bouncing wood cock from the brig
> Where a black quagmire quakes beneath the tread
> The field fare chatters in the whistling thorn
> And for the awe round fields and closen rove
> And coy bumbarrels twenty in a drove
> Flit down the hedgerows in the frozen plain
> And hang on little twigs and start again.[18]

Clare here anticipates William Carlos Williams's celebration of the thing in itself, as well as Gerard Manley Hopkins's sense of the muscular musicality of poetic language. The deliberate strangeness of the poem's language – its jarring mix of sounds, and of familiar and unfamiliar words – is a crucial part of the overall disorienting effect. This effect is produced by distinctness blurred or blended, as in the image of 'old heaths withered brake / Mingl[ing] its crimpled leaves with furze and ling.' Readers of the poem have not seen, and cannot see, this scene, though they have perhaps seen examples of the types of animals described. But Clare wants us to know what specific things *he* has witnessed; the varyingly distinct things he mentions – from a single heron, crow, and woodcock, to a drove of bumbarrels and the vaguer 'field fare' (a wonderfully generic name for a kind of thrush) – suggest a specific and nearly momentary depth of focus. Much of the poem's language would be unfamiliar to many readers; 'awe' for hawthorn and 'bumbarrels' for tits are not in the *OED*, and many other names are colloquial. The grammar and spelling too are idiosyncratic. Combined, these effects produce a sense that the reality described has been perceived by a specific observer, and that that observation is not reproducible. After a first reading of the poem many of us will barely know what has actually been described, though the precise and distinct sound of the poem suggests that something specific has in fact been represented. In the end, only the framing gaze of the observer connects the objects. The thing in itself is the moment of perception, and it is composed of distinct living things (plants, animals, and Clare) whose implicit meaning or relevance is only in their being together in Clare's range of vision. And yet no meaning is made explicit. In the context of the bird poems as a whole, this poem is just another piece of description, a bit of evidence that allows us to see how individual beings live together, how a

The Metaphysics of Classification 141

moment can be complex and complete without any desire to classify or separate. Interestingly too, the subjectivity of each being, including Clare's, seems equally present *and* remote, as alive or merely material as the 'black quagmire' which 'quakes beneath the tread.' (Whose tread? we may wonder.)

Other poems in the bird series are a little more forthcoming, such as 'The Wrynecks Nest':

> That summer bird its oft repeated note
> Chirps from the dotteral ash and in the hole
> The green woodpecker made in years remote
> It makes its nest – where peeping idlers strole
> In anxious plundering moods – and bye and bye
> The wrynecks curious eggs as white as snow
> While squinting in the hollow tree they spy
> The sitting bird looks up with jetty eye
> And waves her head in terror too and fro
> Speckled and veined in various shades of brown
> And then a hissing noise assails the clown
> And quick with hasty terror in his breast
> From the trees knotty trunk he sluthers down
> And thinks the strange bird guards a serpents nest. (213)

There is a wonderful economy in this sonnet as bird-watcher's field-guide – a hybrid indeed. In fourteen lines we learn an astonishing number of facts about the bird: when and where it may be seen, how its song may be recognized, where we may find its nest, what it and its eggs look like, and how it defends its nest. But the central point of the poem is surely to present an argument against egg-snatching. The actions of the peeping idler (as opposed to the patiently monitoring poet) are spurred by ignorance about what he does not really see. Careful observation, the poem implies, is its own reward; seeing the individual animal, noting its particular place and beauty, lead naturally to an ethic of conservation and a powerful egalitarian sense of the individual animal's right to exist. (There is none of the shock in reading Clare, as there is in White, of encountering an animal beautifully observed one moment that is quickly killed in the next to become a still-life object for classification.)

The anthropomorphism of these poems involves a subtle blurring of difference (the clown acts with the same instinct the bird does, for instance). When it is far more blatant, as in 'The Lamentations of Round-

Oak Waters,' in which the brook itself is made to speak, we see more clearly the way in which this language is a kind of hybrid, as James McKusick has noted. Clare's language, McKusick argues, 'strive[s] to attain the opacity and concreteness of natural phenomena while also evoking the sincerity of response that can only emerge from a wild, unpolished idiom' (242). Thus Clare resisted all proddings from friends and publishers to polish his grammar and spelling. The particularized and individual language of the poetry not only reflects Clare as the specific, anti-universalizing observer, but also reveals a kind of shared or overlapping subjectivity of the observer and the observed. Clare in his poems speaks to and for animals, trees, brooks, heaths, and moors, most often as a way of speaking about the loss of a community of specific humans, animals, and 'greensward spots' ('Lamentations of Round-Oak Waters'). Clare's occasional impersonation of these other 'beings' suggests his eagerness to interpret their behaviour, and ultimately his similarity to them. Individuals are distinct, but the birds and animals he sees are enough alike that the poet may imagine their voices, not by a kind of new-age telepathy, but by a sympathetic response based upon careful observation. That the poet can speak for other non-human beings suggests his sense that his own identity and language have been formed by these observations, these other lives. In 'The Eternity of Nature,' for instance, Clare explains his desire to speak for birds as a way of also explaining the assumed absence of an audience of his own:

> And so I worship them in bushy spots
> And sing with them when all else notice not
> And feel the music of their mirth agree
> With that sooth quiet that bestirreth me
> And if I touch aright that quiet tone
> That soothing truth that shadows forth their own
> Then many a year shall grow in after days
> And still find hearts to love my quiet lays (166)

Like Shelley in 'To a Skylark,' Clare sees the bird singing for itself as a grand simile for his own poetic activity, but the bird song is here neither triumphal nor disembodied. Although Clare is working over a romantic cliché, what is striking about the bird poems is how literally they reveal Clare adopting this strategy of singing with the birds. His poetry is a repetition of the bird's song, and is 'quiet' in that it appears to be directed at no other being in particular, and in that it sings of its surroundings, which is what Clare imagines, for instance, about the 'little Robin in the quiet glen' (166). And yet the implicit value of the poetry is also a sense of a profound overlap of tone, that his poetry will 'shadow forth' the voices of the lives that he has observed in the natural world.

I have been arguing that an important component of empiricism is resisting the categorizing tendencies of the naturalists who stress system, and the necessary assumption within such systems that language magically corresponds to real, natural entities. As Locke, Darwin, and Goldsmith (among many others) note, systematists reduce horrendous complexity to a manageable simplicity, but with the loss of detail that distinguishes the real from a mere tracing of the original. Systematists must hide gaps of awareness or push them to the edges (those exotic species as yet unclassified), whereas naturalists like Clare and White expose these gaps in the implied blank spots left between moments of observation, or in explicit inabilities to name (as in Clare's occasional poems simply about a 'bird'). They know that they have seen but little.

The writing of Percy Shelley, though, most clearly reflects a mode of thought that undermines species distinctions, or anticipates the implications of a dissolving of species fixity, which is not quite the same thing. If Clare and White find an openness to individual distinction at the level of the organism, inspired by what in the end seems like almost continual bird-watching, Shelley typically questions the very concept of individuality. He frequently erases boundaries at the abstract level of classification, so that in act 4 of *Prometheus Unbound*, for instance, he can find essential individuality residing at the molecular and the global level (anticipating the concepts of the selfish gene, and of Gaia in contemporary biology), as well as at the species level ('oh Man, and not men' [4.394]).[19] It is perhaps difficult to call Shelley's musings about the natural world empirical, since he is in both prose and poetry relentlessly abstract. Perhaps it makes more sense to call him theoretically empirical, or abstractly anti-essentialist. Though he acknowledges the linguistic construction of classes of being, Shelley imagines, and in his poetry attempts to realize, a reality that is 'equal, unclassed, tribeless' [3.4.195]. Shelley moves beyond or is perhaps largely incapable of the kind of specific observation we see in White and Clare because his perceptions are nearly always informed by a profound historical awareness. In 'Ode to the West Wind,' for instance, though the poem's speaker witnesses an actual storm in precise detail, he gains through his perception a vision of the past (the reflection of Pompeii) and the future (imagined as cataclysmic change). For Shelley, nature is defined by relentless change, by the absence of fixity. This change is materially driven, and is capable of radically altering any order life appears in the moment to have. In *Prometheus Unbound*, deluge and comets are imagined as causing the extinction of 'earth-convulsing behemoths, which once / Were monarch beasts' [4.310–11]; and in the vegetarian tracts, Shelley understands that animals (both human and non-human) are individually altered and redefined by changes in diet.

In broad terms, Shelley's sense of the relation of species to historical change can be interestingly compared to that of Cuvier, who is his contemporary, and whom he read. While Cuvier also imagined the earth's history in terms of cataclysmic change (as opposed to the British uniformitarian geologist James Hutton), he insisted most of all among naturalists of his day that species were fixed. They were defined by type, by the essence of the combined functions of their anatomies, which made them uniquely capable of existing. For Cuvier, species defined the range of possible life; an individual animal could vary from the species, but only to its detriment – it was diseased or malformed to the degree that it departed from the type to which it belonged. Just as individual molecules were replaced during the life of the individual animal without changing the functional identity of the animal, individual animals could vary without changing the essence of the species. Historical change, brought on by catastrophes, only eliminated species. They could not be altered by environmental change (as Erasmus Darwin allowed), and no new ones could be created.[20] As I note above, Cuvier's notion of the essential fixity of species depends on the ability of the scientist to determine type by an examination of generally internal anatomy. This is a science which gives free rein to the power of mental categories to determine the essence of the material, which is why Foucault has argued that Cuvier is the most important of all modern taxonomists.[21]

Shelley's thinking clearly overlaps with Cuvier's at crucial points – Shelley's vegetarianism, for instance, begins with a profound sense of how functional anatomy determines a healthy species ideal. Yet his sense that the ideal defined by function can itself be transformed suggests an important difference that brings us closer to Charles Darwin's sense of the complexity of the process of life, and the irreducible artifice of our attempts to categorize it.[22] Cuvier suggests a final harmony between the very ideal of order, discernible and reducible to abstraction by human consciousness, and a virtually static nature (his catastrophes do not actually threaten the ultimate order). That is, in Cuvier's fixed system, nature becomes equivalent to our reduction of it to *a priori* concepts, and our language conforms with arithmetical regularity to the external order. In 'Mont Blanc,' on the other hand, Shelley radically challenges these assumptions. This most empirical of Shelley's poems works to undermine both the sense that there is a static order in the physical world and the sense that our consciousness is capable of grasping whatever more complex order there might finally be.

The 'power' that Shelley aims to perceive and reveal is made present only through the 'everlasting' and 'clear' 'universe of things [that] flows through the mind.' Both in and utterly remote from perceived nature (like consciousness itself), this shadow can be thought of as a kind of abstraction for what cannot be classified. It is an order that lies beyond what we think we see or name.[23] The speaker finds it reflected in the overwhelming diversity of what he sees, from that blankness of the glacier and the 'flood of ruin' it creates, the chaos of the raving and bursting river, to the 'pines, and crags, and caverns,' over which 'sail / Fast cloud-shadows and sunbeams.' Indeed, part of what is most striking about the description of Mont Blanc is the chaotic mixing of classes of things. Foucault notes that it is not until the kind of organic functionalism of Cuvier that the 'antithesis of living and non-living' becomes a fundamental ground for all classification (231–2). What is mysterious about the power the speaker searches for is that it seems present in both organic and inorganic matter; he seems unable to find a clear boundary even between life and death. Glaciers, rivers, waterfalls, rainbows, and rocks seem instinct with life and meaning; broods of pine, predators (eagles and wolves), and the race of man seem bound with death, or are merely impermanent, barely a part of the elements he can scan. Mont Blanc is not exactly a synecdoche for the entire material realm, but it appealed to Shelley, as it did to thousands of other tourists, because it seemed to allow one to see the effects of geologic time compressed. Here one could see first hand the powerful geologic forces that shaped the very face of the earth.[24] The power of the material world is manifested in its ability to have changed so much. The speaker seems able to anticipate catastrophes that are not cyclical, but simply bring massive change, wiping out temporary forms of life, like eagles and wolves and humanity.

> ... the rocks, drawn down
> From yon remotest waste, have overthrown
> The limits of the dead and living world,
> Never to be reclaimed. The dwelling-place
> Of insects, beasts, and birds, becomes its spoil;
> Their food and their retreat for ever gone,

> So much of life and joy is lost. The race
> Of man flies far in dread; his work and dwelling
> Vanish, like smoke before the tempest's stream,
> And their place is not known. (ll. 111–20)

This power makes all classification temporary, a feeble and grandiose attempt by consciousness to create order out of what is inherently chaotic. Even in discerning the order of the moment, however, the speaker is inevitably baffled. He is indeed entranced by the chaos. The poem argues that he who sees the world most clearly must recognize, as Shelley suggests too in the *Defence of Poetry*, that language is creative and metaphoric, rather than itself being tied to some precise and fixed order. The most open-eyed view of the material realm reveals both the incongruity between consciousness and the chaotic external order, and the paradoxical dependence of the former on the latter. The physical world is nature's 'deep eternity'; in attempting to see its 'clear universe' the poet's 'human mind' becomes his 'own separate fantasy.' That is, consciousness seems to produce also an illusion of its own coherence and separateness, created by 'passively ... render[ing] and receiv[ing] fast influences' from 'the clear universe of things around.' The poem is a self-reflective account of the fact that the means of producing this inevitable separation, those fundamental classifications by which the universe is ordered, is language itself. It is as though we see most when we are filled with 'one legion of wild thoughts,' and it is only in the 'still cave of the witch Poesy' that some of these interchanges are reduced to shadows and ghosts of any ultimate order by being transformed into words. The *Defence*, and the poem itself, do not suggest that a discourse about the order of things is necessarily wrong; indeed, it is a necessary and creative act, part of the way in which Linnaeus, Buffon, and Cuvier became legislators of the world. The poem does suggest, though, that it is necessary to recognize the ephemeral nature of this legislation (which Cuvier, at least, did not). The complexity, the infinite density, of the physical world is its 'mysterious tongue / Which teaches awful doubt' – doubt, for instance, about our ability to perceive a totality, a complete order. I am not going to argue that Shelley thought of taxonomy as one of the 'large codes of fraud,' but I am suggesting that he may as well have. The emphasis of the poem is clearly on the incommensurate nature of our ability to recognize and reproduce external order. In contrast to Shelley's usual perfectionism, for instance, evolutionary change in 'Mont Blanc' is as physical, and unteleological – and thus as apparently lacking in order – as Shelley is capable of imagining.

What Shelley reminds us of here is what Charles Darwin also argued: that we see more clearly, we see more of the world, when we allow classification to be only a heuristic device, when we resist creating semantic objects that we quickly come to assume have an independent value. It requires a dexterity of focus, an ability continually to change the magnifying power of our microscopes or telescopes (or simply to pick them up), lest we become convinced that there is only one scale in nature. This is what both good science and good nature writing do. Each reminds us that there is more to know and see than can be known or seen by one person, one perspective, one set of categories.[25] Such writing attempts to reproduce the experience of perceiving nearly limitless detail, showing that we can dissolve our vision of the external realm, our patterning of it, into a focus of ever more particular objects. This finally suggests an empiricism that can remind us of Spinoza's ringing dictum that 'the more we understand singular things, the more we understand God' (165). Spinoza's God, like Shelley's 'power,' is not an ultimate order, a detached force, but a presence felt through the apprehension of limitless form. Both are 'beings' that are fully in and of the world, representing the unreachable potential of our consciousness to know that world.

V

Moving through the Environment: Travel and Romanticism

I have to this point focused my attention almost exclusively on romantic depictions of the natural world in poetry of the period. We think of poetry as the most refined, the most literary and thus mediated, of literary genres, and thus perhaps the least well suited to anything like the kind of empirical awareness that I have been arguing is a consistent impulse within the period – an attempt to look through culture and artifice at whatever is really there in the physical world, whether that presence is threatening or comfortingly similar to human being. Part of my argument has been that lyric poetry in the romantic period itself allows writers and readers deliberately to approach the limits of language, so that one might recognize that language itself distorts and reproduces what it represents. It is precisely this kind of self-consciousness that is crucial to a sound empiricism, allowing us to negotiate our desire to see the world empirically with the simultaneous awareness that that world is truly beyond our reach.

In this chapter I shift gears somewhat, and turn to another broad and loosely defined genre. In the context of romantic-period *readers*, the kind of writing which would most directly represent the natural world, and do the most to nurture a desire for encountering the diverse material presence of nature, was not primarily the nature lyrics of Wordsworth, Shelley, Coleridge, or Clare (though for modern readers they can do this very well), but rather the journalistic travel writing of William Gilpin, William Bartram, Alexander von Humboldt, Mary Wollstonecraft, and scores of others. I argue for three related points. First, that in travel writing of the romantic period we find an interest in the documentation of the particularity of the physical world. Second, that though the desire for knowledge of the physical world itself has ideological repercussions, this desire can nonetheless be understood as an end in itself. I am keen to show how the interest on the part of a writer and her audience in writing about travel and landscape cannot simply be reduced entirely to forms of imperialism and class distinction, as is frequently done in contemporary accounts of it. Third, that an examination of some of the formal features of writing about travel and landscape can help to explain its widespread popularity. Thus I hope to be able to ground my sense that the romantic period sees the development of an interest in the material otherness of landscape by showing that such an interest exists in texts beyond those of traditional, 'high culture' romanticism. I begin with some theoretical reflections, move on to a survey of a few kinds of travel writing at the turn of the century, and conclude with closer readings of the relation of travel and landscape in writing by Dorothy and William Wordsworth.

In attempting to define the genre of travel writing, Tzvetan Todorov, in a rhetorical equivalent of throwing his hands in the air, poses the question, 'What is *not* a journey?' For Todorov, the journey is a fundamental metaphor and one of the primary motivators both of narrative and an idea of narrative: 'As soon as one attributes an extended figurative meaning to the world – and one has never been able to refrain from doing so – the journey coincides with life, no more, no less: is life anything more than the passage from birth to death? Movement in space is the first sign, the easiest sign, of change ... Narrative is also nourished by change; in this sense journey and narrative imply one another. The journey in space symbolizes the passing of time; physical movement symbolizes interior change; everything is a journey, but as a result this 'everything' has no specific identity' (287). Todorov is right to note that the idea of travel, both as a quest for a particular goal and as goalless wandering, informs literary history from its origins. His question points us to the nebulous boundaries of writing about travel, that it is at once at the centre and the periphery of conceptions of the literary. Anyone seeking to write about travel must survey the field and stake out clearly what portion of it one hopes to define. Todorov's contribution to this act of definition is, however, tellingly abstract and ahistorical. Journeys, he argues, are primarily either about the traveller, or about the worlds the traveller encounters; 'the two kinds of travel narratives are opposed as autonomy and heteronomy, finding one's raison d'être inside or outside oneself' (292). One should add that they can be fictional or non-fictional (or both), teleological (and thus truly narratives) or open-ended and digressive, and written in the form of journals, epistles, or recollections. They are motivated and consumed by desires such as profit, pleasure, instruction, and conquest, to name but a few. Travelogues can involve varying degrees and kinds of observation; they may rely on other texts, reports of other travellers, or on flights of fancy. They can involve travel to places very near or very far, known or unknown, exotic or ordinary. All we may safely say, from the outset, is that travel produces texts, and texts produce travel, and that the relations between them are myriad.

In spite of these complexities, Todorov's bipartite division remains useful. The journey may focus inward or outward, and for Todorov the ideal travel narrative develops 'a certain tension (or a certain balance) between the observing subject and the observed object ... on one side, the boundary is science; on the other autobiography' (293). Yet Todorov construes the observable object only in human terms, as travellers seek to witness other people and their societies, and thus defends a nostalgia for travelogues of the colonial period, when writers were highly conscious of the cultural impact of such balancing acts. This focus on travel and travel writing as inevitably a mode of acculturation dominates criticism on the topic; James Buzard's excellent recent study of tourism and travel writing defines his topic strictly as a complex process of cultural negotiation, and notes early on that he will ignore 'types of tourism focused mainly on natural settings' (14). For the romantic period, this excludes an enormous amount of material, and a significant component of almost all travel writing. I will focus on the ability of travellers to observe and represent also the non-human world, especially the otherness inherent in landscape – the material sublime revealed through extensive, detailed description. The writing I am interested in is non-fiction, is in the first person, and involves a more or less daily exploration of new worlds, generally because the writer is moving through new physical environments. It includes travelogues and guidebooks, though the distinction between these two genres had not clearly been established during the period. This writing generally purports to reveal moments of discovery, whether the discovery is understood in scientific, cultural, or personal terms. It is challenging and rewarding because its negotiations between perception and representation, between differing cultures, and finally between consciousness and the physical world are frequently complex and explicit. Part of its appeal, like that of lyric poetry, is its apparent spontaneity, its ability to portray seemingly unpredetermined slices of the lives of travellers, and those places, people, and cultures which are encountered. Among the multiple motivations of travellers to travel must surely be the desire for the unexpected. It is precisely the open-endedness of travel that allows the complexity of the real to enter into discourse.

In terms of genre, travel writing is an explicit and continuous struggle between the ordering structures of narrative and the disordering, fragmenting tendencies of the (lyric) desire to reproduce the present moment (and the balance between these varies somewhat according to whether the writing occurs during or after the travel). The impulses of narrative are supplied by the itinerary, the route of travel, and the various personal and cultural ideologies the traveller engages in order to make sense of what she sees. Those of lyric are presented by the chaos of the real, the ability of the new to escape preconceived categories. To put it as abstractly as one can about a kind of writing which must continuously confront the realm of the particular, such travel writing may be defined as an attempt to put place into discourse. One travels in part to escape cultures and environments one already knows, or to seek new ones, or simply because one has the opportunity to put oneself in motion. At its most self-conscious, as Alison Hickey has argued for Johnson's *Journey to the Western Islands of Scotland*, travel is a matter of exchange and negotiation between the various systems one is familiar with and those one encounters. Regardless of intention, the effect of travel is to put the world in motion, and this inevitably involves noting the changing physical presence of that world.[1]

The popularity of travel writing – that it is a continuous presence in the history of books and reading, and that it enjoys a kind of explosion in the late eighteenth century – is due to the productive tensions between place and text that I have been describing. John Glendening argues more specifically that for tourism in general, and romantic travel writing in particular, 'what tourists sought in their travel readings and their own journeys was something that seemed more real and substantial, and thus more moving, than what they had known in their increasingly tense and disrupted lives ... a quest for authenticity, for real "experience" that lets us know we exist in some fundamentally valid and meaningful way.'[2] For Glendening, the desire for 'authenticity' that motivated tourism is consonant with much of what we call (increasingly neutrally, it should be said) the 'romantic ideology.' When a tourist seeks to overcome the inadequacy of his immediate life and environment, a sense of his contingency or incompleteness, 'the romantic imagination invokes, in privileged sites and experiences, an authenticity that can be arrogated to oneself, as a sought-for alterity validates the person capable of recognizing and feeling it ... With their escapist overtones, romanticism and tourism readily reinforce one another in a nostalgia-tinged attempt to recapture the freedom, simplicity, and intensity of experience associated with childhood and former times' (7).

Glendening's argument is powerful and suggestive. Tourism and travel invoke a romantic paradigm in that moving into unfamiliar territory isolates the self, allows it to recognize and recreate its own autonomy, which is more or less the same thing as a sense of authenticity. However, authenticity is produced not only through social disruption, which put notions of identity related to class and nation into play, but also through a growing sense of the difference of the physical world itself. This sense can also be produced by travel writing, informing readers of landscape beyond the familiar backdrops of their own lives. And while this may involve a desire for an escape or release from cultural constructions of identity, it can involve as well a more objective, or at least a more open and complex, perception of the physical world. Confronting landscape suggests noting it as a category – an object in itself – and recognizing both that it has obvious if murky relations to being, and that its existence alienates consciousness in the sense that its scope, solidity, and seeming permanence make it radically unlike human or animal existence. Landscape resists description and understanding. It may be made meaningful, but its meaning is not like that of texts. We may read landscape, but generally only when it is converted to text, and in that conversion we easily recognize an act of transformation, in which much is lost and gained.

Travel, then, reveals landscape as having a kind of authenticity, a presence unto itself, unspoken and unspeakable, which produces a yearning in us to recognize and attempt to know it. Whether or not one pays particular attention to one's local landscapes, as Wordsworth did, the yearning for authenticity seemingly inscribed in landscape is revealed in the movement from the familiar to the unfamiliar. Such movement indeed tests one's familiarity. Seeing unfamiliar landscapes makes one aware of the limits of one's knowledge. New landscape seems alien and authentic because it seems consistent only with an awareness of the larger permanence and materiality of the natural world. So too the familiar can seem unfamiliar, as it comes to be seen as part of this larger realm rather than merely as a backdrop onto which one has projected one's own small history. Reinforcing the notion of landscape's authenticity during the romantic period was the growing geological awareness fomented by the scientific debates between Cuvier and Hutton. These debates, as John Wyatt has recently shown (152–6), revealed to Wordsworth and other nineteenth-century travellers that landscapes had common and nearly inscrutable histories – of unimaginable physical forces in relentless cycles of flood and volcanic activity that stretched over millions of years. Indeed, that accounts of such forces were very much in the avant-garde of science during the romantic period would only have added to the general sense of landscape's mysteriousness.

That travel writing is vitally concerned with depicting the materiality of nature is perhaps now so obvious that it scarcely needs saying. It is worth saying, and examining, however, because we inevitably think of travel writing as revealing primarily cultural, political, and representational obsessions. It is equally obvious, but to literary critics much more in need of decoding, that travellers travel in order to encounter other people, cultures, and nations, and to put them in their proper places. Travellers risk the apparent comfort of whatever conformity exists at home, either to reproduce that conformity on a larger scale (to the degree that a traveller discovers underlying similarity), or to identify difference as 'other'; both, as Edward Said (among many others) has argued, are inevitably imperialistic procedures. The circle of the journey and the traveller's ability simply to survive his encounters mark the eventual stability of the traveller's voice and perspective. This stability in turn demonstrates – to the degree that readers can participate vicariously in the writer's experience, and take the traveller as a national or cultural representative – the resilience and power of the home nation or culture. The powerful assumption here is that putting place into discourse reveals how discourse controls and possibly pre-empts understanding of place. This discourse, as recent examinations of colonial and postcolonial writing have persuaded us, works powerfully to reproduce codes of cultural, racial, and gender superiority. Raymond Williams argued in *The Country and the City* that this can happen within nations (or cultures) as well as between them, that English tourists of even their own natural landscapes placed themselves into a separate class from those who inhabited the landscape they gazed upon. 'The self-conscious observer,' Williams writes, is 'the man who is not only looking at land but who is conscious that he is doing so, as an experience in itself, and who has prepared social models and analogies from elsewhere to support and justify the experience' (121). Criticism of travel writing has suggested, by focusing exclusively on how it works always to shape our understanding of place in terms of national, cultural, and epistemic dominance, that travel writing ought never to be thought of as mimetic.[3] Writing necessarily reduces the world to the human struggle for power. Even romantic and psychologizing readings of travel literature, like that of Dennis Porter, who argues that 'the most interesting writers of non-fictional travel books have managed to combine explorations in the world with self-exploration' (5), suggest that the landscapes confronted in travel writing are primarily symbolic and subjective.

I don't wish to suggest a strategy for reading the diverse genre of travel literature that skirts or downplays the obviously political and subjective component of this writing. Rather, I want to point to travel writing as a genre which, like lyric poetry, can draw readers' attention at least in part to the materiality of the physical world. I will thus demonstrate how specific examples of travel writing allow for negotiations not just between cultures, classes, genders, and races, but also between consciousness and the physical world, which encourages the attempt or desire to think through the problems of perception and representation to reveal a primary, physical, reality. Such desire is central, for instance, to the kind of experience contemporary travel and nature writer Barry Lopez explores:

> relationships in the exterior landscape include those that are named and discernible, such as the nitrogen cycle, or a vertical sequence of Ordovician limestone, and others that are uncodified or ineffable, such as winter light falling on a particular kind of granite, or the effect of humidity on the frequency of a blackpoll warbler's burst of song. That these relationships have purpose and order, however inscrutable they may seem to us, is a tenet of evolution. Similarly, the speculations, intuitions, and formal ideas we refer to as 'mind' are a set of relationships in the interior landscape with purpose and order; some of these are obvious, many impenetrably subtle. The shape and character of these relationships in a person's thinking, I believe, are deeply influenced by where on this earth one goes, what one touches, the patterns one observes in nature – the intricate history of one's life in the land, even a life in the city, where wind, the chirp of birds, the line of a falling leaf, are known … The interior landscape responds to the character and subtlety of an exterior landscape; the shape of the individual mind is affected by land as it is by genes. (*Crossing Open Ground*, 65)

Lopez suggests that even if (like Wordsworth's Boy of Winander) we are unaware of the impact of landscape, the physical enters and alters our consciousness. It is because culture does this so much more obviously that its influence is always threatening to drown out that of landscape. If we begin by recognizing that no unmediated response to landscape is possible, we can still allow that actual landscape makes a difference, and has a marked effect on consciousness. While a traveller may be in search of authentic unfamiliarity, an experience that allows for an objective glance at culture or nature, she probably cannot escape the fact that she is at some level merely a tourist, inevitably enslaved by conventional expectation, and 'mov[ing] toward the security of pure cliché.'[4] Yet, as Lopez suggests, the exterior landscape is as real as the interior one, and even the most myopic of tourists (who in the eighteenth century might be marked by his use of the Claude-glass, and who today is found taking in the new through the viewfinder of a video-camera) is still physically *in* a specific environment, and can be affected by it. Travel is not just about encountering other cultures, or imposing culture and consciousness, but also about recognizing the contingency of consciousness, and perhaps even the relative fragility and impermanence of consciousness and culture.

Barbara Maria Stafford has argued that travel writing that is self-consciously scientific, and illustrated with representations of the new lands 'discovered,' is the only kind which truly strives to 'grapple with real things. This conscious rejection of certain established mental constructions became part of the larger Enlightenment struggle to avoid the conventionality of verbal and visual languages in pursuit of an unmediated nature' (1). The explorer's enterprise, like that of the scientist, was 'predicated on the belief that he could discover a tangible (not an illusory) world exuberant with details and alive with the individualities that would withstand customary patterning, generalization or schematization' (1–2). She argues that accounts of scientifically motivated travel stand self-consciously in contrast to the vogue for the 'picturesque,' which she characterizes as thoroughly abstract, generalizing, and artificial, interested only in an aesthetics of representing nature, rather than the object itself (3–7). Yet her examples of the 'illustrated travel account' are in fact far less consistent, far more mediated by an astonishing array of conventions and conflicting interests, than she allows. William Bartram, William Bligh, and Horace Benedict Saussure, for instance, authors of three very different and relatively popular accounts of travel, exploration, and survival, mix stories of personal heroism, the exotic, the oriental, and the macabre with minute observations of fauna, flora, and terrain, and philosophical speculation. For example, Bligh takes careful note of tidal variations even as he and his crew are only days away, they think, from death by starvation. And Bartram regularly stops his narrative to speculate on such matters as the consciousness of plants and animals, and God's beneficence. Each is punctuated too by descriptions of landscape that are clearly informed by popular (though not necessarily consistent) notions of the picturesque and/or the sublime. Impressive scenery occurs everywhere. Part of the larger impact of travel writing is to confirm that while individual details of the natural world differ from place to place, the larger aesthetic, moral, and political order can be reassuringly stable. This is certainly how Helen Maria Williams, an avid reader (and sometime writer) of travel literature, sees the significance of Alexander de Humboldt's *Personal Narrative of Travels to the Equinoctial Regions of the New Continent*, which she translated into English, and for which she wrote an enthusiastic preface, part of which I quote here:

> Happy the traveller, with whom the study of Nature has not been merely the cold research of the understanding, in the explanation of her properties, or the solution of her problems! who while he has interpreted her laws, has adored her sublimity, and followed her steps with passionate enthusiasm, amidst that solemn and stupendous scenery, those melancholy and sacred solitudes, where she speaks in a voice so well understood by the mysterious sympathy of the feeling heart. With what soothing emotions, what eager delight, do we follow the traveller, who leads us from the cares, the sorrows, the joys of ordinary life, to wander in another hemisphere! to mark unknown forms of luxuriant beauty, and unknown objects of majestic greatness – to view a new earth, and even new skies! from which the stars known from childhood, the stars of home, have disappeared, and are succeeded by a foreign firmament ... What sympathy does the traveller excite, while he imprints the first step, that leads to civilization and all its boundless blessings, along the trackless desert, and, struggling within the savageness of the untamed wilderness, obtains a victory that belongs to mankind. (vi, xii)

Williams's wonderfully vicarious response to Humboldt points first of all to the passion travelogues could invoke in readers. The desire for escapism is explicit, of course, but so too is the desire for knowing about new places. The passage suggests as well the congruence between the paradox of the picturesque and the ideology of travel; Humboldt's voyages of discovery are a first step, as Williams says, to the civilizing of 'the untamed wilderness,' and yet this same travel takes the reader out of the worries of cultured life into a virginal nature which is at once utterly foreign and instantly recognizable as luxuriant, beautiful, and majestic. Such voyaging discovers new knowledge, and imposes old.

As Buzard notes, early travel books 'were apt to be the rather hybrid, discursive production of an individual, rambling from accounts of the author's own travels to facts and opinions on manners and customs, to commentary on the classical texts germane to the tour' (67). It is precisely the necessarily hybrid nature of travel writing that I wish to dwell on here, since it inevitably allows room for the inclusion of the materiality of nature. This diversity and complexity are apparent even in the romantic-period picturesque tour, which Stafford characterizes as numbingly abstract, and necessarily uninterested in the actual substantiality of the material. Wordsworth characterized the movement similarly in *The Prelude*, as a 'strong infection of the age,' which, though it interrupted his own 'deeper feelings,' was

> ... never much my habit – giving way
> To a comparison of scene with scene,
> Bent overmuch on superficial things,
> Pampering myself with meagre novelties
> Of colour and proportion; to the moods
> Of time or season, to the moral power,
> The affections and the spirit of the place,
> Less sensible.   (11.156–64)[5]

Contemporary criticism has had easy work deriding the vogue for the picturesque as assembling the very worst aspects of artifice, appropriation, and taste; yet such derision is inevitably reductive. Wordsworth acknowledges this in his own criticism of the picturesque in admitting that it is fuelled not just by matters of 'judgement,' but also

> another cause,
> More subtle and less easily explained,
> That almost seems inherent in the creature,
> Sensuous and intellectual as he is,
> A twofold frame of body and of mind.
> The state to which I now allude was one
> In which the eye was master of the heart,
> When that which is in every stage of life
> The most despotic of our sense gained
> Such strength in me as often held my mind
> In absolute dominion.   (11.166–76)

That is, the appetite for picturesque landscape that Wordsworth experienced was not just a matter of succumbing to popular taste, but also, it seemed to the poet, an appetite for *seeing* the world that is inherent in the act of perception itself. It is an appetite which, Wordsworth here argues, keeps the additive and projective abilities of the intellect too much at bay, preventing him from that 'deepest feeling that the mind / Is lord and master, and that outward sense / Is but the obedient servant of her will' (271–3). As Wordsworth himself recognizes, then, the 'picturesque' is not readily reducible to one theory or taste; its cultural popularity is not purely a matter of fashion, a product solely of the age, but is a manifestation of, or development from, some more essential need to see the world, a 'craving' for 'combinations of new forms, / New pleasure.'

Recent studies have argued that the picturesque is a primarily aesthetic category which performed the cultural work of detaching landscape from its particular connections to political or ecological orders, turning it into a commodity which might bestow class distinction. Elizabeth Bohls describes it as the ability to 'detach the viewer from the concrete particularity of the place he saw ... in order to assert the subject's distance from those social groups associated with the sense and their disorderly desires: the laboring classes and women.'[6] Certainly the enthusiastic use of the Claude glass – a tinted convex mirror which could produce from nearly any landscape an instant approximation of a heavily varnished painting of it – neatly and amusingly reveals the transparency of the desire to turn landscape into a mechanically reproducible aesthetic artifact. The picturesque, through its primary theorists William Giplin, Uvedale Price, and Richard Payne Knight, frequently involved a fetishizing of land, a practice which we don't need Bourdieu to realize is part of a process of class distinction and demarcation. I have no wish to deny the picturesque's political genealogy; it is as guilty of inducing cultural and social stupidity as any form of modern tourism. But, as Bohls notes, the practice of scenic tourism could not fail to note actual landscape, even as it desired to produce deracinated abstractions, and the picturesque was in any case ill defined and open-ended enough that all manner of interests could be included under its very large banner.[7] Travel and travel writing have the effect of deconstructing the 'station' – the paradigmatically pre-fixed perspective – revealing the artifice and shallowness of the image produced from a single vantage point.[8]

Indeed, Gilpin and Knight particularly are explicit about how arbitrary and limited their own aesthetic interests are, how there interests are a matter of evolving and merely personal *taste*. That is, they are all too aware that there is a 'real' and objective nature, which their viewing, painting, and describing mediates – often, and notoriously, by 'improving' it, but often too by failing to capture its 'true' magnificence. There is something nearly postmodern in Gilpin's frankness about how superficial his tour and pictures are (his discussions are generally about 'surfaces' and how they can be conveyed), and how pictures may be manipulated purely for effect. For Gilpin the common-sense difference between the real and the image or copy may be exploited rather than dutifully hidden or theorized. Gilpin is frequently explicit too about how much more impressive an actual 'scene' is than any attempts by language or paintbrush can render, so that the reproducer needs every trick possible simply to hint at the actual beauty of his favourite corners of England.[9] Moreover, the genre of writing that Gilpin defines becomes more, rather than less, diverse as it develops. Writers of picturesque tours of the Lake District such as Thomas West, William Hutchinson, and James Clarke devote themselves not to the production of pictures by travelling artists, which is primarily Gilpin's purpose, but to a more general class of tourist who might be inspired to see this type of scenery, even with the aid of a Claude glass (which West describes and explains how to use). They expand on the freedom for physical and spiritual wandering fomented by Gilpin's explicit mix of the conventions of art, and by self-consciously situating the tourist at boundary-lines of kinds of culture and nature, which allows for a dazzling variety of ways to be excited by *things* in nature. Like Gilpin's, their goals are enthusiastically multiple and contradictory and involve seeing the 'world' as though for the first time, wishfully unaltered, and seeing it as artists have seen it, or imagined it, before them. Such travel would mean being away from the city, in the 'wild,' even as these writers explain the most comfortable means of conveyance, and the most efficient routes. The highest acclaim picturesque travel writers can give a particular view is that it 'surprises,' and yet they give meticulous instructions for how to get to specific 'stations' that will yield exactly the same view they describe in detail, and, indeed, the view that all other tourists who follow the directions will see (which suggests in part an assumption that the actual view will be more impressive than any representation of it). These travel writers are variously interested, too, not just in views but, like Wordsworth, in the personal histories of local residents and travellers, in the human environments created within the natural ones.[10]

In these picturesque travelogues as well, then, having nature as a subject inspires not so much a freedom from all convention and a predilection for empiricism as a relative freedom within inconsistent convention and ideology that allows for the continued presence of a latent empiricism.[11] Part of the success of the travelogue in general is its ability to incorporate a variety of interests, and that of the picturesque in particular is the ease with which it allows readers themselves to recreate experiences of travel and perception, however limited, by practising the techniques for drawing and painting explained and exemplified in them. Such writing can give comfort that the sheer size of the planet, its variety and complexity – as revealed by accounts of increasingly far-flung voyagers – can actually be productively sampled by anyone. One can reproduce such work without wandering too far from home, and thus continue to feel rooted in an environment the edges of which have become increasingly distant and disorienting, even as these writings reveal them to be not categorically different from what one already knows. Thus the very popularity of these works speaks in part of a desire on the part of readers to know more about the physical reality which surrounds them; it is not a matter purely of a hunger for some cultural knowledge. The appetite for a 'complete' knowledge of a place can easily become self-caricaturing, as may be seen in the preface to Thomas Garnett's *Observations on a Tour through the Highlands*, which promises 'a description of the country, manners, and customs of the inhabitants, natural curiosities, antiquities, mineralogy, botany, natural advantages, proposed improvements, and an account of the state of manufactures, agriculture, fisheries, and political economy, with local history and biography. My purpose has been to give as perfect account as possible of every place and every thing I saw' (v). It is striking how frequently factual accuracy is the apparent pre-eminent concern of such writing. For instance, John Bristed's unintentionally farcical account of his 'expedition ... to see and to investigate the manners of the great body of the people, and to obtain a knowledge of their situation,' reveals the traveller as private eye: 'In order to effect this purpose we deemed it necessary to travel in such a condition as would, in all probability, induce the people whom we met to treat us without any disguise or factitious and artificial civility, and show their native character, whatever it may be, in all its outlines and features. We, therefore, assumed the garb of poverty [and] ... we took upon us the character of Americans, because we know that their nation was a favourite with the Scottish' (i).

Pleading for the accuracy of one's observations does not make them accurate, of course, but it is worth noting that writers were conscious that their readers were highly utilitarian. Travel writing had to provide information, a documentation of specific realities that were otherwise unavailable to most readers. The preface of John Stoddart's vaguely picturesque tour, after noting that '*Tours* are the mushroom produce of every summer,' argues that for any one such production to 'live,' it must 'serve as palatable and nutritious food for the mind.' Stoddard's notion of a nutritious text is one that is filled with the telling particularity of the actual:

> The squeamishness of modern taste is too readily disgusted with detail, and feels too little the importance of tracing Nature in her minuter operations. A work, however, which aspires to any permanence, must rest on more solid

merits; it must contain either a communication of important physical facts, and discoveries, or an accurate tracing, and novel illustration of human feelings. Natural philosophers of late have not unfrequently been travellers. They have displayed great talents and industry, they have accumulated much valuable matter, and their labour has richly deserved its reward; but high merit in this, as in all other lines, is rare: it demands a peculiar combination of favourable circumstances, a predisposition toward, and a long pursuit of the requisite studies, a ready eye for observing facts of a particular class, and a well-furnished judgment, to serve at once as their standard and storehouse. (viii–ix)[12]

Because, as he admits, he is no natural philosopher, Stoddart himself will be more 'humble.' Indeed, his preface admirably struggles to find some sort of justification for a kind of writing which he is forced to acknowledge lacks any real method, and will not be empirical in the way that a natural philosopher's writing can be. His vaguely Wordsworthian aim (which came to him while on a tour of the Westmoreland lakes) is to record the development of his own 'taste'; his self-education might lead to the similar education of the reader. 'Whilst I pursued the varieties of Nature and Chance, I strengthened the uniformities of sentiment and reflection. I persuaded myself, that if a just delineation were given of my feelings, together with the actual events, the local scenes, and the personal characters, which are essential to truth of description, it would create no unpleasing interest in the minds of a certain class of readers' (xi). Stoddart seeks to justify, in part, the randomness of his writing, its seeming lack of purpose, which is of course a feature of travel writing in general. Even Bristed's seemingly anthropological intent is overwhelmed by the sheer enormity and uncontrollability of what there is to describe, and his account descends, with unintentional comedy, into descriptions of how his constant need to be writing down his observations is interrupted by over-zealous hosts. The problem, as Sterne had revealed several decades before in both *Sentimental Journey* and *Tristram Shandy*, has to do with the enforced selectivity of narrative. One sees much more than one can narrate, and if it is a traveller's intention to record as much of his perceptions as possible, he soon becomes overwhelmed by the magnitude of the matter that needs narrating. Like Gilpin, most writers acknowledge not just that pictorial representation is inadequate to represent the real but also that written accounts are even more unable to convey the full presence of the real. From the writer's perspective, narrative threads offer coherence and purpose, but artificially reduce the full complexity of the traveller's experience. In general, travel writing avoids extended expectations of narrative except in terms of the route of the voyage, which rarely has anything like a climax or an expectation of closure – the trip ends when time or money runs out, when the circuit of the journey has been made, and so on; return trips are generally given scant attention. Moreover, the travel writer, as Stoddart's sensitivity makes clear, could also be aware of the problem from the reader's perspective. What value are the traveller's perceptions, and his recording of them, to a reader? What interest can there be in mere recording of facts as they are encountered along the essentially arbitrary route, and by what could easily seem like the random gaze, of the traveller? This is the pre-eminent question about such travel writing, I think, which is only partly explained by accounts of how such writing produces some sense of class, nation, or gender distinction. No amount of vicarious experience can yield such subsidiary effects if that experience is not *in itself* of some value.

Whatever their explicit or implicit intentions, travel writers are obliged to describe, in widely varying degrees of detail, the physical environment that is encountered; and they attempt to be precise about the route of their travel (especially when the books are offered not merely as travel accounts, but as guidebooks, which are intended to be used by tourists retracing the routes of the original). Frequently, they include little else. Indeed, these two matters form so much the core of travel writing that much of it is straightforwardly in the form of epistles or journal entries. Thus John Leyden, for instance, begins his *Journal of a Tour in the Highlands and Western Islands* without any kind of preface, but launches straight into the following, extraordinarily uninviting, account of the first day of the journey:

> *July* 14, 1800. – From Edinburgh to Linlithgow we traversed a flat uninteresting district, where the hills which confined our view presented nothing picturesque, and the groups which the valleys exhibited were extremely insipid. A distant prospect of the Ochil hills on our right, and the occasional glimpses of the Forth, were all that diversified the scene; so to relieve its uniformity we talked of the wild districts of Germany and Bohemia, and enjoyed a comfortable degree of that wise passiveness which is undisturbed by reflection, and suffers the uninterested images of things to glide over the mind as over a mirror. The ruin of Niddry Castle, situated beyond Kirkliston at the termination of a clump of trees, is the only picturesque object. (1–2)

There is nothing like an introduction here. We know where the travellers are, and, vaguely, where they are headed on this day. We have no idea, except from the title, what the purpose or destination of the trip is. We know nothing about the traveller and his companions. This information is supplied by the conventions of the genre, which include the discovery of picturesque scenes and simply the description of travel for its own sake. The very first line reveals the writer's intent to provide such 'interesting' scenery by his immediate announcement of the lack of it. Travel is revealed to be a diversion, a search for stimulating experience, even though Leyden is already so bored that he needs to discuss the exciting prospects of his German companions' previous travels. Part of Leyden's aim is a conspicuous display of his own touristic taste. He records only those elements which produce 'diversity,' and, as though sensing the need to provide evidence for the possibility of such diverting travel, before the second paragraph is done he has presented 'the most unequivocal proofs' of the journey of a Scottish laird to Ethiopia: 'besides numerous drawings of animals, birds, fishes, and plants which have never before been engraved, we saw twenty-four vols. MSS in Ethiopic, with some very elegant specimens of Ethiopic writing by Mr. Bruce.' Leyden travels to see the evidence of the travels of tourists. We can agree with Raymond Williams and many others that such travel is a dramatic signal of a kind of leisure class, marketing itself as a commodity of urbanity, of world-knowledge, a way of presenting travel to the public as a merely consumable item. Travel, and knowledge of it, confer a status of simple cultural accumulation. This commodification here literally turns foreign discourse into a collectable object, a 'specimen' of something exotic and meaningless.

While Leyden voyages for exotic specimens and landscapes that will fit his conventionally aesthetic demands for diversity, he nonetheless reveals the pleasure of traversing the land, of encountering new things. While we may reduce his motive for writing the book to the need to display his world-experience and leisure, it is harder to reduce the interest of Leyden's publishers and readers entirely to the same motive. Certainly readers could fantasize their own worldliness through the pretence of his own, but there remains an aura of the authentic otherness of what Leyden has seen and wants to see. He too will pause before landscapes, be surprised by them, and attempt to record them. Indeed, travel writing like Leyden's shows that we always learn more about how travellers react to landscape than about the landscape itself. The appealing paradox of such writing is that landscape remains as the real that escapes representation, and gains an allure as something primary because it fails to be represented. Reading such works can also yield the pleasure of catching a specific moment in real time, of co-imagining the space of one's land, nation, or globe. Thus such narratives open with the voyage beginning in some familiar place, to facilitate the transition into the relatively unfamiliar. However mediated and socially useful such travel writing and reading were, they nonetheless produce and reproduce the experience of moving through landscape. That this writing was repetitious and often strikingly *un*-detailed, and yet remained popular, suggests a yearning for an encounter with something real, for a desire to measure and connect with the diversity not just within single landscapes, as the picturesque required, but in landscape itself. Travel writing could produce an awareness of the depth of the natural world, giving a sense of scale to one's own spot of ground, and it is against such depth that we can measure the shallowness of the writer's own ambitions.

As Helen Maria Williams's response to Humboldt's travelogue suggests, part of the pleasure of such reading is in vicariously tracing one's own way through unknown landscape. Such an act involves following or imagining a map of these 'remote' regions, often helpfully supplied by the publisher. Not surprisingly, the increased interest in tourism, tour-guides, and travel writing during this period is matched by an increased interest in maps and atlases.[13] Map-making is itself a highly figurative act, of course, but maps aim for a functional precision (which can be political and topological), rather than primarily an aesthetic one. That is, one knows in reading a map that its intention is not to deceive by superficiality, but to allow one a basis in simplicity, in deliberate two-dimensionality, as it were, for beginning to know unfamiliar terrain. To put it another way, although maps are transparently reductive and can have a 'hidden [as well as fairly obvious] agenda of social power which operates on the reader as an unconscious force and through the symbolic meaning of the image,' they aim nonetheless to reproduce something of the factuality of the land they represent.[14] That maps are essential in the demarcation and ownership of land as well as of political organization (and are thus central in the creation of nationhood) is not irrelevant, but maps cannot be reduced simply to that function either. That travel writing encourages a curious repetitive meticulousness in locating oneself in physical space suggests the underlying yearning for knowledge of the physical. Part of the pleasure of these texts is the constant activity of situating the writer, where the reader's progress through the text is marked by the writer's progress through the landscape, and vice versa.

The payoff for following such writers is found in those moments when the pace of travel slows for the reader because something has caught the traveller's attention – that is, when she stops to provide detail. It is virtually a law of this kind of writing that degree of detail suggests the degree of the observer's interest. Indeed, most writers are far more attentive to landscape than Leyden. Here, for instance, is a not untypical description by the naturalist and cartographer Thomas Pennant, of cliffs at Flamborough-Head, from his popular *Tour in Scotland*:

> The cliffs are of a tremendous height, and amazing grandeur; beneath are several vast caverns, some closed at the end, others are porous, formed with a natural arch, giving a romantic passage to the boat, different from that we entered. In some places the rocks are insulated, are of a pyramidical figure, and soar up to a vast height; the bases of most are solid, but in some pierced through, and arched; the color of all these rocks is white, from the dung of the innumerable flocks of migrating birds, which quite cover the face of them, filling every little projection, every little hole that will give them leave to rest; multitudes were swimming about, others swarmed in the air, and almost stupefied us with the variety of the croaks and screams; I observed among them cormorants, shags in small flocks, guillemots, a pure black guillemots, very shy, auks, puffins, kittiwakes, and herring gulls ... (14–15)[15]

In this passage we have detail minutely rendered, giving a sense both of the size of the cliffs and of the proximity of the viewer to them. This is a scene not typical of either sublime or picturesque aesthetics; there is a sense of being overwhelmed by the variety of sights and sounds, but the point is not to inspire a sense of fear or bland harmony. It provides, rather, a sense of the novelty of the site – few readers will have seen such a spectacle – and reveals the natural world as complex, full of life, filled with environments which we might travel to see but in which humanity plays no real role. This description does not speak of a modern ecological ethos so much as it reveals the simple desire travellers and readers have for observing the intricacies of the natural world. Moreover, in contrast to much of the lyric poetry I have examined in preceding chapters, moments of this kind of detail celebrate the ability of language actually to represent something of the real. The use of catalogue suggests a faith that the fullness of nature can at least be approached through language. Such description is indeed the hallmark of much travel writing. It works to reproduce the presence of the real by enacting a kind of interchange between landscape and text, where the objective fixity of each form (the materiality of the land, the physical presence of the book, spreading the word) lends support and interest to the other. Most of all, such writing can breed a not insignificant desire to perceive this new, complex physical reality for oneself, to move, finally, beyond the text and representation, to see the world itself.

I am not arguing that the desire accurately to record perceptions of the landscape, of the physical presence of the world, is free of ideology, that there are no 'visual ideologies' (Rose, 87) at work in the recording of landscape. Neither do I wish to suggest that these texts should be treated as being simply representational. But the idea that ideology is inescapable has become a critical club, used tautologically to enforce the notion of the all-pervasive power of 'discourse,' which is always about modes of distinction and domination. The social conditions that frame the gaze of the traveller and his or her readers are of course important, as is the substantial cultural work that these texts perform. And there are certainly important differences of class, gender, nationality, and so on, which can be noted in the manner by which the traveller's gaze is framed, and differences too in the epistemological and aesthetic intentions of the writer. Yet such criticism allows us too quickly to lose sight of the constancy, and the similarity, of interest in the materiality of nature that travel writing frequently expresses. As critical readers, all *we* see about such writing is that it expresses cultural forces at work. Opposed to this, and equally persuasive in explaining the genre's popularity, is the ability of travel writing to register the existence of a natural world that could be seen as an end in itself, symbolic of nothing, filled with the intense complexity of the real. This interest in the physical produces, and is produced by, a desire for pure observation which travel encourages and reflects – a desire that is significant even if it is never fulfilled.

The evidence I have presented thus far for my claims about travel and the desire for the presence of the material has been relatively cursory, culled from an extensive if somewhat random survey of travel writing from the romantic period. I turn now to a more intensive examination of travel and landscape as reflected in writing by William and Dorothy Wordsworth. Dorothy Wordsworth's *Recollections of a Tour Made in Scotland* is a direct example of the kind of travel writing I have been surveying, and close reading of its depiction of landscape will provide substantial evidence for many of the claims I have been making about travel writing thus far. Examining Wordsworth's poetry of travel allows us to explore more fully the relation of movement to lyric and the representation of immediacy. Wordsworth's poetry reveals a self-conscious awareness of the effect of travel on the perception of landscape that is similar to the travel writing that I have been investigating.

It has not been sufficiently noted, except in the work of Byron, how important travel is within the traditional canon of romantic texts, particularly in the writing of William Wordsworth. Indeed, it is tempting to think of Wordsworth's most celebrated poetry as stemming less from a fixation upon the 'spot,' as Hartman has argued, than from movement. Hartman's famous thesis is that the prototypical Wordsworthian stance is symbolized by the 'halted traveller;' meaning floods in when the poet stops to meditate on the single object or place.[16] Yet the converse of this is also plausible: that movement rather than stasis produces Wordsworth's understanding of the physical world. The spot is only known as a specific 'place' through the perspectival triangulations that are necessarily produced by travel. A quick survey reveals that many of the great episodes of Wordsworth's autobiographical poetry are connected with travel. Wordsworth returns to the Wye on a walking tour, and the momentary stasis that 'Tintern Abbey' celebrates is punctuated as much by the spatial relocation as the temporal one; the poet has been to France and London in the intervening years, and has had to travel to return to a spot he has only ever known as a tourist. Though we think of Wordsworth as a poet of the Lake District, writing intensively about a small portion of familiar landscape that we imagine as almost continually available to the poet, most of the definitive episodes of *The Prelude* involve travelling to or away from such landscape. Indeed, much of the poem is taken up with accounts of the poet's walks and journeys, his encounters with new people and new landscapes. Its incipient moments, for instance, present the poet not just as a potentially professional poet, but more directly as a potentially professional traveller:

> Now I am free, enfranchised and at large,
> May fix my habitation where I will.
> What dwelling shall receive me? in what vale
> Shall be my harbour? underneath what grove
> Shall with its murmurs lull me to rest?
> The earth is all before me. With a heart
> Joyous, nor scared at its own liberty,
> I look about; and should the guide I choose
> Be nothing better than a wandering cloud,
> I cannot miss my way.   (1.9–19)

Part of the importance of *The Prelude* is that it is an extraordinary piece of travel writing. It explicitly presents the analogy between travel and self-discovery, suggesting both the idea (made icon and cliché by the paintings of Thomas Cole) that life is a voyage, and the idea that the poet's own growth came inevitably through travel.

What is important for my purposes is that travel in *The Prelude* is a crucial part of the poet's connection to the natural world. Much of the experience that Wordsworth records in his poem consists of his response to specific landscapes to which he has travelled, as well as the 'bliss of walking.'

> I love a public road: few sights there are
> That place me more; such object hath had power
> O'er my imagination since the dawn
> Of childhood, when its disappearing line,
> Seen daily afar off, on one bare step
> Beyond the limits which my feet had trod,
> Was like a guide into eternity,
> At least to things unknown and without bound.   (12.130, 145–52)

Wordsworth is filled with the desire, that is, to see the unfamiliar, which is here neatly described as that which lies just 'one bare step' beyond the horizon of what one already knows. Part of the restoration of his imagination, this book of the poem argues, comes not from escaping into meditative seclusion, but from his practice of

> ... wandering on from day to day
> ...
> ... [to] teach the sound
> Of poet's music to strange fields and groves,
> Converse with men, where if we meet a face
> We almost meet a friend, on naked moors
> With long long ways before, by cottage bench,
> Or well-spring where the weary traveller rests.   (12.137–44)

Many of the central episodes of *The Prelude* present the poet explicitly seeking unfamiliar landscapes, such as in crossing the Alps and Sarum's plain, and ascending Snowdon. As many commentators have noted, in these and other episodes of travel (such as the first of the 'spots of time') voyaging is characterized by disorientation, by losing one's guide or one's way, which reveals both an unexpected reality and an unexpected relation of consciousness to that reality. In crossing the Alps, for instance, this disorientation is initially the result of the power of the real to overwhelm subjective experience:

> That day we first
> Beheld the summit of Mont Blanc, and grieved
> To have a soulless image on the eye
> Which had usurped upon a living thought
> That never more could be. (6.452–6)

In part, Wordsworth records here the disappointment of a tourist's expectation; Europe's most celebrated sublime view is supposed to produce, as Coleridge's manufactured response in 'Hymn before Sunrise' suggests, a cathartic mystical revelation. The real Mont Blanc, the 'image on the eye,' is 'soulless' because its physical presence *must* take priority over subjective desires, and because it suggests no immediate relation or meaning to those desires. It is thus cold, austere, and sharp. One suspects the weather was too fine, the image too perfect. Or, perhaps, its scale is simply too large for Wordsworth, who is more used to the walkable hills of England. Its detail is too remote, and so only with the more specific detail of 'The wondrous Vale / Of Chamouny,' with its 'dumb cataracts and streams of ice, / A motionless array of mighty waves, / Five rivers broad and vast,' can the poet be 'reconciled ... to realities' (6.456–61). The latter produces moments of discrete vision, including spotting 'small birds' and 'eagles' which seem at home in this environment, allowing Wordsworth to overcome the sense of isolation that results from the monumental 'otherness' of the mountain itself.

This experience of the anticlimax of travel is reproduced in more detail with the account of his unwitting crossing of the Alps, a truly classic moment of touristic confusion and anxiety:

> Erelong we followed,
> Descending by the beaten road that led
> Right to a rivulet's edge, and there broke off.
> The only track now visible was one
> Upon the further side, right opposite,
> And up a lofty mountain. This we took
> After a little scruple, and short pause,
> And climbed with eagerness, though not at length

170 Romanticism and the Materiality of Nature

> Without surprise, and some anxiety
> On finding that we did not overtake
> Our comrades gone before. By fortunate chance,
> While every moment now encreased our doubts,
> A peasant met us, and from him we learned
> That to the place which had perplexed us first,
> We must descend, and there should find the road,
> ...
> Hard of belief, we questioned him again,
> And all the answers which the man returned
> To our inquiries, in their sense and substance,
> Translated by the feelings which we had,
> Ended in this, that we had crossed the Alps.   (6.501–24)

Though Wordsworth finds ample recompense for lost opportunities in the *non sequitur* on the imagination that has been seen as the climax of the episode, this passage presents with wonderful irony the crucial problem of finding one's way. Finding the right route here means approaching transcendence, reaching a climax or end that will bestow upon the whole voyage a sense of final significance. The traveller has yearned for the ultimate view, one which would put the whole complex place (the Alps?) into some purposeful order, and place the traveller (as in Casper David Friedrich's painting of that name) above the chaos produced by nature's own vertical reaching. It is a common enough touristic desire, I think. (Who has not been tempted, when faced with some too-large spectacle like the Grand Canyon, or the Rockies, to take one of those helicopter tours offering the possibility of a ready and total view of *the whole thing*?) The poet's bumbling and insistent search, his reluctance to accept the fact that he has crossed the Alps without any kind of significance being revealed, suggests the humbling of his desires. The ode to the imagination which follows aims to make the opposite point, as though Wordsworth learns from this anticlimax to forget about voyaging through nature to find such meanings, and to turn instead to the 'invisible worlds' of his own imaging. Yet this climactic addendum is itself undermined by the descent into a valley that is the actual continuation of the voyage, which 'dislodge[s]' the 'dull and heavy slackening that ensued / Upon those tidings by the peasant given' (6.549–51). In one of the most celebrated passages of the poem, Wordsworth returns to more discrete realities, just as he had after confronting the numbing image of Mont Blanc, though now the new realities are of a kind of permanent disorder.

> The brook and road
> Were fellow-travellers in this gloomy pass,
> And with them did we journey several hours
> At a slow step. The immeasurable height
> Of woods decaying, never to be decayed,
> The stationary blasts of waterfalls,
> And everywhere along the hollow rent
> Winds thwarting winds, bewildered and forlorn,
> The torrents shooting from the clear blue sky,
> The rocks that muttered close upon our ears,
> Black drizzling crags that spake by the wayside
> As if a voice were in them, the sick sight
> And giddy prospect of the raving stream,
> The unfettered clouds and region of the Heavens,
> Tumult and peace, the darkness and the light ... (6.553–67)

The description of Gondo Gorge, as I noted in chapter 2, gives little in the way of particular detail; it strives rather for a realism of effect. Indeed, the passage presents primarily the effect of various perceptions of the natural world on consciousness, with an apparent acceptance of their oppressive or turbulent power. Rather than being turned away from physical reality, Wordsworth has, by becoming lost, turned towards more specific ones, which are less able to produce some durable order. He sees on the way down what he presumably had not been able to notice on the way up because then he was looking for a vision in which consciousness would find some natural home, some full revelation that would speak directly to spirit. The episode as a whole suggests that travel reconciles us to realities by frustrating expectations and by forcing multiple perspectives upon us (both represented by the anxiety of being lost). We are made to feel the interaction of self and the physical world by noting the rapid changes of consciousness as we pass through rapidly changing landscape, which is precisely the effect this passage duplicates.

The episode may be interestingly contrasted to the ascent of Snowdon, a drama which supplies a much more direct climax, both because it is the poem's final episode and because it is an ascent which yields a more direct kind of transcendence. Here too the poet is on an 'excursion' with a specific aim in mind – 'to see the sun / Rise from the top of Snowdon' (13.4–5) – a singularity of purpose that is mocked by the interruption of the trek by the 'shepherd's cur,' whose own singular purpose is only the 'small adventure' of unearthing a hedgehog. (It knows precisely what there is to find on such hikes.) The specific vision the poet receives – and it matters that Wordsworth is talking about real phenomena here, something actually perceived rather than imagined – is again partly the product of disorientation. He is expecting a sunrise that would illuminate the earth and sea, revealing perhaps an Edenic order, and sees instead, as the climbers suddenly penetrate the mist that blankets the base of the mountain, a kind of instantaneous moonrise that illuminates a sea of clouds. The earth itself is reduced to the dimly lit peaks that protrude through the clouds and the sounds that appear to rise out of the chasm in the clouds. It is a richly symbolic scene, which Wordsworth spends the next sixty lines reinterpreting as evidence of the essential harmony between mind and nature; 'it appeared to me / The perfect image of a mighty mind' (13.69–70). One of the immediate implications of the event is again the heightening of sensory perception produced by the apparently necessarily disorienting effects of travel (here represented both literally and metaphorically), of being out of one's environment, as it were. Wordsworth argues that the scene showed him how 'Nature thus / Thrusts forth upon the senses' a power which is the 'genuine counterpart' (13.85–9) to our imagination. A more literal reading of the event reveals that it is not nature doing the thrusting, but the act of travel itself, which brings the poet to an unexpected reality, the 'universal spectacle' (13.61).

Travel in Wordsworth's poetry is less obvious, but equally important, in those passages describing the poet's walks to familiar places in the Lake District, often returned to after long absences (as with the Grasmere fair, which the speaker appears to approach from the road, symbolically representing the poet's return 'home'), or needing to be revisited in order to be understood (as in the 'spots of time' episodes). The Lake District, one learns in *The Prelude* as well as Wordsworth's *Guide to the Lakes*, is not just a place one travels to, but a place one travels within. It must be toured because it is too large to see at once, and because the views change so dramatically as one travels through it and as the weather changes. This is one of the central points of Wordsworth's *Guide*, whose descriptions he hopes will lead to 'habits of more exact and considerate observation than, as far as the writer knows, have hitherto been applied to local scenery ... Yet, though clustered together, every valley has its distinct and separate character: in some instances, as if they had been forced in studied contrast to each other ... In common also with other mountains, their apparent forms and colours are perpetually changed by the clouds and vapours which float round them: the effect indeed of mist or haze, in a country of this character, is like that of magic' (*Prose Works*, 2:170–6). Getting to know this region involves putting oneself in it in such a way that one is forced to recognize both its magnitude and the subtlety of its particular characteristics. In the *Guide*, Wordsworth objects to changes to buildings and landscapes made by recently arrived landowners because they have failed properly to perceive its existing beauty:

> But, in truth, no one can now travel through the more frequented tracts, without being offended, at almost every turn, by an introduction of discordant objects, disturbing that peaceful harmony of form and colour which had been through a long lapse of ages most happily preserved ... All gross transgressions of this kind originate, doubtless, in a feeling natural and honourable to the human mind, viz, the pleasure which it receives from distinct ideas, and from the perception of order, regularity, and contrivance. Now, unpractised minds receive these impressions only from objects that are divided from each other by strong lines of demarcation ... Moreover, a new habit of pleasure will be formed opposite to this, arising out of the perception of the fine gradations by which in nature one thing passes away into another, and the boundaries that constitute individuality disappear in one instance only to be revived elsewhere under a more alluring form. (*Prose Works*, 2:210)

Wordsworth objects to a version of the desire for 'outrageous stimulation' that he deplores in the 'Preface to *Lyrical Ballads*' – a need for order and pattern that are, from Wordsworth's perspective, too obvious and heavy-handed – resulting for instance in new houses that stand out too much against the landscape, and overly neat plantations of trees. Wordsworth's counter-aesthetic is one that reveals the deeper harmonies of what already exists, perceived through the deliberate observation of the District afforded by careful travel. The touring that Wordsworth recommends counters, that is, the fixity of the single view, which tends towards the stylized demarcations idealized in examples of picturesque landscape painting.

It is worth noting that experience produced by travel is represented in many of the *Lyrical Ballads*, as well as *Descriptive Sketches*, 'The Old Cumberland Beggar,' 'Resolution and Independence,' and, obviously, *The Excursion*. Travel in Wordsworth's poetry is a direct route to new experience, not just in seeing new landscape, but also, as Alan Bewell has argued, in observing people from the perspective of the Enlightenment anthropologist, actively seeking the unfamiliar in order to add to a detailed knowledge of a specific locality. Excursions offer new data, fresh encounters with 'unknown modes of being.'[17] For Wordsworth, travel allows a confrontation with the new and unexpected while enforcing the recognition that any observation is necessarily partial. As Bewell, Garber, and others have noted, the *Lyrical Ballads* present people from the margins of society in a remarkably non-judgmental way, suggesting a profound openness to the 'otherness' and interiority of otherwise unregarded representatives of the social world. Moreover, the observational mode that Wordsworth adopts in the course of representing his encounters is an attempt to work through ideology, rather than merely reproducing it. Ideology can be understood as those forces, ideas, and prejudices that necessarily frame the gaze of the observer and secure the fulfilment of expectation. Ideology reproduces visions of familiarity and helps to reduce or eliminate any kind of disorientation. All data is to be fitted into the same preconceived pattern; meaning is known before it is perceived. That Wordsworth's response to the people and scenes he encounters is frequently surprise and reflection suggests how the act of travel at least puts pressure on existing ideology in so far as it brings our gaze to something new, and asks for new kinds of attention.

Wordsworth is consistently concerned with the habits of consciousness, those practices that have become 'second nature,' which are to be trusted in so far as they are based on self-conscious nurturing, and to be suspected when they are not deliberately fashioned.[18] I have been arguing that he is particularly concerned with habits of perception, and that he represents travel as having the ability to shake him into a necessary self-awareness or mindfulness about the habits of taking in the world. He is aware, as it were, of the tyranny and arbitrariness of the observer's gaze, which we have noted already in his discussion of the picturesque – that what the eye lights on takes on its own special significance, completely apart from some necessary relation to a larger context. This is a double-edged power, on the one hand providing the observer with the creativity needed to find unfamiliarity in an otherwise familiar setting, and on the other allowing the observer to produce a private significance disconnected from the diverse orders of the real. These ambiguities are neatly depicted in a series of poems that present the observer in the metaphorical terms of a lover seduced by the object of his attention. Such, for instance, is the sonnet 'With Ships the Sea Was Sprinkled':

> With Ships the sea was sprinkled far and nigh,
> Like stars in heaven, and joyously it showed;
> Some lying fast at anchor in the road,
> Some veering up and down, one knew not why.
> A goodly Vessel did I then espy

> Come like a giant from a haven broad;
> And lustily along the bay she strode,
> Her tackling rich, and of apparel high.
> This Ship was nought to me, nor I to her,
> Yet I pursued her with a Lover's look;
> This Ship to all the rest did I prefer:
> When will she turn, and wither? She will brook
> No tarrying; where She comes the winds must stir:
> On went She, and due north her journey took.   (PW, 3:18)

The main question of interpretation is how far to press the poem's metaphor of the ship as lover: is the poem about the arbitrariness of the act of observation, or of the act of choosing a kind of mate, an object that is in some sense sympathetic or kindred? That the answer to this question is also arbitrary (suggested as well by Wordsworth's careful account of the poem to Lady Beaumont) suggests how neatly the poem exposes the dilemma of interpretation – that it depends apparently in equal parts on the object and the observer, the ship which thrusts itself 'like a giant' upon the view and the observer who 'pursue[s] her with a Lover's look,' who deliberately creates an interest in the object, making it special and different. Is it the gaze that produces her power, 'where She comes the winds must stir' (suggesting that the gaze, once drawn, takes in specific details that are otherwise passed over)? Or is the power her own prowess – this ship is simply bigger and faster, with more purpose, than the rest of the boats on the water, and thus has a natural 'right' to draw the gaze of the speaker? An 'actual' empirically discernible reality is here left deliberately open, suggesting an awareness of the complexity of the gaze that characterizes Wordsworth as observer. The poem points to the problem of how we give priority to objects: 'The mind can have no rest among a multitude of objects, of which it either cannot make one whole or from which it cannot single out one individual, whereupon may be concentrated the attention divided among or distracted by a multitude.'[19]

We cannot pass over the gendered terms of the poem, since their implications are both rich and troubling. The feminizing of the boat as object is more than nautical jargon; that her 'tackling [was] rich, and ... apparel high' points to the explicitness of the female personification. The poem is about a gaze that recognizes the boat as object, whose actual purpose and meaning are unknowable and yet to some degree projected and manipulated by the speaker. The poem thus seems an example of the kind of masculine, self-creating ego identified by Anne Mellor and many others, in which women and nature become instruments for self-definition. On the other hand, the power of the ship / woman is also its own; it moves unhindered by the gaze, and indeed quickly moves free of it, as though of its own volition, 'lustily' moving across the water. In the poem, perception is characterized by the wandering of the eye, and the search for something new and of interest, which piques rather than satisfies desire. The speaker is explicitly presented as a kind of voyeur, but the object of his gaze is utterly unaffected by it. The feminizing of the object suggests the romance of perception, and perhaps of travel in general – the objects that come to attention, which are singled out, or seem singular of their own account, appear destined in hindsight to have brought something of personal significance. The object that yields meaning counters the indifference or inimicalness of the landscape. Yet the allegory in this poem is so overt that it seems to highlight, rather than hide, the essentially arbitrary nature of the selected object. Indeed, what is perhaps most evident here is the desire of the observer, his need for some way to frame or give priority to what amounts to an infinite field of vision.

There are a number of other poems written around the same period which present a similar constellation of themes. Wordsworth's 'love' poem about Mary Hutchinson, 'She was a Phantom of Delight,' is indeed uncomfortably like the sonnet; here the traveller's gaze has become a metaphor for the lover's (rather than the other way round). The woman becomes 'A dancing Shape, an Image gay, / To haunt, to startle, and waylay'; she is an 'apparition' of the dawn, which seems only at first to be 'a moment's ornament' (*PW*, 2:213), This spirit, however, reveals itself 'upon nearer view' to be real after all – 'I see with eye serene / The very pulse of the machine; / A Being breathing thoughtful breath.' The poem borrows the image of the startled innocence of the traveller to supplement the classic trope of the godly or angelic woman; the gaze here seems literally to reconstitute the actual person of Mary Hutchinson. Yet the poem alerts us to the problem of desire and control intrinsic in regarding both landscape and a desired person. Selecting a mate and viewing nature are made alike throughout Wordsworth's *œuvre*, as a number of feminist critics have pointed out. For instance, Daniel Watkins suggests that the overlap between Wordsworth's desires for women and for nature is part of a coherent ideology in which women and nature are part of a 'frame within which the poet creates himself,' a process of 'constructing a masculine subject position with power over a feminine idealized object [that] is inherently an act of violence.'[20] There is no doubt that Wordsworth fails to render the full liberty of the 'objects' that are 'viewed' in these poems. The question both poems pose, however, especially when seen in the context of the traveller's gaze, is how it might be possible ever to do so. The problem is not so much with Wordsworth as with the very act of representing the act of perception. Such an act is always a kind of romance, reflecting the desire of the gazer, even when the gaze is turned on objects that seem inimical to desire (as I discussed in chapter 2). The love poem reveals the depth of this need, whereas the sonnet shows that Wordsworth is fully conscious of the arbitrariness of the gaze, that perceiving must necessarily be selective and reduce a field to an object. Infinite matter escapes notice, and so one must, in a sense, make love with what has come to stand out, to define the field of view or moment of perception. This is an inescapably reductive act, but to call it a violent one is hyperbole. Because in both poems the act of framing or centring the gaze is so explicitly an act of desire or delight on the part of the speaker, the 'object' itself is explicitly under-represented. It is not in itself reduced because it escapes the poem.

We see the romance of perception in the context of travel as well in such poems as 'Solitary Reaper,' 'Stepping Westward,' and 'I Wandered Lonely as a Cloud.' In each of these poems, the speaker is more or less explicitly a traveller, someone wandering or passing by, who has been brought to attention ('halted,' in Hartman's phrase) by a woman or a feminized object (the 'fluttering and dancing' host of daffodils). In each poem, a momentary vision or event seduces the traveller. The women and daffodils seem to arouse a sudden and unexpected desire that transforms the speaker, or rather, awakens him to the moment. In travel writing in general, we have seen, there is a constant struggle between simply trying to record everything one can, and finding significance in specific events and sights. Indeed, there is a kind of ennui in the former; the barrage of the new and unfamiliar brought on by travel can bore as easily as it can excite, because traveller and reader have no means of finding interest in any one object or event. In this context, Wordsworth's poems can be seen as depicting those moments when the traveller is prodded out of passivity, and his desire to find meaning is aroused. In 'Stepping Westward,' for instance, the cheerily symbolic greeting transforms the 'strange Land' from 'dark and cold' to a 'region bright.'

> The voice was soft, and she who spake
> Was walking by her native lake:
> The salutation had to me
> The very sound of courtesy:

>   Its power was felt; and while my eye
>   Was fixed upon the glowing Sky,
>   The echo of the voice enwrought
>   A human sweetness with the thought
>   Of travelling through the world that lay
>   Before me in my endless way.   (PW, 3:76)

The seduction of the speaker by the object of attention is here more subtle than in the other poems, but it is clear that for Wordsworth travel produces moments of value only when some connection can be established, when the possibility of meaning (produced in the interaction of self and other) arises. Such meaning is not produced by the narrative of a journey or quest, but is a matter of finding use, of converting landscape or objects within it into symbols as they are encountered. Wordsworth must personalize the moment and the place, must see a value in it for him, but such meaning is never made explicit; there is a sense that it is not even clear to the poet. These moments begin a process of interchange between the inner and outer landscapes, as suggested in 'Stepping Westward' by the way in which the courtesy of the greeting gives the speaker a 'spiritual right' to travel towards the setting sun. The transformation is one in which the landscape becomes more than a mere backdrop; the fact that the woman offers a greeting 'without place or bound' makes the place no longer unreal, merely picturesque. It is as though recognizing that this place is in some sense ordinary for some people takes it out of the realm of merely passing scenery and allows the speaker to confront it as something more actual, a place that is already familiar to others. Stepping westward, 'a kind of *heavenly* context' as the speaker puts it, suggests progress forward, an advancement, as opposed to the circuitous route of the tourist.

As I noted at the outset of this chapter, Wordsworth's poetry is not typical of what readers of the period turned to in their appetite for travel writing, though it is interestingly reflective of some of the concerns of travel writing in general. It is, most obviously, poetry rather than prose; it aims to present moments of heightened perception rather than the full course of the tour itself, and so somewhat idealizes the experience of travel. The poet's copious wanderings are reduced to those relatively few moments which bear obvious meaning, which have been personalized, as it were, by his having made use of them. He has husbanded and reworked them, adding the complex sheen of literary value. Most travel writing is by its nature uneconomical, recording an excess of fact, whose significance is clear to neither the writer nor the reader. (For this reason too, it is primarily prose, though several travelogues, particularly those by women, include both prose and poetry.) Indeed, travel writing, as I suggested earlier, generally provides this excess because the writer has no clear idea of what might, in the end, be significant. The voyage often appears to be recorded during the voyage itself, and the meaning of experience tends not to reveal itself in the present. Even recollections of travel (as opposed to journals, which one assumes are written more or less during the travels themselves) aim for the fullness of the present; the totality aimed for is not that of the coherence of a completed narrative, but of the fullness suggested by the diversity and detail of reality encountered. Wordsworth converts travel into lyric, and so typically records his moments of travel far after the event. Indeed, it is the ability of a specific moment to endure in his memory (as in 'I Wandered Lonely as a Cloud' and 'Solitary Reaper') that tautologically reveals its value to him. Because the selectivity of lyric is precisely opposite to the norm of travel writing, which strives for maximum inclusiveness of detail, my discussion of Wordsworth might seem beside the point, or show that his interest is always in his own consciousness rather than the physical world itself. Yet it has been my intent to show how travel as an actual phenomenon is important to Wordsworth, that travel in itself, apart from the generic and ideological processes involved in representing it, is thematically central to Wordsworth's understanding of the material realm, and that it cannot help but be. As I suggested at the outset, the enthusiasm for travel, in spite of its cultural and political trappings, necessarily enforces an awareness of the immensity, the primacy, the reality, of physical environments. Wordsworth's own interest in the physical world is necessarily a product of his own travelling experience.

William Wordsworth did much of his travelling with his sister Dorothy, and relied on her journals as an aid to his memory. There is a virtual critical consensus, however, that she reveals herself in her journals (including her travel writing) to have a fundamentally different sense of her ability to reflect, and reflect upon, the physical world. For instance, Margaret Homans states that in her prose, Dorothy Wordsworth typically 'denies her participation in visionary or poetic moments,' and so 'tend[s] to offer a view of nature not dominated by the viewer's consciousness' (86). Similarly, Susan Levin argues that 'her writing does not engage the world in the usual manner. She often appears to be a mere cataloguer of irrelevant detail, a person strangely fixated on the minutiae around her' (4). Anne Mellor argues that Dorothy Wordsworth is concerned to represent herself in a way that is 'relational ... and physically embodied – not a "mighty mind" but an organic body that feels heat and cold and hunger.' Mellor finds in Dorothy Wordsworth's writing a vision of a self that is 'interactive, absorptive, constantly changing, and domestic.'[21] Perhaps because the focus here is relentlessly psychological, the difference in genre is largely overlooked. For these critics, the differences between the two Wordsworths are fundamentally an expression of gender, especially in the sense that a woman necessarily reacts differently to the physical world from a man, but also in the sense that women are forced to regard the world, and write about it, differently from men because of obvious and invidious cultural constraints.

The latter argument is undoubtedly true, and can partly explain the hesitancy of Dorothy Wordsworth's entry into the realm of published writing and her reluctance to write explicitly self-exploratory poetry of the kind engaged by her brother. As Marlon Ross has argued, there can be no question that the idea of writing as a career, especially one in which the writing self could be revealed to the public in acts of self-producing authority, was a largely masculine project, defined explicitly as such by William. Yet much of the apparent difference in the way the two Wordsworths present their encounters with new worlds is a matter of the difference of genre rather than gender, an ancillary product of the form of their writing, and not indicative of an essential sexually differentiated response to landscape. Certainly the kind of cultural limitations that Dorothy Wordsworth faced must have made the writing of journals seem far more available than a career as a poet. And Dorothy Wordsworth's journals are indeed more particularized and detailed than William's poetry. Yet neither fact necessarily proves or suggests that women are by nature more open to landscape, more aware of the particularity of their environment, than men, as Anne Mellor suggests. No doubt genre is itself a gendered category; lyric is understood by, and available to, men and women differently during the romantic period. Thus, that Dorothy Wordsworth writes journals rather than poetry is a matter of cultural constraints, including Dorothy's sense that her observations and writing could serve her brother's labour as a poet. However, most of the features of her writing identified by these critics as distinguishing it are in fact consistent with much travel writing of the period. Travel writing clearly makes far different claims to the vague but crucial category of literariness than poetry does. It is utilitarian and aimed at reflecting external realities, and during this period is generally only incidentally autobiographical. The author of the travelogue displays herself unavoidably, but the interest of the audience and the writer is clearly directed elsewhere, thus producing an appealing and accessible mode of expression for women writers. While not wishing to downplay Dorothy Wordsworth's skill and dedication to a faithfulness to detail, I want to suggest that it is a typical feature of travel writing, encouraged, even necessitated, by the act of travel itself. Similar devotion to detail is found in Thomas Pennant's *Tour in Scotland*, as well as Mary Wollstonecraft's *Letters Written During a Short Residence in Sweden, Norway and Denmark*, Anna Jameson's *Summer Rambles in Canada*, and most of the examples of travel writing I mentioned in the first part of this chapter. An obvious convention of this travel writing is an attempt to reproduce the specific variety, the detailed foreground, found in the picturesque views that such travellers seek out and attempt to record. For a writer to reproduce the contrasts, depth, and irregularity of the picturesque, careful listing of detail is required. However, recorders of the picturesque can follow varying formulae to differing degrees. Ann Radcliffe's scenic interludes in *The Italian*, for instance, play on the uneasy relation between touristic description and a Gothic code for the exotic and mystery. Her set-piece accounts of Italian scenery borrow literally from travel writing a sense of the actuality of setting, which becomes a formulaic strategy for grounding the symbolic, supernatural, and psychological realities that are the primary subject of her novels. Indeed, what we see clearly in Dorothy Wordsworth's travel writing is the ability to communicate the sensation of discovery or personal revelation – the reality, we might say, of moving through unfamiliar landscape – through the reproduction of detail.

What remains to be shown is that underlying attitudes to landscape and environment in Dorothy Wordsworth's *Recollections of a Tour Made in Scotland* are not categorically different from those of her brother. That all her journals are so regularly punctuated with her observations of the physical world around her reveals in the first place that she felt herself to be engaged in an activity of perception and appreciation that was an essential component of her shared life with her brother. Her writing could be of service to him because in the process of steady observation, of alertness to the environment, moments of profundity could be discovered and / or rediscovered. My preceding discussion of William's poetry aimed to show the relation of travel to his own poetry, that travel reveals simultaneously one's longing for knowledge of the land and an estrangement from it. I need now to show that Dorothy Wordsworth's writing reveals a similar relation between landscape and travel.

Dorothy Wordsworth titles her travel account a *Recollection*, and it was composed after the actual tour through Scotland.[22] Yet her text presents itself as a journal, offering descriptions of each day of the trip in a fragmentary past tense, and with such a surfeit of detail that each account appears to be that evening's production rather than a recollection several months after the event. Also like a large number of travel journals, it begins at the moment of departure:

> William and I parted from Mary on Sunday afternoon, August 14th 1803; and Wm., Coleridge, and I left Keswick on Monday morning, the 15th, at twenty minutes after eleven o'clock. The day was very hot; we walked up the hills, and along the rough road, which made our walking half the day's journey. Travelled under the foot of Carrock, a mountain covered with stones on the lower part; above, it is very rocky, but sheep pasture there; we saw several where there seemed to be no grass to tempt them. Passed the foot of Grisdale and Mosedale, both pastoral vallies, narrow, and soon terminating in the mountains – green, with scattered trees and houses, and each a beautiful stream. At Grisdale our horse backed upon a steep bank where the road was not fenced, just above a pretty mill at the foot of the valley; and we had a second threatening of a disaster in crossing a narrow bridge between the two dales; but this was not the fault of either man or horse. Slept at Mr. Younghusband's publick-house, Hesket Newmarket. In the evening walked to Caldbeck Falls, a delicious spot in which to breathe out a summer's day – limestone rocks, hanging trees, pools, and waterbreaks – caves and caldrons which have been honoured with fairy names, and no doubt continue in the fancy of the neighbourhood to resound with fairy revels. (*Journals of Dorothy Wordsworth*, 1:195)

The writing here is not very different from Dorothy's journals. Like them, there is a dramatic absence in *The Recollections* of a sense of interiority; even in this first paragraph there is no suggestion of her motivation for the trip, her ambitions, or almost of any feelings at all. Even the 'threatening of disaster' cannot produce a self-reflective pause in this narrative. Her personal pleasure in response to natural beauty is suggested by the brief hint of the figurative in her language, and a transference of that pleasure onto the place itself: 'Caldbeck Falls, a delicious spot in which to breathe out a summer's day.' There is instead an interesting meticulousness, even a conspicuous display of it; they set out at 'twenty minutes after eleven.' The precision denotes the beginning moment of the tour, suggesting the importance or anticipation of the trip to come. It suggests too something of a scientist's scrupulousness for noting down facts, as though the first moment of a sustained record of observation must itself be noted. Most of all, it figuratively signals an attention *to* the moment. Consistent with the genre, this example of travel writing will appear to depict the world in the immediacy of the present moment, or as near to it as possible. There are no explicit goals; the route of their travel, the sites they hope to see, are given only by the book's title. There is no sense that any part of this account could produce a sense of narrative direction (leading to closure) or a desire for it.

Part of the pleasure of this kind of writing is the reproduction of the present moment, which gives access to the actual. Alan Liu, writing about the Grasmere journals, explains such writing as the process of creating 'an outer form of presence, grounded upon an inner representation by which the working self throws itself into daily correspondence with being.' Liu argues that the journals reproduce the experience of the present, and of presence, because Dorothy defines her being through the act of working ('Autobiographical Present,' 116). Yet in the *Recollections* this presence is not so much of her own being as that of the environments she moves through, and it is not the act of working so much as the act of observing that reveals her purpose (an activity Liu undervalues as work in the journals). In the introductory paragraph we can already note a specific structure or discipline, a surprising regularity of pace produced not just by her walking but also by the tempo of her descriptions. We are told about the major features of the day's journey, the hills, valleys, and towns, in each case with few particularities that begin to point to a complete picture. The account suggests a gaze which aims to be steady and continuous, unable to stop at one point (even if such a thing could be defined) because of the certainty that there is much left to describe. Indeed, seen in this light, the paragraph displays a judicious and efficient strategy for recording observation.

The similarity between Dorothy Wordsworth's journals and the *Recollections* is worth pursuing further. Both the Alfoxden and the Grasmere journals also begin simply by launching into a description of things seen, though the latter begins poignantly with the departure of William and John, with Dorothy remaining behind.

> Wm and John set off into Yorkshire after dinner at 1/2 past 2 o'clock, cold pork in their pockets. I left them at the turning of the Lowwood bay under the trees. My heart was so full that I could hardly speak to W. when I gave him a farewell kiss. I sate a long time upon a stone at the margin of the lake, and after a flood of tears my heart was easier. The lake looked to me, I knew

not why, dull and melancholy, and the weltering on the shores seemed a heavy sound. I walked as long as I could amongst the stones of the shore. The wood rich in flowers; a beautiful yellow, palish yellow, flower, that looked thick, round, and double, and smelt very sweet – I supposed it was a ranunculus ... (*Journals*, 1:37)

What we see in this paragraph, as several commentators have noted, is a straightforward suppression of interiority; she subdues her sense of loss at her brothers' departure by redirecting her attention outward to the world she knows her brothers also know well. She continues with this kind of description for another ten or fifteen lines, until we come to a rare moment of self-reflection – 'I resolved to write a journal of the time till W. and J. return, and I set about keeping my resolve, because I will not quarrel with myself, and because I shall give Wm. pleasure by it when he comes home again' – after which the text immediately returns to a description of her walk home from the lake. The motives for her outward turn are multiple – a means of repressing sorrow, of reminding her of her brother, and of giving him pleasure by both observing the world and writing down those observations. These activities are highly utilitarian, and distinguish her journals from what we typically think of as diaries, which are almost by definition private, written to and for the self. In contrast, Dorothy's journals, like her travelogue, are explicitly intended for an audience, for them to take pleasure in and make use of.

De Selincourt reminds us, however, that Dorothy Wordsworth reworked the *Recollections* substantially, which suggests that she was aware the text would be published, and that she was writing for a relatively public audience, unlike the journals. Yet she began this process only 'for the sake of a few friends, who, it seemed, ought to have been with us,' encouraged by William directly, and presumably as well by his general passion for travel writing (de Selincourt, *Dorothy Wordsworth*, 162, 163). The difference between the journals and this text is largely a matter of the consistency of style and amount of detail, which in turn is a product of the amount of time she allowed herself to devote to the project. Compared to the *Recollections*, in which Dorothy Wordsworth must offer an excuse for the barely perceptible change in the degree of detail offered between parts 2 and 3,[23] the journals are characterized by a substantial variation in the amount she wrote from day to day, an irregularity of attention that is presumably not the mark of a good travel writer.[24] One way in which her awareness of a larger, anonymous audience perhaps makes itself felt is that she scrupulously records every day of travel; the trip gives her a specific frame, and the genre a specific public purpose, for the kind of observing and writing that she had been doing for several years. Yet the function of the writing is substantially the same for both. As texts, they are both intended for consumption by others; with astonishingly few exceptions, the writing of the journals does not open up for her a private space in which she may explore or express notions of her own identity. They are, rather, experiments in recording reality, offering what might be thought of as a Lockean account of the sense impressions of daily experience. This writing would be useful either to her brother, who could and did transform portions of this writing into his poetry, or to the large audience for travel writing, who used them in somewhat different ways.

Writing journals with her brother in mind as a reader, Dorothy writes with a sense of shared experience – that the objects and events described are already known, and that reactions to them could be anticipated and implied. This sense of shared experience must be absent as she considers writing a travelogue for a public audience (as opposed to the few friends she initially considered writing it for). But it is not hard to imagine that these audiences would in effect make similar uses of her work. The value of such writing must lie in the observations themselves, the sense that the experience can be shared because it is grounded in the primary reality of a virtually immutable landscape, and the sense that this experience is itself of fundamental importance to being. In these ways, her writing is like those texts by her brother that I examined above. This is not surprising, because they largely lived and travelled through the same places, and both felt that their writing was in some sense produced by those landscapes. The crucial difference is genre. William's poetry foregrounds self and the deep inability of language to penetrate or reproduce the materiality of the physical world. In finding travel writing coincident with her own purposes, Dorothy eschews epistemological self-reflection in favour of pragmatic reproduction of observed particularity. Dorothy Wordsworth understands the task of her writing not as self-exploration, but as the kind of documentation of external realities that is an essential component of much travel writing. It is an error, I think, to deduce from this generic difference a fundamental and essential difference in modes of subjectivity, as Mellor and Homans have for instance done.[25] That the kind of self-examining, self-creating subjectivity ascribed to William Wordsworth through his poetry cannot be found in Dorothy Wordsworth's writing does not mean that it never existed. Texts cannot be considered the sole evidence for such subjectivity. And that Dorothy Wordsworth found a motivation for her writing in her sense that it would allow her to share something fundamental with her brother and her friends argues strongly for her belief in a profound underlying similarity in their subjectivities.[26] For both writers the daily observation of the external realm was one of the major components of life and consciousness, an activity that each felt was an essential component of existence.

Critical examinations of the *Recollections* have found in it a number of organizing principles. Criticism must make sense of the seemingly chaotic, even when, as is the case for travel writing, some of the arbitrariness and chaos of the writing has its source in the haphazardness of experience itself. John Nabholtz has argued, for instance, that the descriptions of landscape that form the bulk of the text 'are controlled by a basic aesthetic standard derived from the picturesque tradition,' namely, a desire for 'harmonious visual compositions which brought into unity varied and intricate parts' (20). It would have been extraordinary if Dorothy Wordsworth had not been affected by the vogue for the picturesque. However, as I argued above, the picturesque is not so much an aesthetic standard or a strait-jacketing visual ideology as a vague inclusive desire to frame landscape, which allows for both artifice and empiricism. Elizabeth Bohls, who gives the most sustained reading of *Recollections*, likewise argues that the picturesque is relentlessly abstract, denying particularity in order to reproduce a codified aesthetic – a way of *not* seeing the landscape. However, she finds that in the *Recollections* and the journals Dorothy Wordsworth works through and beyond the strictures of the ideology. Bohls feels that Dorothy's femininity necessarily does not allow her easily to assume that this all-powerful discourse could be her own: 'her class privilege qualifies her as an aesthetic subject, even as her gender keeps her at the margin of the aesthetic sphere. She can neither entirely adopt nor entirely resist this powerful way of seeing, but her journals show her maneuvering creatively in its discursive interstices' (177). Though Bohls's reading of the text is full of nuance, the explanation of the possibility of its complexity is based on a reductive logic, since it finds such complexity possible only in the intersection of identities essentialized by class and gender. Like Glendening, on the other hand, I find that Dorothy Wordsworth's text is a good example of a genre that is open to a large range of ideological and aesthetic influences. Glendening, though, argues that the hybrid nature of the text's interests may be reduced to a version of the romantic ideology, that is, to 'erase cultural and historical evidence that would interfere with her program of discovering unspoiled natives and landscapes ... What motivates Dorothy is merely an intense version of what drives tourism generally: the desire to escape not just one's normal social context but the idea that he or she is merely a subject of a context' (124). Texts are only interpretable in social contexts, and both Bohls and Glendening point to these contexts as a way of explaining a travel writer's motive for engaging in what might otherwise seem a random or arbitrary process of documenting one's experience on the road. My argument is that a motive for such writing (and its consumption) can include also the testing of social contexts *as such*, an existential project which allows for the possibility of developing an awareness that the physical world is a source or context of being (general as well as individual) as the cultural one is. Travel writing like Dorothy's does not aim directly to express individual identity, but to explore the physical context of human being that must be the ultimate ground for all social context. Thus travel writing involves a loss of consciousness and identity because it allows for the self to be flooded by an awareness of this physical context. This surplus of the actual must occur all the time anyway, but we become more intensely aware of it when we travel, encountering unfamiliar landscape, and people for whom that landscape is familiar. For travel writers like Dorothy Wordsworth, this grounding of being is simply assumed to be universal, an activity and interest that can be shared not just by her brother but by anyone who takes up the book.

Critical evaluations of the *Recollections* make their case on relatively few examples, where, for instance, Dorothy Wordsworth uses the term 'picturesque,' comments on features of the land and people that strike her as Scottish, makes comparisons to the Lake District, or distinguishes her travel from that of other tourists. These examples, while interesting in themselves, fail to register both the diversity of kinds of perception that Dorothy engages and the range of objects perceived. It is in fact difficult to discern a truly modal experience in the text. Most of all, critical accounts sell short the sheer quantity of physical description in the text. Travel and the passage of time are both marked primarily by descriptions in varying detail of new landscapes and the objects that inhabit them. Descriptions of the physical world form by far the bulk of the text, and critics can do little to reproduce a sense of just how continuous a presence the concern for the external is, short of persuading other readers to read *Recollections* directly. I offer the following example as a random sampling – part of the entry for 21 August, when they saw falls along the Clyde:

> The banks of the Clyde from Lanerk to the Falls rise immediately from the river; they are lofty and steep, and covered with wood. The road to the Falls

is along the top of one of the banks, and to the left you have a prospect of the open country – corn fields and scattered houses. To the right, over the river, the country spreads out, as it were, into a plain covered over with hills, no one hill much higher than another, but hills all over; there were endless pastures overgrown with broom, and scattered trees, without hedges or fences of any kind, and no distinct footpaths ... We walked, after we had entered the private grounds, perhaps two hundred yards along a gravel carriage-road, then came to a little side gate, which opened upon a narrow gravel path under trees, and in a minute and half, or less, were directly opposite to the great waterfall. I was much affected by the first view of it. The majesty and strength of the water (for I had never before seen so large a cataract), struck me with astonishment, which died away, giving place to more delightful feelings; though there were some buildings that I could have wished had not been there, though at first unnoticed ... The waterfall (Cora Linn) is composed of two falls, with a sloping space (which *appears* to be about twenty yards) between, but is much more. The basin which receives the fall is enclosed by noble rocks, with trees (chiefly hazels, birch, and ash) growing out of their sides whenever there is any hold for them; and a magnificent resting-place it is for such a river; I think more grand than the Falls themselves. (*Journals*, 1:222–3)

Though the Wordsworths and Coleridge have travelled to a spot frequented by tourists, the account is not really an 'adept verbal postcard,' as Glendening puts it, suggesting that much of Dorothy's writing is underwritten by essentially picturesque technique (129). There is little sense of the narrator having achieved the kind of stasis implied by having found a 'station,' which could produce the kind of implicitly framed image that might define the picturesque, even though she is visiting exactly such a station. The description is characterized by movement, and again by a paced regularity, suggestive of both the pace of the walk and the changing view. The description emphasizes fact and includes regular contrasts of scale. The falls themselves, the object of the day's walk, are not described in strikingly more detail than other things seen along the way. Also worth noting is Dorothy's reluctance to give her own reaction; she is 'much affected,' but provides no more detail than this. So, too, she uses relatively few adjectives in the description, and includes perhaps as an implicit explanation for her reluctance an anecdote about Coleridge's encounter with some other tourists who blandly apply the terms 'majestic,' 'sublime and beautiful' to the scene, the 'precise meaning' of which Coleridge had been trying to distinguish. The anecdote has the effect of placing her own reaction outside that aesthetic debate, and of suggesting that words in any case are reductive and imprecise in rendering the physical world.[27]

My examination of just a few exemplary moments cannot reproduce the effect of a text so thoroughly intent upon reproducing detail. The effect I am concerned with is cumulative. Page after page of such detail points to a project that is overwhelmingly pragmatic, as travel writing must be. One senses a commitment in the author primarily to do what she can in selecting particulars, and an awareness that landscape presents information that can only be roughly reproduced in the text. The information itself is the initial reward, which produces and reproduces a longing for the travel, and the land, which is both aesthetic (and thus subjective) and empirical. The pleasure, as Dorothy Wordsworth describes it, is of 'intricate windings,' as she reveals in the following description of the Loch Long by Arrochar:

> Crossed the bridge, and looked to the right, up the vale, which is soon terminated by mountains: it was of a yellow green, with but few trees and few houses; sea-gulls were flying above it. Our road (the same along which the carriages had come) was directly under the mountains on our right hand, and the lake was close to us on our left, the waves breaking among stones overgrown with yellow sea-weed; fishermen's boats, and other larger vessels than are seen on fresh-water lanes were lying at anchor near the opposite shore; sea-birds flying overhead; the noise of torrents mingled with the beating of the waves, and misty mountains enclosed the vale; a melancholy but not a dreary scene. Often have I, in looking over a map of Scotland, followed the intricate windings of one of these sea-lochs, till, pleasing myself with my own imaginations, I have felt a longing, almost painful, to travel among them by land or by water. (*Journals*, 1:289)

The description is straightforwardly objective, and again displays the pragmatic pattern of contrasting large and small scales to create a circumscribed sense of thoroughness. Though we get a sense of the observer as being slightly overwhelmed by the scale of what she sees, her account is not obviously indebted to the aesthetics of the sublime or the picturesque. The panorama is completely circular, adding to a sense both of the observer's attempt at objectivity and of her own relative insignificance in this landscape. We get a sense here too of the limits of her vision, of the distant horizons along the vale on the one hand and the loch on the other, none of which she can investigate further. The longing she speaks of is not clearly relieved by what she now sees; it is a desire to view complexity in the landscape more clearly and completely, to confront it directly for herself – in a sense to unwind this intricacy. The neutrality of the description is all the more remarkable given that Coleridge had just abandoned the tour, and that Dorothy writes explicitly about the sorrow this caused her. There is a clear sense of her not allowing emotion to colour her vision, or of allowing the scene to add to her melancholy.

Dorothy Wordsworth's pragmatism is marked as well by her repeated ability to reveal that her own perception is necessarily framed and relative, frequently by describing forms of optical illusion. By thus displaying a component of artifice in responding to and reproducing landscape, she is able to give readers a clear sense of the difficulty of the travel writer's task, and points to landscape as the object whose reality is to some degree incapable of being measured or assessed. In one such instance, she notes the effect of an accidental and physical narrowing of her vision:

> While tea was preparing we lolled at our ease, and though the room-windows overlooked the stable-yard, and at our entrance there appeared to be nothing but gloom and unloveliness, yet while I lay stretched upon the carriage cushions on three chairs, I discovered a little side peep which was enough to set the mind at work. It was no more than a smoky vessel lying at anchor, with its bare masts, a clay hut and the shelving bank of the river, with a green pasture above. Perhaps you will think that there is not much in this, as I describe it: it is true; but the effect produced by these simple objects, as they happened to be combined, together with the gloom of the evening, was exceedingly wild. (*Journals*, 1:239)

Even in describing an optical illusion she strives for objectivity, giving the facts of the situation, of what she saw and how she saw it. The effect, she says, is wild, but no details are given about what this specific framed view (or spectacle) meant for her, or how she reacts. Readers are left to guess at the actual image, and its effect, guided only by the very spare language – only the adjective 'smoky' is in itself provocative. (The scene suggests perhaps the 'visionary dreariness' described by William Wordsworth in book 11 of *The Prelude*.) Her reluctance to explain the image, to explore its meaning or her response to it, is probably owing to the obvious, if accidental, artifice involved in its creation. Its meaning would be too clearly a product of the power of the imagination rather than of the objects themselves. Yet the image does hold real power for her, and that power is in the objects themselves as well as the momentary framing of them. The episode points to an interesting self-awareness on Dorothy

Wordsworth's part that the reality she takes in will necessarily be distorted, suggested here by both the exaggerated stasis ('we lolled at our ease') and the exaggerated limiting of her view by the 'side peep' through which we can imagine her peering with just one eye. That the scene is 'wild' and yet narrowly focused argues for her desire to see the landscape widely and thoroughly, that she is not looking for specific, affecting views.

Like her brother, Dorothy frequently finds her gaze drawn to singular objects. She pauses, for instance, before what appears to be a large, levered mine pump, a machine 'it was impossible not to invest ... with some faculty of intellect' (*Journals*, 1:208). The travellers similarly confront a 'huge single stone' near Glenfalloch, which they attempt to measure. The presence of the rock poses for her a number of unanswerable questions, including whether or not 'that obscurity and unaccountableness, that mystery of power which is about it, [had] any influence over the first persons who resorted hither for worship' (370–1). The effect of both these objects is rooted in their materiality – that they have a presence and a definition that cannot be identified, even though the former is in fact manmade. An account of the object's function as a pump would serve to demystify it, but all three travellers prefer to indulge the illusion that it is a part of the landscape rather than something that could be interpreted. This makes sense only if the object is seen as something that is in the first instance material, as the cityscape of London is for William in the poem 'Composed upon Westminster Bridge.'

A similar encounter occurs in their visit to the 'rock of Dumbarton.' Dorothy notes at length, in her account of their wanderings around the base of the rock, the difficulty in assessing it, in figuring out what it is. She explains how it is situated, and that a castle, fortifications, and a house are built upon it. She notes too that the rock is 'deeply stained by time and weather,' and that it is 'of all colours, but a rusty yellow predominates.' It is as though she has difficulty resolving an impression of the rock because of its size and because she is too near to it to see the whole of it at once. A further sense of her disorientation is given through a description of another optical illusion:

> We sat down on one of the large stones which lie scattered near the base of the rock, with sea-weed growing amongst them. Above our heads the rock was perpendicular for a considerable height, nay, as it seemed, to the very top, and on the brink of the precipice a few sheep (two of them rams with twisted horns) stood, as if on the look-out over the wide country. At the

same time we saw a sentinel in his red coat, walking backwards and forwards between us and the sky, with his firelock over his shoulder. The sheep, I suppose owing to our being accustomed to see them in similar situations, appeared to retain their real size, while, on the contrary, the soldier seemed to be diminished by the distance till he almost looked like a puppet moved with wires for the pleasure of children, or an eight years' old drummer in his stiff, manly dress beside a company of grenadiers. I had never before, perhaps, thought of sheep and men in soldiers' dresses at the same time, and here they were brought together in a strange fantastic way. As will be easily conceived, the fearlessness and stillness of those quiet creatures, on the brow of the rock, pursuing their natural occupations, contrasted with the restless and apparently unmeaning motions of the dwarf soldier, added not a little to the general effect of this place, which is that of wild singularity, and the whole was aided by a blustering wind and a gloomy sky. (*Journals*, 1:240–1)

This account may well owe something to Dorothy's familiarity with her brother's poetic descriptions of disorienting singularity in his examples of 'visionary dreariness,' which I discussed in chapter 2. Dorothy's account, though, is much more explicit than William's about an awareness in the present moment of the involvement of her imagination, that the image she sees is in some sense artificial. This one is interestingly produced not by the mechanical means of a 'peep' as the previous one is, but by an unusual combination of the familiar and the unfamiliar, and by coincidence. The image is fantastic because it is momentary – an accident of looking up at the right time and from the right place – and a product of the habits of her own perception. Again, too, there is no obvious aesthetic code at work here. The image is explicitly a kind of picture, but it suggests the surreal rather than the picturesque, as Bohls has noted (197). It is clearly not objective or of the landscape itself. Dorothy here too refuses to specify the meaning of the image, even though she begins an interpretation, suggesting that its effect was more than simply one of oddity. Its key element is the contrast of the normal and natural sheep with the dwarfed and artificial soldier, both seen on the edge of a rocky precipice. The contrast interestingly reflects her own situation, her inability to align her perspective with that which the scale of the rock seems to demand. The sheep remain natural because they are such a common sight that they can easily be imagined as being a part of the landscape rather than being dwarfed by it, like the solider and Dorothy. Like the soldier, Dorothy's own wandering before the rock (and during her tour) has in a sense been stiff and aimless, an arbitrary traversing of ground. Furthermore, the soldier's position on the rock suggests a caricatured version of the tourist's gaze – looking mechanically from the highest point for a complete vision. His dress and his repetitive motion mark him as out of place, and as someone who is not able to pay the right kind of attention to the landscape. The episode thus mutely suggests Dorothy Wordsworth's sense of her alienation from the materiality of landscape, a sense that is nonetheless fuelled by a desire to see it as clearly as possible.

Dorothy Wordsworth describes another illusion during her unusually long and detailed account of their climb up the hill of the island Inch-ta-vannach, on Loch Lomond. The description of the views she remembers goes on at unusual length (roughly three pages), and is characterized by the intricacy and complexity of the changing mix of islands, lake, and hills she sees as she ascends. This landscape too is unresolvable, even though her perch seems to be neatly at the centre. Interestingly, her recollection centres on the views from the climb up the hill, rather than from the top, suggesting a preference for a view that is still in some sense incomplete and disoriented. She characterizes these views as being 'like a flash of images from another world ... it was an outlandish scene – we might have believed ourselves in North America' (*Journals* 1:251–2). She begins methodically trying to describe the islands, the most singular objects before her, but their outlines become lost; they are 'intermingled with the water, I might say interbedded and interveined with it ... There were bays innumerable, straits or passages like calm rivers, landlocked lakes, and, to the main water, stormy promontories.' As though troubled by the maze, the indefiniteness of objects, Dorothy attempts to look beyond 'the intricate view [to] Dumbarton rock with its double head.'

> There being a mist over it, it had a ghost-like appearance ... Right before us, on the flat island mentioned before, were several small single trees or shrubs, growing at different distances from each other, close to the shore, but some optical delusion had detached them from the land on which they stood, and they had the appearance of so many little vessels sailing along the coast of it. I mention the circumstance, because, with the ghostly image of Dumbarton Castle, and the ambiguous ruin on the small island, it was much in the character of the scene, which was throughout magical and enchanting – a new world in its great permanent outline and composition, and changing at every moment in every part of it by the effect of sun and wind, and mist and shower and cloud, and the blending lights and deep shades which took the place of each other, traversing the lake in every direction. The whole was indeed a strange mixture of soothing and restless images, of images inviting

to rest, and others hurrying the fancy away into an activity still more pleasing than repose. (*Journals*, 1:253)

The other-worldliness of the scene hints at transcendence; it is a view that seems to reveal nature as more than material, as mutable, fleeting, and including human constructions. Dorothy's description suggests a version of nature that is somehow complete in itself, defined by both movement and fixity, solidity (weirdly figured by the ghostly presence of Dumbarton rock) and fluidity. The impression seems to allow human perception a momentary and tantalizing access to a total vision of the external world. Yet it is clearly marked as artificial, based on her subjective perspective, allowing for a series of 'optical delusions' – not just of the floating trees, but also of the moving shadows of the clouds, and the mist hovering over the distance.

The effect is not so much of alienation, a sense of remaining outside and disconnected from the physical world, as of stalled insight. The image, she says, is 'intricate and homeless, that is, without lasting abiding place for the mind ... Wherever we looked, it was a delightful feeling that there was something beyond.' The inadequacy of her perception is suggested as well by the failure of the view from the top of the mountain to deliver a clearer sense of the place. 'Looking backwards, [we] saw the islands below us as on a map. This view, as may be supposed, was not nearly so interesting as those we had seen before.' The landscape is now resolved, as it were, into something clear and orderly, an image that reveals the solidity and fixity of the place at last, and one which we might expect to confer upon the viewer a sense of completion and knowledge. From the top, the travellers are able now to distinguish as seemingly discrete objects the islands, shoreline, and hills they had seen as oddly mutable, but this view now seems as unreal as the flux of images that they had encountered on their ascent. It is, in a sense, just one more view, not one that is more real than the others. Dorothy's dissatisfaction with this view is suggested not simply by the relative brevity of her description of it but also by the fact that they spend their time trying to pick out familiar houses along the shore, something 'comfortable.' In sharp contrast to the earlier views, the 'whole scene,' as she puts it, is 'beautiful' but also characterized by 'barrenness, or rather bareness.' The complete view here reveals a natural world that remains isolating, where human habitation seems insignificant, and where too little is actually revealed. The sense of connection through the perception of intricacy that precedes this view, which offered a sense of the complexity and scope of the natural world, is revealed to have been an illusion, based on seeing things incompletely rather than in more detail. And yet, while revealing the order of things, the view from on high sacrifices many orders of detail. Dorothy Wordsworth suggests here again how landscape inevitably avoids being seen. The episode neatly presents the dilemma of the romantic impulse to 'know' the natural world, one that ends inevitably in a sense of alienation. The craving for an intimate knowledge of the natural world, figured by the simultaneous desire for pursuing intricacy and for seeing individual objects resolved, is doomed to failure. Travel reveals that the world is always too large and too intricate, too interconnected, to comprehend. The natural world exists as the super-real, that which cannot be escaped, is always immediate and available, but is incapable of being resolved to distinct objects, or of being understood as an amalgamation of objects. This aura of dissatisfaction permeates the *Recollections* and, by implication, most travel writing that does pay serious attention to the landscape. Such writing presents an awareness of the inability of the traveller to have seen enough, and of the writer to have reproduced even that portion of world that was encountered.

I have been arguing that Dorothy Wordsworth is relatively pragmatic in her descriptions of landscape. She gives what information she can, and her accounts reveal the limitations of her perception. Moreover, she experiments with various ways of making sense of what she has seen, engaging conventional categories for putting her impressions into some kind of order. Thus, as many commentators have noted, she occasionally attempts to characterize what she has seen in more obviously picturesque or nationalistic terms. For instance, exhausted by her experience climbing the hill on Inch-ta-vannach, and, one suspects, by her attempt to describe it, she notes that on the long and uneventful walk to Tarbet, they 'saw a very craggy-topped mountain amongst other smooth ones; the rocks on the summit distinct in shape as if they were buildings raised up by man, or uncouth images of some strange creature. We called out in one voice, "That's what we wanted!" alluding to the frame-like uniformity of the side-screens of the lake for the last five or six miles' (*Journals*, 1:256). In yielding to convention, it is as though she senses that this is what readers might want too (a neatly limited contrast between order and irregularity); she does not bother with the kind of detail that is far more typical of descriptions of those scenes which draw her attention. Dorothy Wordsworth occasionally explores the idea that her impressions of the places and the people she has seen add up to idea of a nation, or perhaps vice versa, that an idea of a nation might allow her impressions to cohere. The idea of nationality is of a collective identity, which can literally incorporate a diverse set of particulars into a kind of super-entity. Travel to a foreign country naturally invites the sense that the nation can in part be defined geographically by its landscape, that the nation *is* the land on which a culture has developed. This encourages both an additive approach, in which all of the things one sees add up to a version of the whole, and a selective one – that a particular scene can be representative of that whole. Both strategies require finding something characteristic, an underlying order or essence of the landscape. One can assert that a landscape is Scottish, and one's idea of the nation is perhaps substantially composed of images of specific places that are at once distinct and characteristic. This is certainly an early intention of the Wordsworths, as is evidenced by this account during the fifth day of their trip:

> After ascending a little while we heard the murmur of a stream far below us, and saw it flowing downwards on our left, towards the Nith, and before us, between steep green hills, coming along a winding valley. The simplicity of the prospect impressed us very much. There was a single cottage by the brook side; the dell was not heathy, but it was impossible not to think of Peter Bell's Highland Girl.
>
> We now felt indeed that we were in Scotland; there was a natural peculiarity in this place. In the scenes of the Nith it had not been the same as England, but yet not simple, naked Scotland. (*Journals*, 1:205)

This is a curious passage. The impression of Scottishness is clearly an early, untested one, based on expectation rather than experience, and, weirdly, on a reference to William's not very Scottish poem, 'Peter Bell,' the eponymous hero of which has wronged a

> sweet and playful Highland girl
> A light and beauteous as a squirrel
> ...
> Her dwelling was a lonely house,
> A cottage in a heathy dell.   (*PW*, 2:374)

We might be forgiven for suspecting irony in Dorothy's reference. The poem's description does not inspire a very compelling image of a landscape (or of a Highland girl, for that matter). That Dorothy picks up the poem's clumsy use of the word 'heathy' (only to note that the scene before her is not, in fact, covered in heath) and urges strenuously that it 'was impossible not to think' of her brother's poem points to the self-evident shallowness of her feeling of having identified something characteristic in the landscape. What seems characteristic at this early moment is barrenness, attesting to an idea of 'simple, naked Scotland,' a patently naïve belief that, as the examples I have examined suggest, is not borne out by the landscape she comes to examine in detail. In the end, Dorothy Wordsworth's intimations of Scottish identity have little to do, in fact, with landscape. She comes to discuss national identity most frequently in descriptions of houses and people, particularly in connection with the 'highlands,' which she considers, not unusually, another marker of national identity. And her occasional comparisons of Scottish places to the Lake District are most often done simply as a kind of shorthand, to suggest substantial similarity.

As we have seen already, the land refuses to cooperate, to yield a meaning that overlaps somehow with that of the people and culture that abide there. In searching for an idea of the nation in landscape, the former comes to appear like the ghostly image of Dumbarton hovering over the landscape – as illusion, something insubstantial and temporary, a human construct feebly laid out over something comparatively substantial and material. This is the hope – one might almost call it an instinct – of much writing about landscape; as the quotation from Lopez that I discussed at the outset of the chapter argues, the land may shape consciousness, just as people may shape a landscape. A corollary of this argument (one that Lopez explores at length) is that experience with a common landscape necessarily produces in a people a distinctive, collective, identity. But how might one test such an assumption? Familiarity with a particular landscape may make that place comfortable, and allows the possibility of connecting one's own history with that place, as William Wordsworth documents in much of his poetry. Yet travel reminds one of the possibility that the meaning we create through such familiarity is itself contingent, a construct rather than something essentially there. An awareness of this possibility is suggested in an interesting exchange near the end of the *Recollections*. The two Wordsworths ask a Scot for directions:

> He answered in an intelligent manner, being perfectly acquainted with the geography of Scotland. He told us that the village which we saw before us and the whole tract of country was called Appin. Wm. said that it was a pretty wild place, to which the man replied, 'Sir, it is a very bonny place if you did but see it on a fine day,' mistaking Wm.'s praise for a half-censure; I must say, however, that we hardly ever saw a thoroughly pleasing place in

Scotland, which had not something of wildness in its aspect of one sort or other. It came from many causes here: the sea, or sea-loch, of which we only saw as it were a glimpse crossing the vale at the foot of it, the high mountains on the opposite shore, the unenclosed hills on each side of the vale, with black cattle feeding on them, the simplicity of the scattered huts, the half-sheltered, half-exposed situation of the village, the imperfect culture of the fields, the distance from any city or large town, and the very names of Morven and Appin, particularly at such a time, when old Ossian's old friends, sunbeams and mists, as like ghosts as any in the mid-afternoon could be, were keeping company with them. William did all he could to efface the unpleasant impression he had made on the Highlander, and not without success, for he was kind and communicative when we walked up the hill towards the village. He had been a great traveller, in Ireland and elsewhere; but I believe that he had visited no place so beautiful to his eyes as his native home, the strath of Appin under the heathy hills. (*Journals*, 1:320)

The misunderstanding between William and the Scot turns exactly on familiarity with landscape, and the lesson that Dorothy draws is more complex than at first perhaps appears. The familiarity of the Scot with the landscape allows him to know that the scene before them can be 'a very bonny place.' He presumably understands William's use of the word 'wild' to suggest something both primitive and inhospitable, which is insulting for a place that one considers home, necessarily linked to one's culture. That he is himself a traveller enforces this point; he has encountered all degrees of wild places, and he is defensive precisely because he can make and has made these kinds of comparisons for himself. This sense of wildness is insulting because it suggests either that human existence in that place must necessarily be degraded – that the landscape brutalizes its inhabitants – or that its inhabitants have failed to make the landscape sufficiently reflect human development and culture. The assumption here is that knowledge of a place alone can tame this wildness, make it completely lose its seeming otherness, which involves overcoming the fact of its materiality by projecting onto the landscape various orders of culture and consciousness. A place then becomes so familiar that its meaning is either that of one's own life in the place, or of one's own life in spite of the place, when landscape fades to mere backdrop. Dorothy is, however, developing her own contrast between wildness and beauty, and her notion of wildness consists not simply of the kind of primitiveness inferred by the Scot (and suggested by her description of the state of the village and its agriculture). We are indeed very far from an idea of 'simple, naked Scotland' here. Dorothy offers a virtual potpourri of causes for wildness, from the immediate presence of a sense of nature's immensity, produced by the sea-loch and the ranges of hills, and the area's relative isolation, to the specific weather conditions, which she identifies as being favourites of Ossian.

What is pleasing to both the Wordsworths, I have been arguing, is the ability of landscape to defy imagination, to refuse to reveal itself. Wildness here has an almost modern sense of the ability of some aspect of landscape to be beyond human perception (or activity, exploitation). This includes a sense of Dorothy Wordsworth's failure actually to identify an *idea* of Scotland as a nation in the landscape. Wildness is thus the inability of a natural landscape to reflect or hold such meaning, so that the land figures only itself, its own materiality, its connection to the larger materiality of the physical world. In this way it fails to offer a purchase for culture. Dorothy's sense of wildness might be thought of too as her recognition of having failed to find such coherence or meaning – of not, in the end, having paid attention to the political idea while roaming the landscape. The land comes to speak less of human identity than of its own impenetrability. This is an awareness produced, as I have suggested throughout this chapter, by moving through the landscape, attempting to focus on various scales of particularity and recognizing the inevitable partiality of one's perspectives. Consciousness may take in a vast selection of images and have them become part of the language of memory, but the landscape remains exterior and other, unaffected by our gaze.

Conclusion

Conclusions are appealing for readers but frustrating for writers. The scientific model is for conclusions to present the essential kernel of what has been learned, that which has been shown to be true. A good conclusion reveals the single underlying argument that ultimately holds all the preceding material together. What reader does not welcome it? Such a conclusion is all we really need to remember of the work in general. On the other hand, it is a tried but tired rhetorical gesture for writers in the humanities to forego even the possibility of such a conclusion. We often feel that our work is by its nature open-ended, speculative, inconclusive. We aim to suggest rather than conclude, to put ideas into play. I am torn between the two modes of concluding. I have assembled a diverse set of arguments intended, as I said at the outset, to show a variety of responses to the natural world, and that the careful study of nature must lead to complexity and even contradiction. A consistent thread of my argument, though, has been to suggest the value of resisting abstraction (which has the contradictory good sense of Blake's witty aphorism that to generalize is to be an idiot). I thus repeatedly point to how romantic writers celebrate the particular moment of perception as well as the specific moment of producing and interpreting the literary representation of that act of perception. In my survey of romanticism, as in my sense of the exemplary mode of romantic nature-watching, the moment is more important than the system.

There clearly is practical value in attempting, in the end, to offer a few even merely heuristic generalizations, to try to remind oneself and one's readers of the key arguments and implications of one's work. I have just offered one in pointing to the moment of perception as an end in itself, pre-empting theory and ideology. It follows from this, and thus much of my work here has attempted also to show, that romantic-period writers desire to perceive and know the natural world as clearly and truly as possible, through individual and particularized observation. Moreover, they frequently strive to understand the natural world as a realm distinct from consciousness and culture. Any kind of environmentalist ideology must begin not simply in attempting to find pleasure (aesthetic or otherwise) in the natural world, but in the desire to know it, to perceive it as it is. This is necessarily a dialectical process, contrasting the built and the unbuilt, the wild and the partially or wholly domesticated, the permanent and the transient, the objective and the subjective, the human and the non-human, and the familiar and the unfamiliar. In this sense, of course, we have always been environmentalists. But the strain of romantic thought I've examined here remains fixated on the material, the concrete particularity of the natural world that exists purely and simply apart from our conscious interest in and active alteration of it.

The primary evidence I've presented for this case is the sheer amount of interest taken in the natural world and the variety of ways that writers attempt to perceive and represent that world. The texts I've examined are characterized by the novel ways their authors put themselves into nature and make a careful exercise of studying it. This involves physical and mental work. The Wordsworths, we are too apt to forget, travelled an extraordinary amount, much of it on foot, solely with the intention of observing the physical world around them. They were both equally capable of seeing the grand vista and the flower at their feet. Astonishingly, Stubbs spent a year studying the anatomy of horses by dissecting them, carefully recording the many layers of their flesh. Gilbert White and John Clare made themselves intimately familiar with particular counties, seeing what was hidden to virtually everyone else. Shelley grounded his relentless desire for abstraction, for seeing totalities, with extraordinary moments of awareness of his particular connections to the physical world around him. All these writers as well observed the behaviour of animals.

This sheer appetite for the infinite physical presence of the world is itself worthy of analysis. However, a central paradox that my work returns to is that even as this interest in the physical was reflected in the work of these writers, and spurred by advances in geology, biology, medicine, and travel, it led also to the contrasting awareness that the physical world was less comprehensible and more alien than these writers hoped it would be – that as nature becomes increasingly the object of attention, as well as the avenue of escape, it becomes increasingly strange and unknowable. This is one of the ways in which romanticism heralds modernism and contemporary environmentalism. Even as we grow more capable of analysing and manipulating the physical world, and aware of the irreparable damage we do it and the potential harm we do ourselves, we recognize too that the physical will always be other. We are at once subsumed by it and remote from it, as Shelley and Wordsworth repeatedly reflect.

For me one of the most interesting signs of the change that the romantic period represents in the understanding of the physical world is that geology becomes a specialized discipline during this period. It had been the assumption of systematists like Linnaeus and Coleridge (and Pope too, for that matter) that everything was instinct with life because it was created by God, so that all the matter of nature was essentially the same stuff, a part of the same system. Thus they aimed to include both organic and inorganic 'species' in their conceptions of what Coleridge would call the 'one life.' But the very act of observing the world and reflecting upon our relation to it, as well as the profound sense of 'earth time' revealed by geology, showed that there were myriad different processes at work over different time scales. Thus nature could not be summed up as a single abstraction, or be imagined all at once. Moreover, as Shelley suggests in 'Mont Blanc,' geology shows that rocks are in a sense more 'real' than organisms of the biosphere because their cycles are longer and deeper, and because they are the most remote from consciousness. The development of geology, that is, suggests that nature may be, to borrow from Paul Fry once again, grey rather than green, inert and inimical to consciousness, rather than open to and productive of it.

It makes sense, my book argues, that this alienation from the material should occur in the period when Foucault identifies science developing into a powerful discourse. It is when we begin formally and systematically to study the natural world, to develop a discourse powerful enough to represent it, that poets sense the failure of discourse to bridge the gap between consciousness (perception) and the material. Life springs from the ground and returns to it, but the ground remains. The earth is a source and reminder of life, and exists separately from it, having its own far longer and deeper cycles which seem to mock the rapid rise and fall of individual organisms and species. In both 'The Ruined Cottage' and 'Michael,' stones feebly assembled mock human life even as they memorialize it. Whereas in Pope readers are urged to study nature to uncover a profound but readily accessible order which confirms a Panglossian view of human affairs, the natural world as it is known by the writers I've examined here becomes alien in new and profound ways. As more is known about its specific systems, cycles of generation and decay, orders of beings and things, the more it seems unknowable, fundamentally different from consciousness. The natural world is thus less capable of being an abstraction, or of being subsumed under one name.

My work thus counters the optimistic and idealist version of the literary interactions with science recently articulated by Philip Kuberski and Mark Lussier. Both authors use an understanding of the theories of twentieth-century cosmology and particle physics to reimagine the historical opposition between science and the humanities. Lussier argues for a 'synchronistic' view specifically of romanticism and nature, in which the seemingly fundamental uncertainties of modern physics provide an opening for a both a truly intersubjective universe, and a genuinely material consciousness.

> Romantic poets, in an effort to resist the alienation of mind and matter within Enlightenment epistemology yet preserve political liberalism, overturned mechanistic metaphors and articulated a symbolism of symmetry, of mental and material rhythmic cohesion in a universe best described as having an 'implicate order'; the material (historical, social, anthropological and scientific) and the mental (perceptual dynamics, cultural structuration and creative events) shape a founding symmetry based in complementary principles of mutual integrity. And in 'any Romantic natural science,' the practitioners reject 'mechanical metaphors in favour of organic ones.' Holism, then, is a feature of romantic theories of poetry and physics.[1]

This is a rhetorical idealism bred by a confidence in the multiplicity of metaphor to overcome historical and material difference. Lussier's speculations about the 'harmonies' between romantic idealism and the ability of modern physics to bridge the divide between consciousness and materiality are explicitly a kind of thought experiment, a poetic criticism that offers the thrill of resemblances. Its implications are green in the sense that they posit a natural world in which all is one, and from which we can never truly be alienated. For Lussier the paradigmatic moment of romantic poetry, as well as his own criticism, is when 'the divide between mind and matter, mental function and sensate experience, subject and object, is eradicated in the processes of perception' (35).

Romanticism has often been defined by such moments of idealistic reverie, in which consciousness 'becomes one' with nature one way or another, and Lussier provides here more modern and seemingly hard-edged rhetoric for this species of romanticism. But this typology is artificial not simply because it applies specifically twentieth-century (scientific) terminology to nineteenth-century poetry, but also because it takes the part for the whole. Undoubtedly there are moments in romantic-period writing where the desire to overcome the divide between subject and object – for consciousness and the material to inhabit each other – is paramount, as well as where consciousness projects versions of itself onto the landscape. However, my argument throughout has presented examples that stand exactly counter to these forms of idealism, where subject and object are not eradicated, where the intention is to see the object as clearly as possible, and where, in a sense, consciousness and the material remain mysterious to each other. The version of romanticism I've presented in this book shows how we exist outside the physical world even as we stand within it.

In the first chapter, I suggested that this resistance to idealism is in itself proto-environmentalist. It results in part from recognizing that the natural world does not exist for our existence, that its reality is 'other' and of a scale that is beyond human measure. I make this argument not so much to find an origin for this way of thinking about the natural world in romanticism as to counter a prevailing sense that romanticism is instead aligned with the idealist environmentalist stance that nature and human existence may be easily reconciled by positing some all-encompassing system or harmony, an 'ecology' or 'chaosmos' in which balance and order may be achieved at multiple levels (evolution, progress, population, imagination, perception, subjectivity). I've shown throughout the book as well that the merit of this resistance is primarily to keep in check – literally to test and limit – the reality we necessarily construct for ourselves, individually and culturally, physically and mentally. The physical world is the first and last site of the human impulse to colonize; we claim land, animals, territories as our own; we rule, remanufacture, and give meaning to them. The strain of thought I have been investigating attempts to recognize this practice as built on nebulous ground because it assumes that substance is malleable and transparent, somehow easily continuous with consciousness.

The most consistent dialectic of this strain of thought lies in an examination of the relation of the individual to the collective or class, the ability to perceive distinctness. It is a vexed topic, seemingly neutral, but rife with moral, ontological, and epistemological implications. For the most part, I have argued for a preference for recognizing distinctness in the perception of the natural world, that perceiving class, species, or group identity, seeing forms of common identity, whether through harmony and oneness, or clear hierarchies, allows for the distortion of abstraction and generalization, which involves a disconnection from the immediate reality of the physical realm. This world is seen closest, most accurately, when the observer is fuelled by a desire to see 'nothing that is not there,' as Wallace Stevens put it, which involves looking as well for what is uniquely there, allowing perception to be overwhelmed by the sheer volume of data. This is a fundamentally humbling posture, bringing us to the 'nothing that is.'

Dancing in my memory throughout discussions of this theme, however, are Wordsworth's lines from the 'Intimations Ode':

> – But there's a Tree, of many, one,
> A single Field which I have looked upon,
> Both of them speak of something that is gone. (*PW*, 4:280)

The desire to take note of particularity or detail (it can become a fetish) is precisely the ability exemplified in these lines of directing one's attention from many to one, an act figured in Wordsworth's poem as part of what precipitates the fall from a childhood state of visionary innocence into ordinary adult experience. The fall is defined in the poem as a failure of perception:

> It is not now as it hath been of yore; –
>   Turn whereso'er I may,
>   By night or day,
> The things which I have seen I now can see no more. (*PW*, 4:279)

This change of state is characterized by the loss of a special form of knowledge about the natural world. Indeed, the child's vision of the world is defined by the ability to see through the illusion of materiality in the world; the child sees the world as suffused with 'celestial light' that is immediate evidence for the abiding spirituality that is apparently present everywhere, and tells literally of a transcendent state, beyond that of the temporary succour provided by the 'homely Nurse' of nature. Seeing the one tree of many is in part a metaphor for the dawning of the child's own self-awareness, his sense that he is himself one, a distinct existence, a consciousness inhabiting a specific body and no longer a part of the collective activity of spring, in which

> ... Earth herself is adorning,
>   This sweet May-morning,
> And the Children are culling
>   On every side,

> In a thousand valleys far and wide,
> Fresh flowers; while the sun shines warm,
> And the Babe leaps up on his Mother's arm. (*PW*, 4:280)

The 'Intimations Ode' presents Wordsworth at his most idealistic and nostalgic, and prefigures the environmental dream for a world so deeply suffused with spirit that we are somehow reunited with it, which is the hope the poem ends with. But the poem also argues that the fall is inevitable and necessary, and not without its own rewards. Perception and consciousness must be *of* the world and its objects, and that act enforces a recognition of the separation not just between objects, but between consciousness and the object. Resolving the one (or the specific) from the many (the different or the similar) simply is a function of awareness. Each step downward to more specific oneness seems to reveal a more primary reality, even as it dissolves identity. Even that which seems only momentarily distinct or individual can have the effect of revealing the collective as merely an epiphenomenon. Recreating or synthesizing oneness at a larger scale is no doubt a crucial activity as well, and Wordsworth and Coleridge typically value it especially as an act of the creative imagination. However, it is an act motivated by an awareness of absence produced by the perception of specificity, of attempting to resolve the one. Indeed, it stems from the failure to make the resolution clear in the first place. The possibility of distinctness, oneness, fades as every 'one' is revealed to be itself pixellated at all scales (including the oneness of consciousness or identity, as Hume argued) the more resolutely we attempt to focus our perspective. The one becomes the many, and each component of the many is further constituted by other components. Nature too quickly overwhelms our ability to take it in, and so, for instance, the natural sciences are determined as disciplines in part through a somewhat arbitrary limitation of scales of perception and conception.

The fall the 'Intimation Ode' describes is about the discovery of the otherness of the physical world, a 'blank misgiving.' 'Otherness' is a bland, catch-all word, though it has been part of my aim in this book to reveal that it can be given nuance in specific contexts. The otherness I have been after, that Wordsworth and Shelley primarily have seemed to me to reveal, is that of meaninglessness, of a gap between nature and consciousness that is finally unbridgeable, a presence that is inimical. This otherness is revealed by a deconstruction of perception, especially when the perceiver seeks the kind of solace that nature is often thought to provide. It is the result of the impulse to know and see more clearly. The recognition of this otherness, the ability to perceive it, is indeed a mark of maturity, as Wordsworth suggests, the result of having taken in enough data. It is produced by noting the existence of forms of wildness, chaos, and death. A recent essay by Annie Dillard, 'The Wreck of Time,' presents a barrage of data that makes a similar point from the relation of the many and the one, exploring, as she does as well in the chapter on fecundity in *Pilgrim at Tinker Creek*, the sheer volume of death in nature. The essay focuses on human death, exploring the 'disquieting and possibly universal sentiment,' apparently uttered by Joseph Stalin, that '"a single death is a tragedy, a million deaths is a statistic."' The dead outnumber the living by 85 billion to 5.8 billion. Someone calculated that the entire human population, 'arranged tidily, would just fit into Lake Windermere.' It is estimated, Dillard reports, that there are nine galaxies for each living human, and each galaxy has a hundred billion suns. Her data work to show that 'we arise from dirt and dwindle to dirt, and the might of the universe is arrayed against us.' Her argument suggests that we still have difficulty, in fact, moving between the many and the one, that large enough collectivities lose all meaning for us, so that we do not shed a tear when we learn that 'on April 30, 1991 – on that one day – 138,000 people drowned in Bangladesh.'

Dillard drives home the point that we collectively subscribe to the hyperreality of our own existence, blithely ignoring massive evidence of our insignificance in the natural order, the scales of time and distance, and the fact of death. The essay is perhaps a satire aimed against our resolute self-absorption, our profound lack of desire genuinely to shift between scales of the one and the many, within the human world as well as outside it. Dillard's moral impetus is to force us to recognize at once that the physical world is the ground of our being and that we are profoundly disconnected from it. A reader's response may be a momentary humility, or conversely, a renewed zeal for seizing the day. The former response includes a recognition of how thoroughly we have allowed ourselves to define reality purely in terms of culture, of meaning determined by human desire. In this realm, the other is not radically other, and the one and the many are in some sense interchangeable. Neil Evernden argues that we have so completely domesticated nature that 'we are effectively alone, and must build our world solely of human artifacts. The more we come to dwell in an explained world, a world of uniformity and regularity ... the less we are able to encounter anything but ourselves' (*Social Creation*, 116).

Being aware of the irreducibility of the material helps us to explode abstraction and metaphor when we gaze at the land, enables us to scrutinize with a nearly Poe-like sensitivity the inimical difference of the physical world from our own. It is worth pointing out briefly that this privileging of the physical reality of nature characterizes such contemporary nature writers as Edward Abbey and Barry Lopez as well. Abbey signals this radical openness to the materiality of nature throughout *Desert Solitaire* by destabilizing human meaning and consciousness before the actuality of the material. The clarity of the desert air and light, the scarcity of life, and most of all the sheer overwhelming presence of the other-worldly desert rock are the features which Abbey most frequently notes. For Abbey, transcendence and metaphor are signs of the weakness of perception and imagination, required to turn the stuff of the world into the stuff of language and human desire. He defends his book against charges that it 'deals too much with mere appearances, with the surface of things, and fails to engage and reveal the patterns of unifying relationships which form the true underlying reality of existence. Here I must confess that I know nothing whatever about true underlying reality, having never met any ... For my part I am pleased enough with surfaces – in fact they alone seem to me to be of much importance' (xiii). Abbey too feels the urge to reveal the infinity of minute details that can become the object of our attention, claiming that ideally he would be able to write an entire book about a specific juniper tree in his camp (27). Like Wordsworth, Abbey fails to achieve the ambition of yielding personality to actuality, yet his explicit aim to resist these tendencies marks much of his writing, and allows the presence of the actual to be felt through it. Abbey recognizes that language, texts, and consciousness prevent us from seeing what is real, from recognizing the profound strangeness of the physical world.

Lopez is more sophisticated and self-conscious about the problem of how to represent and address the natural world. Part of what makes *Arctic Dreams* such a good book is that it solves some of the problems posed by Abbey's strain of anti-transcendentalism, in which it seems impossible actually to write about nature. Lopez returns repeatedly to the problem of how to find meaning and how to represent the natural world in such a way as not to lose a primary awareness of its physicality, its ultimate remoteness from consciousness. His solution is a relentless dialectic of perspectives that mixes personal epiphany and observation, journalistic accounts of scientific discovery, and narratives of aboriginal understanding. The subjective and personal is continually mixed with large doses of data, collected from a variety of sources. In the explicit mixing of these perspectives, the materiality of nature remains the object on the text's

Conclusion 209

horizon, the fundamental reality that can only be fleetingly rendered. Though he clings to an Emersonian sense that 'the very order of the language, the ecology of its sounds and thoughts, derives from the mind's intercourse with the landscape,' so that our perceptions and understandings of the environment may actually have some ontological validity, he returns repeatedly to the notion that 'the physical landscape is an unstructured abode of space and time and is not entirely fathomable' (257) – that our stories, our visualizations, our science, cannot penetrate the physicality of the world in which we find ourselves. Lopez's characteristic bowing before particular objects of his gaze signals not just reverence for them, but also a sense that consciousness can no more escape being 'interpellated' by landscape than it can by social forces. *Arctic Dreams* argues that our desire for the landscape to reveal certain kinds of meaning (about ourselves, about our relation to nature) cannot be divorced from our actual perception of landscape.

I am not here trying to trace a genealogy of environmental thought. I want simply, in ending the book, to suggest the value of the shock of the material, seeing it as a genuine tonic, and to suggest here the enduring vitality of this theme within the tradition of 'nature writing.' My final example is from Thoreau, who, if we are interested in genealogy, bridges the gap between British romanticism and American environmentalism.

> We need the tonic of wilderness, – to wade sometimes in marshes where the bittern and the meadow-hen lurk, and hear the booming of the snipe; to smell the whispering sedge where only some wilder and more solitary fowl builds her nest, and the mink crawls with its belly close to the ground. At the same time that we are earnest to explore and learn all things, we require that all things be mysterious and unexplorable, that land and sea be infinitely wild, unsurveyed and unfathomed by us because unfathomable. We can never have enough of Nature. We must be refreshed by the sight of inexhaustible vigor, vast and Titanic features, the sea-coast with its wrecks, the wilderness with its living and its decaying trees, the thunder cloud, and the rain which lasts three weeks and produces freshets. We need to witness our own limits transgressed, and some life pasturing freely where we never wander. We are cheered when we observe the vulture feeding on the carrion, which disgusts and disheartens us, and deriving health and strength from the repast. There was a dead horse in the hollow by the path to my house, which compelled me sometimes to go out of my way, especially in the night when the air was heavy, but the assurance it gave me of the strong appetite and inviolable health of Nature was my compensation for this. I love to see that

> Nature is so rife with life that myriads can be afforded to be sacrificed and suffered to prey on one another; that tender organizations can be so serenely squashed out of existence like pulp, – tadpoles which herons gobble up, and tortoises and toads run over in the road; and that sometimes it has rained flesh and blood! With the liability to accident, we must see how little account is to be made of it. The impression made on a wise man is that of universal innocence. Poison is not poisonous after all, nor are any wounds fatal. Compassion is a very untenable ground. It must be expeditious. Its pleadings will not bear to be stereotyped. (*Walden*, 216–17)

Thoreau too revels in the fact of death, when matter is transformed. The tonic of wildness is that it allows us to see genuine otherness of the material, beyond individual or cultural identities. The oneness we locate in our own individuality is threatened and undermined by confronting the tangle of life and death, organic and inorganic, that composes the natural world. It is a tonic to see that the meaning our existence generates for ourselves is radically contingent, that we are inevitably just a part of this, although our glimmers of understanding bring with them a shock of horror.

Notes

Introduction

1 See Motion, 244–7.
2 'We have, then, three forms of belief about the action proper to human beings, all apparently justified by the insights of ecology. We can live "in harmony" with nature, which to some is clearly the "natural" thing to do; or we can expand our domain by direct competition with other species, which certainly seems (at least since Darwin) a "natural" enough thing to do; or we can endorse the overexploitation of nature in certain knowledge that through our destruction we are doing nature's work [like forest fires or floods], just as we were "naturally" meant to do ... Nature justifies nothing, or anything. Ecology is today's official voice on natural matters, an institutional shaman that can be induced to pronounce natural whatever we wish to espouse. Ecology is, in this sense, simply being used as a blunt instrument to help implement particular life-styles or social goals' (Evernden, *Social Creation*, 15).
3 Naess, 45–56. See also Abram, who has argued for a necessarily phenomenological view of the relation of consciousness to the external world so that, as he puts it, 'The world and I reciprocate one another. The landscape as I directly experience it is hardly a determinate object; it is an ambiguous realm that responds to my emotions and calls forth feelings from me in turn' (33).
4 For a contrasting and more plausible account of the effect of the enlightenment on understandings of nature, see Allen, 23–4. Allen argues that enlightenment demystifying of nature allowed 'natural objects ... to lose their crude, straightforward power to overwhelm and even terrify, and to gain instead a far more subtle effect, by serving as the reflectors of inner human strivings and intuitions.' Anna Bramwell (16–18) argues for the deep ambivalence within green thinking towards science, an ambivalence we may easily find in Merchant.

5 For a more specific version of this critique, see, for instance, Biehl, 9–20.
6 Lussier, 25. See also Kuberski. Both writers see a profound connection between uncertainty in language and the complexity and indeterminacy of the physical realm, allowing deconstruction to apply to both literary and scientific theory. Both also see literature (of the romantic period for Lussier, and of the twentieth century for Kuberski) as pre-or co-figuring these insights.
7 Liu, *Wordsworth*, 104. Liu's argument is stronger than the quasi-idealist epistemological claim that we cannot escape the limitations of innate categories and modes of perception; there is no nature, for Liu, not because we cannot overcome individual cognitive limitations, but because we cannot escape cultural and ideological boundaries.
8 David Lindley has recently argued that the drive to find the ultimate unit of matter, perhaps as pure a form of materialism as we can imagine, has been driven to Platonic abstraction by the inability of particle physicists to test their mathematically produced theories. This allows them to produce 'a theory of everything [which] will be, in precise terms, a myth. A myth is a story that makes sense within its own terms, offers explanations for everything we can see around us, but can be neither tested nor disproved' (255).
9 I am using 'empiricism' here generally to suggest the importance of observation and experience, rather than in the historically specific sense, defined by Bacon and Locke, about how knowledge is produced. For a clear-sighted account of the latter, see Smith, *Fact and Feeling*.
10 Cf. Bone, 4–6.
11 'That the postmodern initiative has brought with it a revival of localist rhetoric is not, I think, in question. The local and the particular are now commonly identified as determining the only subject positions that are ethically and epistemologically allowable within a society whose fundamental fracturings are a sort of given' (Simpson, 118).
12 Our empiricism of 'literal' matter, as Liu frequently reminds us, isn't free of fuzziness either. It is only a similar rhetorical factitiousness that keeps physicists in the hunt for an ultimate particle. Richard Lewontin makes a similar case for the rhetoric of versions of particle physics and evolutionary biology, arguing that empiricism is sustained by a theory of evidence which predetermines its own facts, or details (Lewontin, 145).
13 Bate argues, for instance, that 'Wordsworth's localness, his capacity to make poetry out of his native region, was a necessary prerequisite for Clare's' (*Romantic Ecology*, 108). Kroeber sees Wordsworth's intimate knowledge of Grasmere as a crucial part of his holistic sense of place. 'Romantic individuality is a singleness incompatible with isolation. Essential to this perspective is the recognition of each specific element of the whole, not as equal to every

other but as equally necessary in its special fashion to the integrity of the entire system' (*Ecological Literary Criticism*, 56).
14 Murphy argues, for instance, that 'the other, in its various manifestations, including parole, culture, place, class, race, and gender, participates in the formation of a self. The individual occurs as a chronotype within the story of human interaction with the rest of the physical world, but that narrative is only a historical fiction organized by means of a limited perspective through which beginnings, middles, ends, and motivation are substituted for the non-human-centered, contiguously structured universal story that allots us only episodes – the self in and as part of the other ... Conceptualizing self/other as interpenetrating part/part and part/whole relationships rather than dichotomy is fundamental for apprehending the mutually constitutive character of the dialogics-ecology-feminisms triad' (9). Simpson finds the appeal of Haraway's argument in 'its bridging the gap between human and nonhuman by focusing on the cybernetic organism, both as a metaphor for a new concept of identity and as a literary description of what identity is more and more coming to be ... When it proposes that "organisms have ceased to exist as objects of knowledge, giving way to biotic components, i.e., special kinds of information processing devices," it seems to offer not only a newly positive use for technology but a socialized and deindividuated model of the self' (166). See also Haraway.
15 See, for instance, the 'social environmentalism' of Murray Bookchin, which argues for seeing cultural evolution as arising out of, but progressing beyond, biological evolution, thus allowing us to see culture, and the new environments it creates, as themselves natural. For an introduction to Bookchin's ideas, see his 'What Is Social Ecology?'
16 Liu hazards that in the case of cultural detailism 'there is an essential *et cetera* or similar stigma of incompletion far in excess of the margin-of-error requirements of normal science' ('Local Transcendence,' 86).
17 Johnston, 40–1. Johnston is working with Bill McKibben's idea from *The End of Nature* that 'We have deprived nature of its independence, and that is fatal to its meaning. Nature's independence *is* its meaning; without it there is nothing but us' (quoted in Johnston, 41).
18 See Allen, 71ff.
19 Quoted in Prickett, 129–30.
20 Dimock argues for a kind of criticism in which, 'besides locating a text in its original context (only one entry to that ongoing sequence), readers might want to dislocate it, relocate it, and line it up against competing voices – the natural sciences, the visual arts, law, economics – to see how it sounds and resounds' (1065).

21 Wallace Stevens, *The Collected Poems of Wallace Stevens* (New York: Alfred A. Knopf, 1968), 9–10. Used by permission of Alfred A. Knopf, a division of Random House, Inc.

1: The End of the World

1 Liu, *Wordsworth*, 104; see also 11–12. Agreement or disagreement over the phrase became a kind of statement of belief and political position at the session on 'Green Romanticism' organized by Liu in the 1992 MLA Convention in New York.
2 Herbert, 189–93. Neumann does not go as far as Berkeley, referring primarily to subatomic reality; moreover, the act of perception is not said actually to create materiality, but rather its dynamic subatomic attributes (which are, though, the essence of what is 'real' for particle physicists).
3 Baudrillard, *For a Critique*, 200–1. That for evolutionary biologists the possibility of design is anathema suggests the gulf between the two materialisms. For Baudrillard, as for Foucault, materiality is so mediated by the fact of language – its slippery relations, and its real effects in political affairs – that discussions of 'nature' as unmediated materiality are, simply, naïve. That Baudrillard has more recently argued for a theoretical rebalancing of culture and nature points to the unnecessary absolutism of his earlier viewpoint.
4 See Eichner.
5 Davie, 106–8. John Barrell in *The Idea of Landscape* argues that, as opposed to John Clare, 'Wordsworth's idea of nature was always more or less platonic, and the "spirit" of a place was something, for him, to be found by looking through the place itself' (182). McGann and Levinson have made this case most notoriously, arguing that Wordsworth's 'turn to Nature' is a delusory escape from social and moral problems he had been grappling with.
6 Paul Fry is the only critic I am aware of who has made this case in terms similar to mine ('Green to the Very Door?'). Drummond Bone makes a similar case for the theoretical importance of attempting to recognize a true materiality, but he implies that Wordsworth is precisely the wrong poet to look at, because in his poetry 'every turn to particular materiality [is] followed by a swing of greater moment in the opposite direction' (8).
7 'Tintern Abbey,' ll. 100–2. Unless otherwise noted, Wordsworth's poems are quoted from *The Poetical Works of William Wordsworth*, ed. de Selincourt and Darbishire, cited hereafter as *PW*. I shall refer to the text by volume and page number.
8 Fry, 548. Frederick Garber has also importantly argued for Wordsworth's 'object-consciousness,' his 'need to protect the integrity of the object' (6).

9 After offering a strikingly detailed imagining of the decomposition of John Wordsworth's body, Liu states: 'In the vision of the universe-as-assemblage no organisms die to be redeemed in a transcendentally-organic One Life. There are only assemblages passing into other assemblages.' I disagree with Liu, however, in his view that this vision of life, and death, is simply unavailable to Wordsworth because it is entirely the product of the postmodern moment ('The New Historicism,' 553–4).
10 See, for instance, Worster, 3–18.
11 This is a topic for another essay in itself, but to give simply a taste of this diversity, I offer the first quarter of the list of 'Contents' to canto 2 of Erasmus Darwin's *The Temple of Nature*, which covers only the first 165 lines of the canto, and does not account for the roughly 100 lines of footnote material generated by these lines: 'Brevity of Life; Reproduction; Animals improve; Life and Death alternate; Adonis emblem of Mortal Life; Solitary reproduction Buds, Bulbs, Polypus; Truffle, Buds of trees, how generated; Volvox, Polypus, Taenia, Oysters, Corals are without Sex; Storgè goddess of Parental Love; First chain of Society; Female sex produced; Tulip bulbs, Aphids; Eve from Adam's rib; Hereditary diseases ...' (38).
12 John Thelwall provides a succinct example of how defining nature is itself a central subject in political debate in his pamphlet against Burke, *The Rights of Nature* (1796): 'Mr. Burke's nature and mine are widely different. With him everything is natural that has the hoar of ancient prejudice upon it; and novelty is the test of crime. In my humble estimate, nothing is natural, but what is fit and true, and can endure the test of reason' (32). We are very far here from any kind of empiricism.
13 See Wu.
14 Roe, 3–9. Roe argues too that Wordsworth exploits the complexities of the picturesque to show that the 'view' is always one in a specific moment of history, rather than a universalizing one. Bate, *Romantic Ecology*, 54; Bewell, 275, 240ff. Bewell's work overlaps mine in connecting Wordsworth's poetic projects to the diverse range of natural history writing of the period. Another recent critic who examines the centrality of ideas of nature in Wordsworth's poetry is Marshall Brown, who traces the symbolism of the stone in Wordsworth's 'great decade' (310–61).
15 Quoted in Coles, 237.
16 An important dimension of this poem lies in its making absolute a distinction that was increasingly becoming blurred during Wordsworth's day. That is, while Wordsworth often thinks of the material – the rocks and stones and trees of the final line, for instance – as permanent compared to our mortality, he must also have been aware that the material world itself is characterized by

change and malleability. Indeed, as Marilyn Gaull has noted, the turn of the century marked the beginning of the 'golden' age of geology, a field of knowledge in which, in later life at least, Wordsworth expressed considerable interest. The debate that sparked the rise of geology was not about whether the global landscape was subject to dramatic change, but what forces produced such change, and the speed at which it could occur. Cycles within organic life had been observed for millennia, and formed a cornerstone, for instance, of Erasmus Darwin's visions of the natural world; that even the rocks were subject to processes of decay and rebirth was an astounding and much-resisted discovery, threatening, as it did, biblical accounts of creation and world history. John Wyatt has substantially filled in the possible sources for Wordsworth's knowledge and expression of geology, though he concentrates heavily on the final forty years of the poet's life.

17 That trees are organic seems relatively unimportant in this poem. They are fixed, rooted to the earth, and are not, say, a part of a forest, some larger life or being, as they are in 'Nutting' and 'Tintern Abbey.' On Wordsworth's imagining of forests, see Harrison, 156–64.

18 Though the ground covered by Bewell's discussion of the poem is similar to mine, our emphases are different; he argues that 'the absence or disappearance of Lucy's corpse, combined with our inability to place her physically in the grave, prevents us from locating her symbolically in the Underworld and frees us to imagine her afterlife in ways that our sense deny us' (207).

19 Cited in Levere, "'The Lovely Shapes and Sounds Intelligible,'" 89.

20 The new geological sciences generally countered biologically oriented visions of the 'economy' of nature, in being able to envision cycles of decay and destruction, rather than cycles that produced something essentially static, or in equilibrium. See Wyatt, 150–68.

21 As Hartman suggests about the poem, 'All symbols ... point to an exclusion of modes intermediate between birth and death, of human life as such' (*Wordsworth's Poetry*, 146).

22 Hartman, *Wordsworth's Poetry*, 350. Also, see Fry ('Green to the Very Door?') for a concise critical history of this de-idealizing strain within Wordsworth criticism.

23 Quotations from *The Prelude* are from the 1805 edition, ed. Wordsworth, Abrams, and Gill.

24 I take it that it is Locke's version of materialism, which would reduce language and consciousness to instruments of physical laws, that Wordsworth objects to in the Fenwick note to the 'Intimations Ode,' where he calls it the 'subjugation,' contrary to childhood idealism, that he has come to deplore. To be fair, one gets a similar sense *from* Locke himself that language is incapable of

accounting for sensations or ideas produced by materiality. See, for instance, his account of the 'Simple Idea of Solidity' and 'Of the Signification of Words' in *An Essay Concerning Human Understanding*. On the similarities between Wordsworth and Locke see Kharbutli. That consciousness is incapable of understanding its own origins has been made frequently in the contemporary philosophy of the mind-body problem. See, for instance, McGinn, 'Can We Solve the Mind-Body Problem?' (who answers his title's question emphatically in the negative).

25 See Levere, *Poetry Realized in Nature*.
26 Quotations from 'Frost at Midnight' are taken from *Samuel Taylor Coleridge*, ed. Jackson, 87–9.
27 Johnston, 31. As Johnston notes, all the important new historicist books on romanticism and Wordsworth examine the poem as an egregious example of one form or other of escapism.
28 All quotations of the poem are taken from *'The Ruined Cottage' and 'The Pedlar,'* ed. Butler. Line numbers refer to MS D unless otherwise stated.
29 The quotation is from the *Alfoxden Notebook*, f. 20r (p. 121 in Butler).
30 Liu, *Wordsworth*, 381–2. Liu objects here to the fact that the poem cannot recreate the essential individuality of Margaret, being content with a dispersal of her significance into the vague concept of 'humanity.' It is precisely this unity which lyric resists, finding multiple pathways to significance instead of one. I find Liu's objection to the poem remarkable, because in most of his other readings of Wordsworth, he objects to the poet's inability to disperse (his own) individuality into the multiple relations of the social and the communitarian (which is, perhaps, the same thing as 'humanity').
31 See Butler, 261–75. Much of the addendum speaks of how the fading signs of being serve to create a state of meditation in which present consciousness can become actively linked to the 'chain of good' that forms the history of consciousness. Being is built by a selective unification of past being, a science of meditation that 'shall watch / The processes of things and serve the cause / Of order and distinctness / ... So build we up / The being that we are' (Butler, 265–7). This is, as James Chandler has pointed out (121–30), a distinctly Burkean science. It is perhaps deleted from MS D because it offers far too schematized and totalizing a description of meditation; it is narrative because it is end-oriented, suggesting a steady progress and continuity which the abrupt end of MS B, and the Pedlar's images, resist. I thus disagree with Chandler, who finds the MS D version an apt summary of the 'strange discipline' the Poet of the poem is said to have discovered in his meditation on the tale.
32 The poem's multiple layers of revision make it a document for how Wordsworth fled from this idea in later years, turning to a Christian notion that the

material world is a kind of illusion, a temporary home where the 'enlightened spirit' may 'repose / Upon the breast of Faith,' as the Pedlar says in the final version of book 1 of *The Excursion* (*PW*, 5:39).

II: The Meanest Thing That Feels

1 I am not here suggesting that that science which is attempting to ground consciousness in the various processes of nature is necessarily congruent with environmentalist concerns, only that its role in the development of those concerns is expanding, and is not always confrontational, as some ecocritics (such as Carolyn Merchant and Carol Adams) claim. Rather than reducing nature to human nature, as Bruno Latour has argued is the case for Cartesian metaphysics in general, science can aid in connecting human nature to nature, and, when it does not immediately lead to technologies of domination and manipulation (which remains, admittedly, an enormous question in itself), can perhaps reveal the depths of our obligations to it. I should point out here too that the status of animal rights is in no way firmly established within contemporary environmental thinking. Indeed, there is an obvious antipathy between the two 'movements,' in so far as the former tends to argue for the value (and thus the rights) of individual animals, especially those with clear evidence of high degrees of sentience and consciousness, while the latter argues for the value of ecosystems, biodiversity, and species, collectivities within which the life of any individual living being may not matter much. See, for instance, Hargrove.
2 See also Masson and McCarthy.
3 See, for instance, Masson and McCarthy, as well as Donald R. Griffin.
4 For a summary of the controversy, see Deuchar, 79–84, 114–23; Itzkowitz, passim; and Munsche.
5 See also Harwood.
6 Johnson, 2:53–5 (*Idler* no. 17); Thomson, 10–11, 52–3, 103–6; Cowper, 271–7; Rousseau, 153–6; Voltaire, 64–6; Bentham, 412.
7 Linnaeus, 19. Ebenezer Sibly's fourteen-volume expansion of Linnaeus's system begins by arguing that 'under the sensibilities of mind which this pleasing study inculcates, the patient ox is viewed with generous complacency; the guileless sheep with pity; and the sportive lamb raises emotions of tenderness and love. We rejoice with the horse in his liberty and exemption from toil, while he ranges at large though enamelled pastures; and the frolics of the colt would afford unabated delight, did we not recollect the bondage he is shortly to undergo. We are charmed with the song of birds, soothed with the buzz of insects, and pleased with the sportive motions of the fishes, because

these are expressions of the enjoyments we love; and therefore we exult in the felicity of the whole animated creation. Thus an equal and extensive benevolence is called forth into exertion; and having felt a common interest in the gratifications of inferior beings; we shall be no longer indifferent to their sufferings, or become wantonly instrumental in producing them' (1:iii–iv).

8 Harvard's edition of this book measures about twelve by eight inches, is bound in bright red leather, and features prints of really extraordinary colour. The advertisement in the book boasts that 'it will readily be perceived, in perusing the following sheets, the ostensible purpose of which is to treat of Scotland as a sporting country, that it required a gentleman of Colonel Thornton's fortune, added to his knowledge of hunting, hawkery, and fishing, to do, in any degree, that justice to the subject which it evidently merits.'

9 Norris, 3–4. Norris argues, however, that 'Charles Darwin [is] the founder of this tradition, as the naturalist whose shattering conclusions inevitably turned back upon him and subordinated him' (1). Norris argues too that because biocentric thinking seeks to collapse distinctions between culture and nature, it has a very uneasy relationship to 'art,' which is traditionally understood as a repository of highest being of a culture. Thus biocentric thinking 'will require modes that further frustrate communication, that negate their authority, that rupture representation and rebuff interpretation' (2). Obviously, biocentrism need not have such a sophisticated definition or such highbrow effects. Paul W. Taylor defines biocentrism simply as a 'moral attitude' based on a 'respect for nature,' by which he means seeing humanity only as one member of a totality 'seen as a complex web of interconnected elements,' and understanding that each individual organism 'is conceived of as a teleological center of life, pursing its own good in its own way' (105).

10 Burns's poetry is cited by line number from *The Poems and Songs of Robert Burns*, ed. Kinsley.

11 Clare's poetry is cited by page number from *John Clare*, ed. Robinson and Powell.

12 Coleridge's poetry is cited by line number from *Samuel Taylor Coleridge*, ed. Jackson. 'To a Young Ass' originally appeared in the *Morning Chronicle* in 1794.

13 'At the beginning of the 19th century the English would have been surprised to hear themselves praised for special kindness to animals. They were surrounded by evidence to the contrary in a society that exploited animals to provide not only food and clothing, but also transportation, the power to run machinery, and even entertainment. The streets of London were crowded with horses and dogs that served as draft animals and beasts of burden; in addition

passers-by often encountered herds of cattle and sheep being driven to the Smithfield livestock market ... Off the streets, but not hard to find, were slaughterhouses and the knackers' yards where horses no longer fit for work were butchered. Popular amusements included cock fighting, dog fighting, rat killing, bull running and the baiting of wild animals. Few people registered distress at the animal suffering that surrounded them, and many took pride in the doughty national character revealed by its infliction' (Ritvo, 125).

14 In 1809 Coleridge opposed Lord Erskine's first bill against cruelty to animals on the grounds that it was based on the presumably erroneous notion of 'extending PERSONALITY to things' (*Essays on his Times*, 310n). In *The Friend* (of roughly the same period) he states that 'animals possess a share of Understanding, perfectly distinguishable from mere Instinct' (*The Friend*, 1:155), and six years later made the Swiftian argument that 'Mankind ... are *on the whole* distinguished from the other Beasts incomparably more to their *disadvantage*, by Lying, Treachery, Ingratitude, Massacre, Thirst of Blood, and by Sensualities which both in sort and degree it would be libelling their Brother-beasts to call bestial, than to their advantage by a greater extent of Intellect' (*Lay Sermons*, 183–4n). Holmes (*Coleridge*, 138–9) draws attention to a letter by Coleridge in which he humorously agonizes about what to do about the mice in the cottage at Nether Stowey, and suggests that the real moral quandary that Coleridge faced may be a source for the *Ancient Mariner*.

15 It is probably impossible to separate the issue of the 'rights' of animals from their humane treatment. Concern for the latter appears necessarily to imply the former, but many who dealt with the issue in the late eighteenth and early nineteenth century refrained from stating explicitly that animals had rights, because the idea offended the traditional hierarchy. Thomas Young, author of *An Essay on Humanity to Animals* (London, 1798), who argues that the fact that animals can perceive pleasure and pain naturally endows them with 'rights,' begins the essay by stating that he is aware that his topic exposes him 'to no small portion of ridicule ... To many, no doubt, the subject which I have chosen will appear whimsical and uninteresting, and the particulars into which it is about to lead me ludicrous and mean' (quoted in Salt, *Animal Rights*, 152–3). Bentham's brief discussion of animals, noted above, makes a case for the minimal right of all sentient beings not to be subject to the wilful infliction of pain, and John Lawrence makes the case explicit in chapter 3 of his *Treatise on Horses*. Many of those that made the case for humanity to animals did so with the explicit premise that humans are far superior to animals, and that cruelty to animals needs to be avoided primarily because it reflects poorly on our moral supremacy. That animal 'rights' was considered a radical, even an unthinkable, concept then (as it is indeed today) is also suggested by a book by Thomas

Taylor called *A Vindication of the Rights of Brutes* (London, 1792), which used the apparent absurdity of the idea of animal rights to ridicule the idea that humans had rights.
16 Hartman, *Beyond Formalism*, 296. See also Hodgson, 75ff, and Moorman, 454.

III: Shelley's Ideal Body

1 See Morton, *Shelley and the Revolution in Taste*, and Oerlemans, 'Shelley's Ideal Body.'
2 Holmes, *Shelley*, 220; Cameron, 227–32. Newman Ivey White makes many references to Shelley's vegetarianism, concluding that he began the diet in early March of 1813 and essentially continued to be vegetarian for the rest of his life, but offers no real evaluation or explanation of why diet should be important for Shelley. David Lee Clark argues that the essay precedes the note in *Queen Mab* (rather than vice versa) and states that 'the important role which vegetarianism played in Shelley's life and thought' is reason enough to try to ascertain facts concerning the date and sources of his pamphlets, but does nothing to explain this role.
3 Salt, *Percy Bysshe Shelley*, 120–1. Another late-nineteenth century encomium of Shelley's vegetarianism is William Axon's pamphlet *Shelley's Vegetarianism*.
4 This postmodern idealism is apparent too in Morton's more recent article, 'The Pulses of the Body.' Morton here ignores the actual practice of vegetarianism altogether and describes (without explaining) only a 'dietary logocentrism.' Typical of his argument is the assertion that what drives 'vegetarians [and] animal rights writers' is not an attempt to end actual suffering of animals, but 'the disfigural properties of language' (80).
5 The USDA has long supported the meat industry because its mandate is to promote all facets of the agriculture industry.
6 Cheyne wrote a number of guides to diet and health, but see particularly his *Essay on Regimen* (1740). Cheyne argued that since eating animal food creates so much disease, it must be part of God's punishment for our original sin; and so he suggested (rather oddly) that a person should give up animal food for a completely vegetarian diet only if he were sick or old. See also John Arbuthnot, *An Essay Concerning the Nature of Aliments* (1731); A.F.M. Willich, *Lectures on Diet and Regimen* (1799); J. Tweed, *Popular Observations on Regimen and Diet* (1820). John Abernethy was for a time Shelley's doctor, and argued for the importance of diet in understanding the relation of physical and mental ills. See *The Abernethian Code of Health and Longevity* (1829). Tho-

mas Beddoes made a similar case, though, like Cheyne and William Lambe (an important influence on Newton and Ritson), he was especially insistent on the benefits of a vegetable diet. See Beddoes, *Hygeia, or Essays Moral and Medical on the Causes Affecting the Personal State of Our Middling and Affluent Classes* (1802–3), and Lambe, *Reports on The Effects of a Peculiar Regimen* (1809) and *A Medical and Experimental Inquiry, into the Origin, Symptoms, and Cure of Constitutional Diseases, particularly, scrophula, consumption, cancer, and gout* (1805). It was Lambe more than any other doctor of his day who advocated the importance of drinking distilled water, which both Newton and Shelley picked up.

7 Thomas Graham, *Sure Methods of Improving Health and Prolonging Life* (1831), 9–10; William Buchan, *Domestic Medicine, or the Family Physician designed to render the medical art more generally useful, by showing people what is in their own power* (1792, 1840), 56–7. Though we may find the idea of symbolic osmosis amusing, it is largely still with us today, as meat and meat-eating are explicitly advertised, and implicitly felt by many, to be a source of strength, muscle, and power. Similarly, advertisements for milk play on symbolic associations of whiteness and maternity, even as they aim for a scientific aura while making largely obsolete nutritional claims. For an examination of the association of meat-eating, masculinity, and class in the nineteenth and twentieth centuries see Adams.

8 Donald Worster identifies this kind of writing as representing an early kind of 'ecological' thinking (26–55).

9 John Ray, *The Wisdom of God Manifested in the Works of Creation* (1735), 30. This argument was made most famously by Paley (who clearly borrowed from Ray) in the beginning of his *Natural Theology* (1802).

10 For a summary of this genre of theological-scientific writing, see Worster and Willey.

11 Smellie, 376–8. Smellie actually has a great deal of difficulty accounting for the degree of carnage in the natural world, especially the oceans, where there is hardly a herbivore to be found. Animals have to eat something, he suggests rather feebly, and the system of mutual destruction has the final paradoxical effect of preserving species. He argues too that carnivorous competition makes certain animals (humans especially) more intelligent, but he concludes that the reason for extraordinary amount of carnage in Nature must remain a 'mystery' (391).

12 Milton's poetry is cited by page number from *Milton's Poetical Works*, vol. 1, ed. Darbishire.

13 Thomas Trotter, a physician whose most important writing Shelley had read, argued that the art of cookery, in addition to debauchery and the stress of

urban life, was among such excesses (*A View of the Nervous Temperament* [1807] 25–30).

14 Nora Crook and Derek Guiton have argued that the primary motivation for Shelley's interest in diet in particular, and medicine and the connection between spirit and body in general, was a desperate attempt to find a cure for the syphilis they think he had contracted while at Oxford or Eton (69–81). While it is no doubt possible that Shelley did indeed have syphilis, and that he hoped a radical change in diet would cure it, the effect of their argument (inevitable, perhaps, in a book-length inquiry of a single fact) is reductive; it ignores the multifaceted nature of Shelley's vegetarian ecology.

15 Carl Grabo's *A Newton Among Poets* (1930) is still the most comprehensive account of Shelley's knowledge of science, though he takes no note of Shelley's essays on diet. See also Harry White for a more recent account of Shelley's interest in science as complementing, rather than opposing, his idealism.

16 See Young, 19–33.

17 Here is part of Derrida's meditation on eating: 'What is eating? How is this metonymy of introjection to be regulated ... "One must eat well" does not mean above all taking in and grasping in itself, but *learning* and *giving* to eat, learning-to-give-the-other-to-eat. One never eats entirely on one's own: this constitutes the rule underlying the statement, "one must eat well." It is a rule offering infinite hospitality ... This evokes a law of need or desire ... hunger, and thirst ... respect for the other at the very moment when, in experience (I am speaking here of metonymical "eating" as well as the very concept of experience), one must begin to identify with the other, who is to be assimilated, interiorized, understood ideally (something one can never do absolutely without *addressing oneself to the other* and without absolutely limiting understanding itself, the identifying appropriation), speak to him or her in words that also pass through the mouth, the ear, and sight ... The sublime refinement involved in this respect for the other is also a way of "eating well," in the sense of "good eating" but also "eating the good." The Good can also be eaten. And it, the good, must be eaten and eaten well' (282–3). In this complex and clearly incomplete meditation on the subject of the subject, Derrida shifts the question from what one eats to how one eats, arguing that in thinking of the act of sustenance necessarily bring into focus the question of what allows one to take the life of some other living thing, and so also the question of subjectivity, where it located, what produces it, and so on.

18 Morton writes of *Prometheus Unbound* that in it 'Shelley is prepared to say that the liberation of Prometheus from the carnivorous torture he endures can be taken as figure for the reformation of both society and nature' (*Shelley*, 118).

19 Shelley's poetry is cited by act, canto, or section numbers, and line numbers, from *Shelley's Poetry and Prose*, ed. Reiman and Powers.
20 See, for instance, Lappe, Robbins, and Singer, for modern instances of the same vision, as well as a sampling of research into the benefits of a vegetarian diet.
21 There are many accounts the core tenets of a 'deep' or 'biocentric' ecology, but they share a sense that the natural world is to be considered an end in its own right rather than as a resource which exists solely to be plundered by us. Worster argues that Gilbert White's *Natural History of Selborne* is an important early example, which in turn leads to the 'romantic ecology' of Wordsworth, Thoreau, and Emerson. Contemporary definitions are offered by Sessions and Devall, Nash, and Evernden, *The Natural Alien*.
22 Though Bate is right in 'Living with the Weather' to remind us the effects of weather in the poetry of the period (he focuses on Byron's 'Darkness' and Keats's 'Ode'), he is not the first to make this connection. Rampino, Self, and Stothers note that 'the summer months of 1816 in central England were about 1.5°C cooler than during the summer of 1815. The dismal European summer is credited with having inspired Mary Shelley to write *Frankenstein*, and Lord Byron his poem "Darkness"' (85). The most complete account of the 'year without a summer' is Stommel and Stommel.

IV: Romanticism and the Metaphysics of Classification

1 'Could the Red Wolf Be a Mutt?' *NYTM*, 14 June 1992: 30.
2 See Gross for a persuasive revelation of the rhetorical nature of some contemporary taxonomic analysis and description. That is, Gross shows how a particular published paper in taxonomy uses a specific rhetoric of presence to create an impression of essential difference in the creation of a 'new' species.
3 There is an enormous interest in this topic, both within biology, and within the philosophy of biology. Useful in my own thinking are the essays collected in Otte and Endler, and the articles by Stanford, Gregg, and Stevens.
As David Hull argues, 'if species must be eternal and immutable to be "real," Darwin concluded that they are not real. If the boundaries between species ıst be sharp for species to be "real," Darwin concluded that species are not If varieties must be clearly distinguishable from species for species to be " then Darwin concluded once again that species are not real. But species nothing either. After all, they are the things that evolve' (96). Likewise, arrish argues that "Darwin nonetheless recognizes that variation existence of definable species, strictly speaking, a delusion, an arbiition by the naturalist. Where in fact there is only individual varia-

tion, the naturalist classifies discrete groups of species, genera, families, and orders. The decision of where one species or genus ends and another begins can never be definitive, on one level because organisms are ranged on a continuum, but on a deeper level, because that continuum itself is unstable, always changing' (436). See also Levine, 547–8.

5 See Krasner, 33–72.
6 That this is true is aptly reflected in the current debate between pheneticists and cladists about the status of species and taxonomy. The former are, generally, nominalists, who argue for a separation of taxonomy and phylogeny. They argue that the primary reality that ought to be reflected by classification is our sense of the relations of animals based purely on morphological data, not evolutionary history based increasingly on genetic data, as cladists hold. Thus, for instance, a guinea pig is a rodent because it is a small furry mammal with distinctive incisors and jaw muscles, and not, as cladists have recently argued, a separate class because its ancestry appears to be different from that of rats and mice. (See 'Guinea Pigs Not Rodents? DNA Weighing In,' *New York Times*, 13 June 1996). A Dr Honeycutt, a biologist of presumably phenetecist leanings, is quoted as saying 'I could show a guinea pig to my 10-year-old daughter ... and she could tell me it's a rodent.' For a very good account of the controversy between these two contemporary schools of classification, see Hull, 120–40.
7 References to Locke are cited by book, chapter, and section numbers, from *An Essay Concerning Human Understanding*, ed. Fraser.
8 See Lovejoy, 254.
9 Quoted in Lovejoy, 231.
10 These essays can be found in Coleridge, *Shorter Works and Fragments*, ed, Jackson and Jackson (vol. 11 of *The Collected Works of Samuel Taylor Coleridge*). Further references to this volume will be made in parentheses by page number. The editors note Coleridge's heavy indebtedness to the German writers mentioned, as well as to Blumenbach and Kant, but argue (agreeing with Thomas McFarland) that his final goal of asserting the reality of God is different.
11 Barfield, 41–9; Fruman, 121–34. Though Fruman is right to draw attention to a widespread reluctance to acknowledge Coleridge's plagiarism in criticism of *Theory of Life*, he makes virtually no attempt to understand the text as a whole, finding it to be self-evident nonsense. Levere (*Poetry Realized in Nature*, 215–20) argues that *Theory of Life* is to be understood as representative of the culmination of Coleridge's interest and learning in science.
12 This theory does not lead, as Barfield and others have suggested (Barfield, 55–7), to an anticipation by Coleridge of Darwinian evolution. Coleridge's theory, like that of Lamarck, is thoroughly teleological, and thus ontogenetic. For

Coleridge, nature unfolds not through the blind operation of an algorithmic process, but through the fulfilment of an *idea* that leads to a synchronic hierarchy of complexity, rather than a diachronic one.

13 That this point is a major focus of both texts is not surprising, since naturalists like Linnaeus and Bonnet had insisted on the striking similarity between humans and certain primates. Moreover, as Lovejoy notes, Rousseau and Monboddo 'took the further step of asserting that man and the higher apes ... are of the same species' (235). Shelley uses this argument as proof of the fact that humans are really vegetarian. Schiebinger argues that in the debate over the relation between humans and the 'simia' the study of females was used to show the proximity of humans and primates, while that of males was seen to prove human difference (78–99).

14 'The differences are so evidently mere differences of degree, the strongliest marked Varieties melt into each by too imperceptible Shades ... as to leave a doubt that all the prominent-chinned, erect-walking, full-bottomed, tool-making, word-minting bimanous Bipeds of this Planet are of one and the same species' (*Shorter Works and Fragments*, 1390).

15 Even among systematists today the study of animal behaviour is anathema, since (a) animal behaviour is far more difficult to characterize, to reduce to a table of discrete data, than are morphological characteristics; (b) behaviour can vary so much even among individuals of a species; and (c) the observing of behaviour is felt to be inevitably inflected with observer bias – behaviour is necessarily 'interpreted' rather than merely recorded.

16 White, 208. Cf. Worster, 6–9.

17 The strictures against anthropomorphism in science are a direct product of modern systematists who insist on the rigidity of classification, and that the aim of observation should be the establishing of precise and definable points of difference. Charles Darwin could still write an essay on the emotion of animals, and Erasmus Darwin wrote about the desires of plants. A recent biographer of Linnaeus, clearly under the effect of the prohibition and thus embarrassed by his subject's excesses, wrote that Linnaeus, 'when he was in the humor, loved to humanize, to describe nature and its inhabitants in anthropomorphic terms.' He goes on to say, bafflingly, that Linnaeus 'meant nothing in particular by it, but did it out of pure pleasure and because he always wished to be concrete in the highest degree' (Lindroth, 9).

18 Clare's poetry is cited by page number from *John Clare*, ed. Robinson and Powell.

19 Shelley's poetry is cited from *Shelley's Poetry and Prose*, ed. Reiman and Powers, by line number and, for quotations from *Prometheus Unbound*, act number.

20 See Coleman, 141–64.
21 'From Cuvier onward function, defined according to its non-perceptible form as an effect to be attained, is to serve as a constant middle term and to make it possible to relate together totalities of elements without the slightest visible identity. What to Classical eyes were merely differences juxtaposed with identities must now be ordered and conceived on the basis of a functional homogeneity which is their hidden foundation. When the Same and the Other both belong to a single space, there is "natural history"; something like "biology" becomes possible when this unity of level begins to break up, and when differences stand out against the background of an identity that is deeper, and, as it were, more serious than that unity' (Foucault, 265).
22 In the treatises on vegetarianism, Shelley cites Cuvier in arguing that comparative anatomy determines that humans are in fact not carnivores, but herbivores. We have fallen into disease and madness, he argues, because we have fallen from the ideal behaviour determined by our species type ('A Vindication of Natural Diet,' in *Shelley's Prose*, 84). And yet implicit in the essay is the sense that we have made a mental error; we have chosen to eat 'unnatural' food, and if we choose again to eat only vegetable food, we can as a species be transformed into something better. Thus natural laws or types can be overcome and changed by the power of will, by the desire for humans to change. Though these ideas of willed evolution are like those of Lamarck, there is no evidence that Shelley was familiar with Lamarck. More likely these ideas derive from Shelley's reading of Erasmus Darwin. Ironically, the more utopian Shelley gets, the closer he gets to Coleridge's sense of the imminent perfection of human being as a species. The end of *Prometheus Unbound*, P.M.S. Dawson has recently pointed out, suggests a utopia in which the functional potential of the entire world is realized in the final achievement of human beings to realize their potential.
23 Ross Woodman makes a similar point in his recent article 'Shelley's Dizzy Ravine.' Woodman argues that the poem reveals that 'individual identity ... is virtually annihilated by the sheer excess of an empirical reality that cannot be reduced to thought' (313).
24 Cf. Shelley's letters to Peacock of 22–5 July 1816, in which he discusses his trip to Chamounix. Shelley speaks at length about being impressed by glaciers, that their inexorable and slow movement (which seemed to suggest their spreading across Europe) gave evidence as well of the vast stretches of history. Shelley sees the glaciers as proof of a power inimical to humanity, which not only literally threatens our existence but also seems, as he says, to lead to 'the degradation of the human species,' since those living close to the mountain seem to him 'half deformed or idiotic.' The implication is that an environment of such

explicit chaos produces people 'deprived of anything that can excite interest & admiration' (Shelley, *Letters*, 1:500).

25 Philip Kuberski calls this productive flux 'chaosmos,' a productive interplay between empiricism and idealism, order and chaos, literature and science.

V: Moving through the Environment

1 It is worth noting, in this context, that much of the modern genre of 'nature writing' is also rooted in travel, and that one of the most notable and formative of the overlaps between these modes of writing is the work of Thoreau, who read travel writing voraciously. And we should consider too that our own experience of travel begins with processing the fluidity of landscape. Even if we travel to seek only the products of culture – to visit other libraries, art galleries, restaurants, friends – we cannot avoid being confronted by an array of new physical environments.
2 Glendening 3. Also see Buzard, 1–17.
3 Edward Said's *Culture and Imperialism* is an excellent introduction to the necessary connections between cultural production and imperialism. Sara Mills's *Discourses of Difference* offers a good account of the interpretive problems associated with travel literature specifically, from a feminist–cultural studies perspective. Other impressive accounts of the relation of landscape, travel, and ideology are Mitchell, Helsinger, and virtually all of the work of John Barrell, including particularly 'The Public Prospect and the Private View.'
4 Paul Fussell, quoted in Buzard, 2. Buzard's book develops the crucial argument that the touristic and anti-touristic impulses are inescapably intertwined.
5 Quotations from *The Prelude* are from the 1805 edition, ed., Wordsworth, Abrams, and Gill.
6 See Bohls, 95. Also useful are the essays in Copley and Garside. See also Buzard, 10; Liu, 'Local Transcendence,' 91; Andrews; and Fulford.
7 Jonathan Smith has argued that the picturesque remains a powerful cultural force and human desire. In gazing at landscape, 'the displacement of the subject occurs because to the eye that has been properly educated a landscape presents itself as a spectacle, a deportment which in turn creates the position of spectator. Whether depicted in paint, or rolled out as a tableau vivant below a scenic overlook, a landscape situates its spectator in an Olympian position, and it rewards its spectator with the pleasures of distance and detachment and the personal inconsequence of all that they survey ... What this suggests is that we believe ourselves to have stepped out of history when we step into an aestheticized landscape, a landscape that seems pregnant with meaning when, and perhaps precisely because, it omits any reference to that which will follow'

(79–80). Smith argues that gazing on landscape produces an illusion of transcendence. Yet it is easy enough to imagine, or recall, moments in which we aestheticize landscape, in which it becomes 'framed,' and in which we do not abandon an awareness of history altogether. In something akin to Wordsworth's 'spots of time' (an aesthetic gaze which is yet based in memory), the modern 'gaze,' for instance, can easily be produced and qualified by an environmental awareness, which frames landscape as inevitably artificial, as part of a park, for instance, set aside and maintained with a heavy hand, or as doomed in any case to be further despoiled by human parasitism. We can recognize that any seemingly natural and beautiful landscape is reified, even as we understand its tenuousness. An environmental picturesque awareness is inevitably historic in the sense that it inclines us to see every more or less natural landscape as the product of past, present, and future interaction between geologic and biologic processes and human expansion.

8 It is worth noting in this context that much of the criticism of the representation of landscape which finds it to be deeply and necessarily ideological is in fact based on the paradigms of landscape painting (see for instance, the work of Helsinger, Barrell, and Mitchell). Painting landscape, as these critics attest, is a highly conventionalized process, which necessarily decontextualizes the object and the act of perception, as the image is made to seem, inevitably, an end in itself. The textual representation of landscape, I would argue, is necessarily more porous. It allows for an awareness of the movement to and around landscapes, which produces a consequent notion of the relativity of perspective. Moreover, language is clearly incapable of producing the kind of simulacrum that the image strives for, and so the 'reality' that lies beyond the text remains more clearly as an object of attention.

9 In explaining that pencils are better than paints for sketching the picturesque, Gilpin goes on to say that all that language and drawing can produce 'are gross, insipid substitutes of the living scene' (*Observations Relative Chiefly to Picturesque Beauty* 2:10). See also his *Three Essays on Picturesque Beauty*, 22–30, 49–57, and *Five Essays on Picturesque Subjects*, 160–3.

10 Thomas West's posthumously revised *A Guide to the Lakes* (1780) was the most popular, and is most explicitly concerned with reproducible views from specific stations among the hills. James Clarke's *A Survey of the Lakes of Cumberland, Westmoreland and Lancashire* (1789) is deliberately an everyman's guide, and counters the effeteness of West with bawdy jokes, minuscule and random histories of people and places, and detailed and precise maps of roads; Clarke was, after all, a land-surveyor and not a painter or sketcher. William Hutchinson's *An Excursion to the Lakes* (1776) is a more highbrow tour of 'antique remains.' All, however, regularly record how grand views may be

obtained. There is a vast body of critical work on the picturesque. The best recent study is Malcolm Andrews's *The Search for the Picturesque*.
11 Carl Woodring provides a good general account of the complexities I summarize here.
12 Stoddart was the founding editor of the *New Times* in London.
13 As John Brian Harley notes, by the late eighteenth century, more atlases were being published, and at lower prices, then ever before, and increasingly the purchasers of such atlases were 'non-gentry' ('Power and Legitimation in the English Geographical Atlases').
14 Harley, 'Power and Legitimation,' 176. Harley argues elsewhere that 'maps are never value-free images; except in the narrowest Euclidean sense they are not in themselves either true or false. Both in the selectivity of their content and in their signs and styles or representation maps are a way of conceiving, articulating, and structuring the human world which is biased towards, promoted by, and exerts influence upon particular sets of social relations' ('Maps, Knowledge, and Power,' 278).
15 Pennant had already published three volumes of a zoology of Great Britain.
16 Hartman, *Wordsworth's Poetry*. James Buzard offers a useful discussion of Wordsworth's distinction between tourist and traveller in a reading of 'The Brothers' in *The Beaten Track*, 19–31.
17 See Bewell, 1–34.
18 Cf. Chandler, 214.
19 Wordsworth offers this explanation of the poem in his letter to Lady Beaumont (21 May 1807). It is quoted here from Hayden's notes to the poem (*William Wordsworth: The Poems*, 1:992).
20 Watkins, 36. The charge echoes those made by Anne Mellor and many others, that nature for Wordsworth is always gendered, made a passive subject ripe for his manipulation, as I noted in chapter 1.
21 Mellor, 157, 154. Elizabeth Fay comes to the same conclusion, that while Dorothy allows the details of what she sees to 'determine her perception,' William's 'project is to study not nature but the human experience of being in nature. Consequently, the object he needs to keep a steady eye on is not the natural object but himself' (205–6).
22 Ernest de Selincourt notes that Dorothy Wordsworth's memory for detail is astonishing; what makes this 'one of the most readable, because it is the most living, of all books of travel' is that she did not write from notes, but from memory, so that she records only that 'which after a passage of time is still a vital experience' (*Dorothy Wordsworth*, 163). See also Gittings and Manton, 146–7.
23 Returning to the task of producing a complete account of her trip three years

later, Dorothy Wordsworth writes (between parts 2 and 3): 'I am setting about a task which, however free and happy the state of my mind, I could not have performed well at this distance of time; but now, I do not know that I shall be able to go on with it at all. I will strive, however, to do the best I can, setting before myself a different object from that hitherto aimed at, which was, to omit no incident, however trifling, and to describe the country so minutely that you should, where the objects were the most interesting, feel as if you had been with us. I shall now only attempt to give you an idea of those scenes which pleased us most, dropping the incidents of the ordinary days, of which many have slipped from my memory, and others which remain it would be difficult, and often painful to me, to endeavour to draw out and disentangle form other thoughts' (*Journals*, 1:344).

24 Both Bohls and Buzard note the tension in travel writing produced by the writer's attempt to distinguish herself from 'ordinary' tourists. Depth and accuracy of observation are key to a writer's sense of this distinction, as a comparison of Wordsworth's opening paragraph to that of Leyden, quoted above, may suggest.

25 Homans, 86ff. Mellor argues that in Dorothy Wordsworth's journals 'we find a very different concept of self from the egotistical sublime proposed in her brother's poetry' (156). Meena Alexander makes a similar case, as does Susan Levin, 4–7.

26 The same argument applies self-evidently to Wordsworth's poetry of the 'egotistical sublime.'

27 Her aesthetic judgment is foregrounded momentarily when she offers a mild objection to the fact that the land surrounding the falls are 'private grounds,' and this allows her to judge repeatedly how 'injudiciously managed' (224) these grounds are aesthetically – a small cottage being placed haphazardly, and clearings from which to obtain a view of the river poorly placed. But these are matters of the landowner's taste in modifying the landscape, rather than matters of her own desire to reframe the landscape for picturesque purposes.

Conclusion

1 Lussier, 23. Lussier is quoting D.M. Knight, 'The Physical Sciences and the Romantic Movement,' *History of Science* 9 (1970): 54.

Bibliography

Primary

Abbey, Edward. *Desert Solitaire: A Season in the Wilderness.* New York: Simon and Schuster, 1968.

Abernethy, John. *The Abernethian Code of Health and Longevity.* London: J. Williams, 1829.

Arbuthnot, John. *An Essay Concerning the Nature of Aliments ...* London: J. Tonson, 1731.

Bartram, William. *Travels of William Bartram.* Ed. Mark van Doren. New York: Dover Publications, 1955.

Beddoes, Thomas. *Hygeia, or Essays Moral and Medical on the Causes Affecting the Personal State of Our Middling and Affluent Classes.* 3 vols. Bristol: J. Mills, 1802–3.

Bentham, Jeremy. *An Introduction to the Principles of Morals and Legislation.* Ed. Wilfred Harrison. Oxford: Clarendon Press, 1948.

Bligh, William. *A Narrative of the Mutiny on Board his Britannic Majesty's Ship Bounty ...* Philadelphia: William Spotswood, 1790.

Bristed, John. *Anthroplanomenos: or A Pedestrian Tour through part of the Highlands of Scotland, in 1801.* 2 vols. London: J. Wallis, 1803.

Bruckner, John. *A Philosophical Survey of the Animal Creation.* London: J. Johnson, 1768.

Buchan, William. *Domestic Medicine, or the Family Physician designed to render the medical art more generally useful, by showing people what is in their own power.* 1792. Rpt. Hartford: Samuel Slater, 1840.

Burnet, Thomas. *The Sacred Theory of the Earth.* 1684. Rpt. Ed. Basil Willey. Carbondale, Ill.: Southern Illinois University Press, 1965.

Burns, Robert. *The Poems and Songs of Robert Burns.* 3 vols. Ed. James Kinsley. Oxford: Clarendon Press, 1968.
Cheyne, George. *Essay on Regimen.* London: Rivington, 1740.
Clare, John. *John Clare.* Ed. Eric Robinson and David Powell. New York: Oxford University Press, 1984.
Clarke, James. *A Survey of the Lakes of Cumberland, Westmoreland and Lancashire.* London, 1789.
Coleridge, S.T. *Biographia Literaria.* 2 vols. Ed. James Eengell and W. Jackson Bate. Vol. 7 of *S.T. Coleridge's Collected Works.* London and Princeton: Routledge and Princeton University Press, 1983.
– *Essays on His Times.* Ed. David Erdman. Vol. 3 of *S.T. Coleridge's Collected Works.* London and Princeton: Routledge and Princeton University Press, 1978.
– *The Friend.* 2 vols. Ed. Barbara E. Rook. Vol. 4 of *S.T. Coleridge's Collected Works.* London and Princeton: Routledge and Princeton University Press, 1969.
– *Lay Sermons.* Ed. R.J. White. Vol. 6 of *S.T. Coleridge's Collected Works.* London and Princeton: Routledge and Princeton University Press, 1972.
– *Samuel Taylor Coleridge.* Ed. H.J. Jackson. Oxford: Oxford University Press, 1985.
– *Shorter Works and Fragments.* 2 vols. Ed. H.J. Jackson and J.R. de J. Jackson. Vol. 11 of *The Collected Works of Samuel Taylor Coleridge.* London and Princeton: Routledge and Princeton University Press, 1995.
Cowper, William. *The Poetical Works of William Cowper.* Ed. William Benham. London: Macmillan, 1893.
Darwin, Erasmus. *The Temple of Nature.* New York: T. and J. Swords, 1804.
– *Zoonomia, or the Laws of Organic Life.* 2 vols. Boston: Thomas and Andrews, 1803.
Dillard, Annie. *Pilgrim at Tinker Creek.* New York, Harper. 1974.
Garnett, Thomas. *Observations on a Tour through the Highlands.* 2 vols. London: T. Cadwell and W. Davies, 1800.
Gilpin, William. *Five Essays on Picturesque Subjects.* 3rd ed. London: T. Cadell, 1808.
– *Observations Relative Chiefly to Picturesque Beauty ... on ... the Mountains and Lakes of Cumberland and Westmoreland.* London: R. Blamire 1786.
– *Three Essays on Picturesque Beauty.* 2nd ed. London: R. Blamire, 1794.
Graham, Thomas. *Sure Methods of Improving Health and Prolonging Life.* 3rd ed. London: Simple and Marshall. 1831.
Holbach, P.H.T. *The System of Nature; or, the Laws of the Moral and Physical World.* Vol. 1 London: G. Kearsley, 1797.

Humboldt, Alexander de. *Personal Narrative of Travels to the Equinoctial Regions of the New Continent.* Trans. Helen Maria Williams. London: Longman, 1814.

Hutchinson, William. *An Excursion to the Lakes.* London: J. Wilkie, 1776.

Keats, John. *The Poems of John Keats.* Ed. Jack Stillinger. Cambridge, Mass.: Belknap Press, 1978.

Johnson, Samuel. *The Idler and the Adventurer. The Yale Edition of the Works of Samuel Johnson.* Vol. 2. Ed. Walter Jackson Bate and John Marshall Bulllit. New Haven: Yale University Press, 1963.

Lambe, William. *A Medical and Experimental Inquiry, into the Origin, Symptoms, and Cure of Constitutional Diseases, particularly, scrophula, consumption, cancer, and gout,* London: J. Mawman, 1805.

– *Reports on the Effects of a Peculiar Regimen ...* London, 1809.

Leyden, John. *Journal of a Tour in the Highlands in 1800.* Edinburgh: W. Blackwood and Sons, 1903.

Linnaeus, Carl. *Systema Naturae.* 1735. Trans. and ed. M.S.J. Engel-Ledeboer and H. Engel. Nieuwkoop: B. De Graaf, 1964.

Locke, John. *An Essay Concerning Human Understanding.* 2 vols. Ed. A.C. Fraser. Oxford: Clarendon Press, 1894.

Lopez, Barry. *Arctic Dreams: Imagination and Desire in a Northern Landscape.* New York: Bantam, 1987.

Milton, John. *Milton's Poetical Works.* Vol. 1. Ed. Helen Darbishire. Oxford: Clarenden Press, 1952.

Paley, William. *Moral and Political Philosophy.* London: R. Faulder, 1786.

– *Natural Theology.* London: R. Faulder, 1802.

Pennant, Thomas. *A Tour in Scotland.* Chester: John Marle, 1771.

Priestley, Joseph. *Disquisitions Relating to Matter and Spirit.* London: J. Johnson, 1777.

Ray, John. *The Wisdom of God Manifested in the Works of Creation.* 10th ed. London: William Innys, 1735.

Rousseau, Jean-Jacques. *Emile.* Ed. and trans. Allen Bloom. New York: Basic Books, 1979.

Saussure, Horace-Benedict. *Voyage dans les Alpes ...* 4 vols. Neufchatel, 1779.

Shelley, Percy Bysshe. *The Complete Poetical Works of Percy Bysshe Shelley.* Vol. 1. Ed. Neville Rogers. Oxford: Clarendon Press, 1972.

– *The Letters of Percy Bysshe Shelley.* Vol. 1. Ed. Frederick L. Jones. Oxford: Clarendon Press, 1964.

– *Shelley's Poetry and Prose.* Ed. Donald Reiman and Sharon Powers. New York: Norton, 1977.

- *Shelley's Prose: The Trumpet of Prophecy*. Ed. David Lee Clark. Albuquerque: University of New Mexico Press, 1954.
Sibly, Ebenezer. *An Universal System of Natural History*. 14 vols. London: William Lewis, 1794–1807.
Smellie, William. *The Philosophy of Natural History*. Vol 1. Edinburgh: Charles Eliot, 1790.
Spinoza, Benedict de. *The Ethics and Other Works*. Trans. and ed. Edwin Curley. Princeton University Press, 1994.
Stevens, Wallace. *The Collected Poems of Wallace Stevens*. New York: Alfred A. Knopf, 1968.
Stoddart, John. *Remarks on Local Scenery and Manners in Scotland During the Years 1799–1800*. 2 vols. London: W. Miller, 1801.
Taylor, Thomas. *A Vindication of the Rights of Brutes*. London, 1792.
Thelwall, John. *The Rights of Nature*. London: H.D. Symonds, 1796.
Thoreau, Henry David. *Walden*. Ed. Sherman Paul. Boston: Houghton Mifflin, 1960.
Thomson, James. *James Thomson's Poetical Works*. Ed. George Gilfillan. Edinburgh: James Nichols, 1853.
Thornton, T. *Sporting Tour through the Northern Parts of England, and Great Parts of the Highlands of Scotland*. London: Vernor and Hood, 1804.
Trotter, Thomas. *A View of the Nervous Temperament*. 1807. Rpt. New York: Arno Press, 1976.
Tweed, J. *Popular Observations on Regimen and Diet*. Chelmsford: Meggy and Chalk, 1820.
Voltaire. *Philosophical Dictionary*. Trans. Theodore Besterman. London: Penguin, 1972.
West, Thomas. *A Guide to the Lakes*. London: Richardson, 1780.
White, Gilbert. *The Natural History of Selborne*. 1789. Rpt. Ed. Richard Mabey. Harmondsworth: Penguin, 1977.
Willich, A.F.M. *Lectures on Diet and Regimen*. London: Longman and Rees, 1799.
Wordsworth, Dorothy. *Journals of Dorothy Wordsworth*. Ed. E. de Selincourt. Vol. 1. London: Macmillan and Co, 1959.
Wordsworth, William. *The Poetical Works of William Wordsworth*. 5 vols. Ed. Ernest de Selincourt and Helen Darbishire. Oxford: Clarendon Press, 1940–6.
- *The Prelude*. Ed. Jonathan Wordsworth, M.H. Abrams, and Stephen Gill. New York: W.W. Norton, 1979.
- *The Prose Works of William Wordsworth*. 3 vols. Ed. W.J.B. Owen and Jane Worthington Smyser. Oxford: Clarendon Press, 1974.

- *'The Ruined Cottage' and 'The Pedlar.'* Ed. James Butler. Ithaca: Cornell Univ. Press, 1979.
- *William Wordsworth: The Poems.* 2 vols. Ed. John O. Hayden. New Haven: Yale University Press, 1981.

Young, Thomas. *An Essay on Humanity to Animals.* London, 1798.

Secondary

Abram, David. *The Spell of the Sensuous.* New York: Vintage, 1996.
Adams, Carol. *The Sexual Politics of Meat.* New York: Continuum, 1990.
Alexander, Meena. 'Dorothy Wordsworth: The Grounds of Writing.' *Women's Studies* 14 (1988): 195–210.
Allen, David Elliston. *The Naturalist in Britain: A Social History.* Princeton: Princeton University Press, 1976.
Andrews, Malcolm. *The Search for the Picturesque.* Stanford: Stanford University Press, 1989.
Aronowitz, Stanley. *Science as Power: Discourse and Ideology in Modern Society.* Minneapolis: University of Minnesota Press, 1988.
Axon, William. *Shelley's Vegetarianism.* Manchester: Vegetarian Society, 1890.
Barfield, Owen. *What Coleridge Thought.* Middletown, Conn.: Wesleyan University Press, 1971.
Barrell, John. *The Idea of Landscape and the Sense of Place, 1730–1840.* Cambridge: Cambridge University Press, 1972.
- 'The Public Prospect and the Private View: The Politics of Taste in Eighteenth-Century Britain.' *Reading Landscape: Country – City – Capital.* Ed. Simon Pugh. Manchester: Manchester University Press, 1990. 19–40.
Barrish, Philip. 'Accumulating Variation: Darwin's *On the Origin of Species* and Contemporary Literary and Cultural Theory.' *Victorian Studies* 34 (1991): 431–53.
Bate, Jonathan. 'Living with the Weather.' *Studies in Romanticism* 35 (1996): 431–47.
- *Romantic Ecology: Wordsworth and the Environmental Tradition.* London: Routledge, 1991.
Baudrillard, Jean. *For a Critique of the Political Economy of the Sign.* St Louis: Telos, 1981.
- *The Illusion of the End.* Trans. Chris Turner. Stanford: Stanford University Press, 1994.
Bewell, Alan. *Wordsworth and the Enlightenment.* New Haven: Yale University Press, 1989.

Bialostosky, Don. *Making Tales: The Poetics of Wordsworth's Narrative Experiment*. Chicago: University of Chicago Press, 1984.
Biehl, Janet. *Rethinking Ecofeminist Politics*. Boston: South End Press, 1991.
Blunden, Edmund. *Nature in English Literature*. London: Hogarth Press, 1929.
Bohls, Elizabeth. *Women Travel Writers and the Language of Aesthetics, 1716–1818*. New York: Cambridge University Press, 1995.
Bone, Drummond. 'Shelley, Wordsworth, and Byron: The Detail of Nature.' *Wordsworth Circle* 23.1 (1992): 3–10.
Bookchin, Murray. 'What Is Social Ecology?' *Environmental Philosophy*. Ed. Michael Zimmerman. Englewood Cliffs, NJ: Prentice Hall, 1994. 354–73.
Bramwell, Anna. *The Fading of the Greens: The Decline of Environmental Politics in the West*. New Haven: Yale University Press, 1994.
Brown, Marshall. *Preromanticism*. Stanford: Stanford University Press, 1991.
Buell, Lawrence. *The Environmental Imagination*. Cambridge, Mass.: Belknap Press, 1995.
Buzard, James. *The Beaten Track: European Tourism, Literature, and the Ways to Culture, 1800–1918*. Oxford: Clarendon Press, 1993.
Cameron, Kenneth Neill. *The Young Shelley*. New York: Macmillan, 1950.
Chandler, James. *Wordsworth's Second Nature*. Chicago: University of Chicago Press, 1984.
Clare, Johanne. *John Clare and the Bounds of Circumstance*. Montreal and Kingston: McGill-Queen's University Press, 1987.
Clark, David Lee. 'The Date and Source of Shelley's *A Vindication of Natural Diet*.' *Studies in Philology* 36 (January 1939): 70–6.
Coleman, William. *Georges Cuvier: Zoologist*. Cambridge, Mass.: Harvard University Press, 1964.
Coles, Romand. 'Ecotones and Environmental Ethics: Adorno and Lopez.' *In the Nature of Things*. Ed. Joan Bennett and William Chaloupka. Minneapolis: University of Minnesota Press, 1993. 226–49.
Copley, Stephen, and Peter Garside, eds. *The Politics of the Picturesque*. New York: Cambridge University Press, 1994.
Crook, Nora, and Derek Guiton. *Shelley's Venomed Melody*. Cambridge: Cambridge University Press, 1986.
Danby, John. *The Simple Wordsworth*. New York: Barnes and Noble, 1961.
Davie, Donald. *Articulate Energy*. 1955. London: Routledge and Kegan Paul, 1971.
Dawkins, Richard. *The Selfish Gene*. Oxford: Oxford University Press, 1989.
Dawson, P.M.S. '"The Empire of Man": Shelley and Ecology.' *Shelley: Poet and Legislator of the World*. Ed. Betty T. Bennett and Stuart Curran. Baltimore: Johns Hopkins University Press, 1996. 232–9.

Dennett, Daniel. *Darwin's Dangerous Idea: Evolution and the Meanings of Life*. New York: Touchstone, 1996.
Derrida, Jacques. *Points ... Interviews, 1974–1994*. Ed. Elizabeth Weber. Stanford: Stanford University Press, 1995.
de Selincourt, Ernest. *Dorothy Wordsworth*. Oxford: Clarenden Press, 1933.
Deuchar, Steven. *Sporting Art in Eighteenth Century England*. New Haven: Yale University Press, 1988.
de Waal, Frans. *Peacemaking among Primates*. Cambridge, Mass.: Harvard University Press, 1989.
Dillard, Annie. 'The Wreck of Time.' *Harpers Magazine* (January 1998): 51–6.
Dimock, Wai Chee. 'A Theory of Resonance.' *PMLA* 112.5 (1997): 1060–71.
Easterbrook, Greg. *A Moment on the Earth*. New York: Viking, 1995.
Eichner, Hans. 'The Rise of Modern Science and the Genesis of Romanticism.' *PMLA* 97 (1982): 8–31.
Evernden, Neil. *The Natural Alien*. Toronto: University of Toronto Press, 1985.
– *The Social Creation of Nature*. Baltimore: Johns Hopkins University Press, 1992.
Fay, Elizabeth. *Becoming Wordsworthian*. Amherst: University of Massachusetts Press, 1995.
Ferré, Frederick. 'Personalistic Organicism: Paradox or Paradigm?' *Philosophy and the Natural Environment*. Ed. Robin Attfield and Andrew Belsey. Royal Institute of Philosophy Supplement. Cambridge: Cambridge University Press, 1994. 59–73.
Foucault, Michel. *The Order of Things*. New York: Random House, 1970.
Fruman, Norman. *Coleridge, the Damaged Archangel*. New York: George Braziller, 1971.
Fry, Paul H. *A Defense of Poetry: Reflections on the Occasion of Writing*. Stanford: Stanford University Press, 1995.
– 'Green to the Very Door? The Natural Wordsworth.' *Studies in Romanticism* 35.4 (1996): 535–51.
Fulford, Tim. *Landscape, Liberty and Authority: Poetry, Criticism and Politics from Thomson to Wordsworth*. Cambridge: Cambridge University Press, 1996.
Garber, Frederick. *Wordsworth and the Poetry of Encounter*. Urbana: University of Illinois Press, 1971.
Gaull, Marilyn. 'From Wordsworth to Darwin: "On to the Fields of Praise."' *Wordsworth Circle* 10 (1979): 33–48.
Gittings, Robert, and Jo Manton. *Dorothy Wordsworth*. Oxford: Clarendon Press, 1985.
Glendening, John. *The High Road: Romantic Tourism, Scotland, and Literature, 1720–1820*. New York: St Martin's Press, 1997.

Gould, Stephen Jay. *Full House: The Spread of Excellence from Plato to Darwin.* New York: Harmony Books, 1996.

Grabo, Carl. *A Newton among Poets.* Chapel Hill: University of North Carolina Press, 1930.

Gregg, John R. 'Taxonomy, Language and Reality.' *American Naturalist* 84 (1950): 419–35.

Griffin, Andrew. 'Wordsworth and the Problem of Imaginative Story: The Case of "Simon Lee."' *PMLA* 92 (1977): 392–419.

Griffin, Donald R. *Animal Minds.* Chicago: University of Chicago Press, 1992.

Gross, Alan. 'The Origin of Species: Evolutionary Taxonomy as an Example of the Rhetoric of Science.' *The Rhetorical Turn: Invention and Persuasion in the Conduct of Inquiry.* Ed. Herbert W. Simons. Chicago: University of Chicago Press, 1990. 91–115.

Haney, David P. *William Wordsworth and the Hermeneutics of Incarnation.* University Park: Penn State University Press, 1993.

Haraway, Donna. *Simians, Cyborgs, and Women.* New York: Routledge, 1991.

Harding, Sandra. *The Science Question in Feminism.* Ithaca: Cornell University Press, 1986.

Hargrove, Eugene C., ed. *The Animal Rights/Environmental Ethics Debate.* Albany: State University of New York Press, 1992.

Harley, John Brian. 'Maps, Knowledge, and Power.' *The Iconography of Landscape.* Ed. Stephen Daniels and Denis Cosgrove. Cambridge: Cambridge University Press, 1988. 277–312.

– 'Power and Legitimation in the English Geographical Atlases.' *Images of the World: The Atlas through History.* Ed. John A. Wolter and Ronald E. Grim. Washington: Library of Congress, 1997. 171–4.

Harrison, Robert Pogue. *Forests: The Shadow of Civilization.* Chicago: University of Chicago Press, 1992.

Hartman, Geoffrey. *Beyond Formalism.* New Haven: Yale University Press, 1970.

– *Wordsworth's Poetry: 1787–1814.* New Haven: Yale University Press, 1971.

Harwood, Dix. *Love for Animals and How It Developed in Great Britain.* New York: 1928.

Helsinger, Elizabeth K. *Rural Scenes and National Representation: Britain, 1815–1850.* Princeton: Princeton University Press, 1997.

Herbert, Nick. *Quantum Reality.* Garden City, NY: Anchor Press, 1985.

Hickey, Alison. '"Extensive Views" in Johnson's *Journey to the Western Islands of Scotland.*' *SEL* 32.3 (1992): 537–53.

Hodgson, John A. *Wordsworth's Philosophical Poetry, 1797–1814.* Lincoln: University of Nebraska Press, 1980.

Holmes, Richard. *Coleridge: Early Visions.* London: Penguin 1989.
- *Shelley: The Pursuit.* London: Penguin, 1987.
Homans, Margaret. *Women Writers and Poetic Identity.* Princeton: Princeton University Press, 1980.
Hull, David. *Science as a Process.* Chicago: University of Chicago Press, 1988.
Itzkowitz, David. *Peculiar Privilege: A Social History of English Fox Hunting 1753–1885.* Sussex: Harvester Press, 1977.
Johnston, Kenneth. 'The Romantic Idea-Elegy: The Nature of Politics and the Politics of Nature.' *South Central Review* 9.2 (1992): 24–43.
Keith, W.J. *The Poetry of Nature.* Toronto: University of Toronto Press, 1980.
Kharbutli, Mahmoud. 'Locke and Wordsworth.' *Forum for Modern Language Studies* 25 (1989): 225–37.
Krasner, James. *The Entangled Eye: Visual Perception and the Representation of Nature in Post-Darwinian Narrative.* New York: Oxford University Press, 1992.
Kroeber, Karl. *Ecological Literary Criticism: Romantic Imagining and the Biology of Mind.* New York: Columbia University Press, 1994.
- *Romantic Landscape Vision.* Madison: University of Wisconsin Press, 1975.
Kuberski, Philip. *Chaosmos.* Albany: SUNY Press, 1994.
Lappe, Frances Moore. *Diet for a Small Planet.* New York: Ballantine, 1982.
Latour, Bruno. *We Have Never Been Modern.* Trans. Catherine Porter. Cambridge, Mass.: Harvard University Press, 1993.
Levere, Trevor H. '"The Lovely Shapes and Sounds Intelligible": Samuel Taylor Coleridge, Humphry Davy, Science and Poetry.' *Nature Transfigured.* Ed. John Christie and Sally Shuttleworth. New York: Manchester University Press, 1989.
- *Poetry Realized in Nature: Samuel Taylor Coleridge and Early Nineteenth-Century Science.* Cambridge: Cambridge University Press, 1981.
Levin, Susan M. *Dorothy Wordsworth and Romanticism.* New Brunswick, NJ: Rutgers University Press, 1987.
Levine, George. 'Charles Darwin's Reluctant Revolution.' *South Atlantic Quarterly* 91.3 (1992): 525–55.
Levinson, Marjorie. *Wordsworth's Great Period Poems.* New York: Cambridge University Press, 1986.
Lewontin, R.C. 'Facts and the Factitious in Natural Sciences.' *Critical Inquiry* 18 (1991): 140–53.
Lindley, David. *The End of Physics: The Myth of a Unified Theory.* New York: Basic Books, 1993.
Lindroth, Sten. 'The Two Faces of Linnaeus.' *Linnaeus: The Man and His Work.* Ed. Tore Frangsmyr. Berkeley: University of California Press, 1983.

Liu, Alan. 'Local Transcendence: Cultural Criticism, Postmodernism, and the Romanticism of Detail.' *Representations* 32 (Fall 1990): 75–113.
- 'The New Historicism and the Work of Mourning.' *Studies in Romanticism* 35.4 (1996): 553–62.
- 'On the Autobiographical Present: Dorothy Wordsworth's *Grasmere Journals*.' *Criticism* 24.2 (1984): 115–37.
- *Wordsworth: The Sense of History*. Stanford: Stanford University Press, 1989.
Lopez, Barry. *Crossing Open Ground*. London: Picador, 1988.
Lovejoy, Arthur O. *The Great Chain of Being*. 1936. Rpt. Cambridge, Mass.: Harvard University Press, 1964.
Lovelock, James. *Gaia: A New Look at Life on Earth*. 1979. Rpt. New York: Oxford University Press, 1987.
Lussier, Mark. *Romantic Dynamics: The Poetics of Physicality*. New York: St Martin's Press, 2000.
Masson, Jeffrey Moussaieff, and Susan McCarthy. *When Elephants Weep: The Emotional Lives of Animals*. New York: Delacorte Press, 1995.
McFarland, Thomas. *Coleridge and the Pantheistic Tradition*. New York: Oxford University Press, 1969.
McGann, Jerome. *The Romantic Ideology*. Chicago: University of Chicago Press, 1983.
McGinn, Colin. 'Can We Solve the Mind-Body Problem?' *Mind* 98 (1989): 349–66.
McKusick, James. '"A Language That Is Ever Green": The Ecological Vision of John Clare.' *University of Toronto Quarterly* 61 (1991–2): 226–49.
Mellor, Anne. *Romanticism and Gender*. New York: Routledge, 1993.
Merchant, Carolyn. *The Death of Nature*. New York: Harper and Row, 1980.
Mills, Sara. *Discourses of Difference: An Analysis of Women's Travel Writing and Colonialism*. London: Routledge, 1991.
Mitchell, W.J.T. 'Imperial Landscape.' *Landscape and Power*. Ed. W.J.T. Mitchell. Chicago: University of Chicago Press, 1994. 5–34.
Modiano, Raimonda. *Coleridge and the Concept of Nature*. Tallahassee: Florida State University Press, 1985.
Moorman, Mary. *William Wordsworth: The Early Years*. Oxford: Clarendon Press, 1957.
Morton, Timothy. 'The Pulses of the Body: Romantic Vegetarianism and Its Cultural Contexts.' *1650–1850: Ideas, Aesthetics and Inquiries in the Early Modern Era*. 4 (1998): 53–80.
- *Shelley and the Revolution in Taste: The Body and the Natural World*. New York: Cambridge University Press, 1994.
Motion, Andrew. *Keats*. New York: Farrar, Straus and Giroux, 1998.

Munsche, P.B. *Gentlemen and Poachers: The English Game Laws 1671–1831*. Cambridge: Cambridge University Press, 1981.
Murphy, Patrick D. *Literature, Nature, and Other: Ecofeminist Critiques*. Albany: State University of New York Press, 1995.
Nabholtz, John R. 'Dorothy Wordsworth and the Picturesque.' *Studies in Romanticism* 3 (1963): 118–28.
Naess, Arne. *Ecology, Community and Lifestyle*. Trans. David Rothenberg. New York: Cambridge University Press, 1989.
Nash, Roderick. *The Rights of Nature*. Madison: University of Wisconsin Press, 1989.
Norris, Margot. *Beasts of the Imagination*. Baltimore: Johns Hopkins University Press, 1985.
Oerlemans, Onno. 'Shelley's Ideal Body: Vegetarianism and Nature.' *Studies in Romanticism* 34:4 (1995): 531–52.
Otte, Daniel, and John A. Endler, eds. *Speciation and Its Consequences*. Sunderland, Mass.: Sinauer Associates, 1989.
Pennant, Thomas. *A Tour in Scotland*. Chester: John Monk, 1771.
Perkins, David. *The Quest for Permanence: The Symbolism of Wordsworth, Shelley and Keats* Cambridge, Mass.: Harvard University Press, 1959.
Pite, Ralph. 'How Green Were the Romantics?' *Studies in Romanticism* 35.3 (1996): 357–73.
Plumwood, Val. 'Nature, Self and Gender: Feminism, Environmental Philosophy, and the Critique of Rationalism.' *Environmental Philosophy*. Ed. Michael Zimmerman. Englewood Cliffs, NJ: Prentice-Hall, 1994. 284–309.
Porter, Dennis. *Haunted Journeys: Desire and Transgression in European Travel Writing*. Princeton: Princeton University Press, 1991.
Prickett, Stephen. 'On Reading Nature as a Romantic.' *Coleridge, Schleiermacher and Romanticism*. Ed. David Jasper. New York: St Martin's Press, 1986. 126–42.
Rampino, Michael, Stephen Self, and Richard Stothers. 'Volcanic Winters.' *Annual Review of Earth and Planetary Sciences* 16 (1988): 73–99.
Ritvo, Harriet. *The Animal Estate*. Cambridge, Mass.: Harvard University Press, 1987.
Robbins, John. *Diet for a New America*. Walpole, NH: Stillpoint Press, 1987.
Roe, Nicholas. *The Politics of Nature*. New York: St Martin's Press, 1992.
Rolston, Holmes, III. 'Value in Nature and the Nature of Value.' *Philosophy and the Natural Environment*. Ed. Robin Attfield and Andrew Belsey. Cambridge: Cambridge University Press, 1994. 13–30.
Rose, Gillian. *Feminism and Geography: The Limits of Geographical Knowledge*. Minneapolis: University of Minnesota Press, 1993.

Ross, Marlon. *The Contours of Masculine Desire: Romanticism and the Rise of Women's Poetry*. New York: Oxford University Press, 1989.
Said, Edward. *Culture and Imperialism*. New York: Knopf, 1993.
Salt, Henry S. *Animal Rights*. Rpt. Clarks Summit, Penn.: Society for Animal Rights, 1980.
– *Percy Bysshe Shelley: Poet and Pioneer*. 1896. Rpt. London: George Allen and Unwin, 1924.
Schiebinger, Londa. *Nature's Body: Gender in the Making of Modern Science*. Boston: Beacon Press, 1993.
Schor, Naomi. *Reading in Detail: Aesthetics and the Feminine*. New York: Methuen, 1987.
Serres, Michel. *The Natural Contract*. Trans. Elizabeth MacArthur and William Paulson. Ann Arbor: University of Michigan Press, 1995.
Sessions, George, and Bill Devall. *Deep Ecology: Living As If Nature Mattered*. Salt Lake City: G.M. Smith, 1985.
Simpson, David. *The Academic Postmodern and the Rule of Literature*. Chicago: University of Chicago Press, 1995.
Singer, Peter. *Animal Liberation*. New York: Avon, 1977.
Smith, Jonathan. *Fact and Feeling: Baconian Science and the Nineteenth-Century Literary Imagination*. Madison: University of Wisconsin Press, 1994.
Smith, Jonathan. 'The Lie That Blinds: Destabilizing the Text of Landscape.' *Place/Culture/Representation*. Ed. James Duncan and David Ley. London: Routledge, 1993. 78–92.
Stafford, Barbara Maria. *Voyage into Substance*. Cambridge, Mass.: MIT Press, 1984.
Stanford, P. Kyle. 'For Pluralism and against Realism about Species.' *Philosophy of Science* 62 (1995): 70–91.
Stevens, Peter. 'Species: A Historical Perspective.' *Keywords in Evolutionary Biology*. Ed. Evelyn Fox Keller and Elizabeth A. Lloyd. Cambridge, Mass.: Harvard University Press, 1992. 302–11.
Stommel, Henry, and Elizabeth Stommel. *Volcanic Weather*. Newport, RI: Seven Seas Press, 1983.
Tarter, Jim. 'Collective Subjectivity and Postmodern Ecology.' *Interdisciplinary Studies in Literature and Environment* 2.2 (Winter 1996): 65–84.
Taylor, Paul W. 'The Ethics of Respect for Animals.' *The Animal Rights/Environmental Ethics Debate*. Ed. Eugene Hargrove. Albany. SUNY Press, 1992.
Tetreault, Ronald. *The Poetry of Life: Shelley and Literary Form*. Toronto: University of Toronto Press, 1987.
Thomas, Keith. *Man and the Natural World*. New York: Pantheon Books, 1983.

Todorov, Tzvetan. 'The Journey and Its Narratives.' Trans. Alyson Waters. *Transports: Travel, Pleasure and Imaginative Geography, 1600–1830.* Ed. Chloe Chard and Helen Langdon. New Haven: Yale University Press, 1996. 287–96.
Turner, James. *Reckoning with the Beast.* Baltimore: Johns Hopkins University Press, 1980.
Watkins, Daniel P. *Sexual Power in British Romantic Poetry.* Gainesville: University Press of Florida, 1996.
Weiskel, Thomas. *The Romantic Sublime: Studies in the Structure and Psychology of Transcendence.* Baltimore: Johns Hopkins University Press, 1976.
White, Harry. 'Shelley's Defence of Science.' *Studies in Romanticism* 16 (1977): 319–30.
White, Newman Ivey. *Shelley.* 2 vols. New York: Knopf, 1940.
Willey, Basil. *The Eighteenth-Century Background: Studies on the Idea of Nature in the Thought of the Period.* 1940. Rpt. Boston: Beacon Press, 1961.
Williams, Raymond. *The Country and the City.* New York: Oxford University Press, 1973.
Woodman, Ross. 'Shelley's Dizzy Ravine: Poetry and Madness.' *Studies in Romanticism* 36 (1997): 307–25.
Woodring, Carl. *Nature into Art.* Cambridge, Mass.: Harvard University Press, 1989.
Worster, Donald. *Nature's Economy: A History of Ecological Ideas.* Cambridge: Cambridge University Press, 1985.
Wu, Duncan. *Wordsworth's Reading.* New York: Cambridge University Press, 1993.
Wyatt, John. *Wordsworth and the Geologists.* New York: Cambridge University Press, 1995.
Young, Art. *Shelley and Nonviolence.* The Hague: Mouton, 1975.

Index

Abbey, Edward, 18, 208
Abernethy, John, 102, 221n6
Abram, David, 211n3
Abrams, M.H., 37
Adams, Carol, 222n7
Adorno, Theodore, 39
Allen, David Elliston, 211n4
Andrews, Malcolm, 230n10
animals: animal rights, 75, 79, 82, 83, 88, 141, 218n1, 219n13, 220n14, 220n15; consciousness and, 66–7, 82, 138–9; differences from humans, 135, 226n13; Game Laws and, 73–4; hunting and, 72–7, 86, 90–4; otherness and, 66–9, 74, 77; representation and, 65–97; romanticism and, 65–97; vegetarianism and, 103–7. *See also* species
anthropocentrism, 58, 69, 77, 84, 94, 97, 135
anthropomorphism, 65–97, 138–9, 226n15, 226n17
Arbuthnot, John, 102, 221n6
Aristotle, 126, 127
Aronowitz, Stanley, 33
associationism, 56

Axon, William, 221n3
Austin, Mary, 18

Bacon, Francis, 104
Baillie, Joanna, 71
ballad, 90–1, 94
Barfield, Owen, 133
Barrell, John, 18, 33, 214n5
Barrish, Philip, 224n4
Bartram, William, 37, 137, 148, 155
Bate, Jonathan, 3, 18, 34, 38, 43, 57, 71, 78, 121, 212n13, 224n22
Baudrillard, Jean, 12, 32, 214n3
Beddoes, Thomas, 102, 222n6
Bentham, Jeremy, 75, 88, 220n15
Berkeley, George, 31
Bewell, Alan, 3, 18, 38, 50, 57, 173, 215n14, 216n18
Bialostosky, Don, 46
Blake, William, 200; *Marriage of Heaven and Hell*, 70–1
Bligh, William, 37, 155
Blumenbach, J.F., 136
Blunden, Edmund, 34
Bohls, Elizabeth, 158, 186, 192
Bone, Drummond, 14, 22, 214n6

Bookchin, Murray, 213n15
Bradley, A.C., 33
Bristed, John, 160, 161
Brown, Marshall, 45, 215n14
Bruckner, John, 105–6
Buchan, William, 102–3, 222n6
Buell, Lawrence, 3, 18
Buffon, Comte de, 128, 131, 146
Burke, Edmund, 5, 18, 37
Burnet, Thomas, 103, 119
Burns, Robert: animals and, 78–9; 'The Auld Farmer's New-year-morning Salutation,' 78; 'On Seeing a Wounded Hare,' 78; 'To a Mouse,' 78–9
Buzard, James, 150, 156, 228n4
Byron, George Gordon, Lord, 167, 224n22

Cameron, Kenneth Neill, 99, 101
chain of being, 126, 131
Chandler, James, 37, 217n31
Cheyne, George, 102, 103, 111, 221n6
Clare, Johanne, 79
Clare, John, 16, 38, 55, 71; animals and, 79–82; language and, 140–2; taxonomy and, 137–43; 'The Badger,' 80; 'Emmonsails Heath in Winter,' 139–41; 'The Eternity of Nature,' 142; 'The Fox,' 80; 'The Hedgehog,' 80–1; 'The Lamentations of Round Oak Waters,' 142; 'The Marten,' 80, 81; 'The Nightingales Nest,' 81; 'The Woodlarks Nest,' 81; 'The Wrynecks Nest,' 141
Clark, David Lee, 101, 221n2
Clarke, James, 159, 229n10
Cole, Thomas, 168
Coleridge, Samuel Taylor, 13, 17, 22, 202; animals and, 83–8, 220n14; Dorothy Wordsworth and, 188, 190; race and, 136–7; taxonomy and, 133–7, 225n11; *Biographia Literaria*, 49; *Contributions to a Course of Lectures*, 133, 135–7; 'Dejection: An Ode,' 27–8; 'Eolian Harp,' 84; 'Frost at Midnight,' 56–7; 'Hymn before Sunrise,' 169; 'Kubla Khan,' 92; 'The Nightingale,' 27, 84–5; *Rime of the Ancient Mariner*, 70, 85–8; *Theory of Life*, 133–7, 225n11; 'To a Young Ass,' 68, 70, 83–4
Cowper, William, 75
Crook, Nora, 223n14
Cuvier, Baron Georges, 50, 127, 128, 137, 144–6, 152

Danby, John, 95, 97
Darwin, Charles, 108, 125, 128, 139, 144, 147, 219n9, 224n4, 226n17
Darwin, Erasmus, 35, 37, 107, 110, 128, 132–3, 144, 215n11, 216n16, 226n17, 227n22
Davie, Donald, 33
Dawkins, Richard, 22, 124
Delacroix, Eugene, 70
Dennett, Daniel, 22
Derham, William, 34
Derrida, Jacques, 113, 223n17
Descartes, René, 71, 75, 139
de Selincourt, Ernest, 184, 230n22
Deuchar, Steven, 73, 75–6, 92
de Waal, Frans, 66
Dillard, Annie, 207
Dimock, Wai Chee, 24, 213n20

Easterbrook, Greg, 8–9
ecofeminism, 7–8, 18, 19, 36, 67, 176–7, 211n4
elegy, 36, 39, 40–4, 48, 51, 54, 63–4

Emerson, Ralph Waldo, 22, 28, 30, 31
empiricism, 14–21, 43, 139, 143, 147, 148, 159, 212n9, 212n12
environmentalism, 5–9, 31, 37, 47, 65–6, 68, 211n2, 212n13, 213n14, 218n1, 222n8, 224n20; biocentrism and, 77–8, 97, 219n9, 224n21; deep ecology and, 7, 18, 19; existential, 43, 62–4; language and, 21–3; particularity and, 14–21; perception and, 11–12, 21–3, 26–9, 200–10, 229n7; romanticism and, 9–21, 23–6, 28, 200–10
ethology, 66, 68, 226n15
evolution, 66, 107, 108, 128, 131, 132, 134, 146, 225n11
Evernden, Neil, 6, 11, 12, 207, 211n2

Fay, Elizabeth, 230n21
Ferré, Frederick, 7
food chain, 104–5, 112
Foucault, Michel, 126–8, 130, 144, 145, 202, 227n21
Friedrich, Caspar David, 170
Frost, Robert, 26
Fruman, Norman, 133, 225n11
Fry, Paul, 21, 35, 65, 202

Gandhi, Mohandas, 113
Garber, Frederick, 93, 214n7
Garnett, Thomas, 160
Gaull, Marilyn, 216n16
geology, 45, 50, 152–3, 202, 216n16, 216n20
Gericault, Theodore, 70
Gilpin, William, 148, 158–9, 161
Glendening, John, 151, 186–7
Godwin, William, 31, 118
Goldsmith, Oliver, 103, 131–2
Gould, Stephen Jay, 6, 20

Grabo, Carl, 223n15
Graham, Thomas, 102, 222n7
Griffin, Andrew, 94
Gross, Alan, 224n2
Guiton, Derek, 223n14

Haney, David, 62
Haraway, Donna, 19
Harding, Sandra, 33
Harley, John Brian, 230n11, 230n14
Harrison, Robert Pogue, 11
Hartley, David, 56
Hartman, Geoffrey, 10, 30–1, 37, 48–9, 55, 77–8, 89, 167, 216n21
Heidegger, Martin, 11
Heisenberg, Werner, 32
Helsinger, Elizabeth K., 81
Hickey, Alison, 151
Hodgson, John, 93
Hogarth, William, 75
Holbach, P.D., 35, 37, 106–10, 118, 133
Holmes, Richard, 84, 99, 220n14
Homans, Margaret, 10, 179, 185
Hopkins, Gerard Manley, 140
Hull, David, 224n4
Humboldt, Alexander von, 148, 156, 164
Hume, David, 56, 107, 108, 117, 206
Hutchinson, William, 159, 229n10

ideology, 149–56, 163, 166, 174, 187, 214n5, 229n8. *See also* romantic ideology

Johnson, Samuel, 75, 131, 151
Johnston, Kenneth, 20, 57, 60, 217n27

Keats, John, 13; 'Epistle to J.H. Reynolds,' 4; 'Ode to a Nightingale,' 48,

70, 84; 'Ode to Autumn,' 121; 'Sleep and Poetry,' 49
Keith, W.J., 34
Knight, G. Wilson, 33
Knight, Richard Payne, 158
Kroeber, Karl, 3, 10, 11, 18, 19, 34, 43, 212n13
Kuberski, Philip, 10, 203, 212n6, 228n25

Lamarck, Jean-Baptiste de, 128, 132, 134, 227n22
Lambe, William, 111, 222n6
Latour, Bruno, 15, 218n1
Lawrence, John, 220n15
Leopold, Aldo, 18, 137
Levere, Trevor, 225n11
Levin, Susan, 179
Levinson, Marjorie, 10, 33
Lewontin, Richard, 212n12
Leyden, John, 162–3
Lindley, David, 212n8
Linnaeus, Carolus, 75, 80, 125, 127, 128, 129, 137, 202, 218n7, 226n17
Liu, Alan, 10, 11, 15–18, 31–2, 34, 36, 58–9, 62–3, 183, 212n7, 212n12, 213n16, 215n9, 217n30
Locke, John, 31, 41, 56, 137, 216n24; *Essay Concerning Human Understanding*, 129–31
Lopez, Barry, 18, 53, 154–5, 197, 208–9
Lovejoy, Arthur, 126–7
Lovelock, James, 9, 14, 50, 124, 131
Lussier, Mark, 10, 203, 212n6
lyric, 21–2, 39, 57–64, 148, 150–1, 165, 179

Malthus, Thomas, 105
materialism, 35, 214n3, 216n24

materiality, 4–5, 14–21, 34; body and, 40–7, 49, 101–7, 114; consciousness and, 38, 48, 53–7, 60–4, 65–6, 101, 106, 109, 111–13, 119–22, 146–7, 154–5, 200–10, 217n24, 218n1; culture and, 31–4, 51–2; otherness and, 200–10; Shelley and, 100, 119–22; travel writing and, 148–99 passim; vegetarianism and, 100, 111, 112; Wordsworth and, 35, 37, 39, 41–64, 65, 98, 215n16
Mayr, Ernst, 125
McFarland, Thomas, 133
McGann, Jerome, 3, 10, 33
McGinn, Colin, 217n24
McKibben, Bill, 213n17
McKusick, James, 79, 82
Mellor, Anne, 10, 33, 36, 175, 179–80, 185, 231n25
Merchant, Carolyn, 7, 67
Mills, Sara, 228n3
Milton, John, 106, 110
Modiana, Raimonda, 136–7
More, Thomas, 115
Morris, William, 116
Morton, Timothy, 98, 99–100, 113, 122, 221n4, 223n18
Murphy, Patrick, 8, 10, 18, 213n14

Nabholtz, John, 186
Naess, Arne, 7
narrative, 149–50, 161–2, 183
Nash, Roderick, 82
naturphilosophie, 33, 35, 43, 133, 136
Neumann, John von, 32, 214n2
Newton, Isaac, 37
Newton, J.F., 101, 110, 115
Norris, Margot, 77, 219n9

Oersted, Hans Christian, 43

Oswald, John, 82–3
otherness, 201–10, 213n14; animals and, 66–9, 74, 77

Paine, Thomas, 82
particularity, 14–21, 160–1, 165, 204–6
pathetic fallacy, 87
Paley, William, 103, 107, 115, 222n9
Peacock, Thomas Love, 99
Pennant, Thomas, 165, 181
perception, environmentalism and, 11–12, 21–3, 26–9, 200–10, 229n7; taxonomy and, 129–31; travel writing and, 148–99 passim
Perkins, David, 35
physics, 14, 31–2, 212n8, 214n2
picturesque, 155–60, 64, 165, 174, 181, 186, 189, 192, 195, 215n14, 229n8, 229n9
Pite, Ralph, 5, 13
Plumwood, Val, 18
Plutarch, 101, 111
Poe, Edgar Allan, 14, 133
Pope, Alexander, 103, 108, 126, 202
Porter, Dennis, 153
Price, Uvedale, 158
Priestley, Joseph, 35, 37, 40–1, 106, 107, 110

Radcliffe, Ann, 181
Ray, John, 34, 103–4, 137
Ritson, Joseph, 101, 104–5
Ritvo, Harriet, 68, 75, 84
Roe, Nicholas, 38, 215n14
Rogers, Neville, 98
Rolston, Holmes, III, 124
romantic ideology, 3, 10, 15, 31–4, 67, 151–2, 153, 157, 186–7. *See also* ideology
Rose, Gillian, 166

Ross, Marlon, 180
Rousseau, Jean-Jacques, 37, 75, 103
RSPCA, 75, 79, 80

Said, Edward, 153, 228n3
Salt, Henry, 99
Saussure, Horace Benedict, 155
Schelling, Friedrich von, 35
Schiebinger, Londa, 128, 136, 226n13
Serres, Michel, 5, 12
Shelley, Mary, 224n22
Shelley, Percy Bysshe, 13, 22, 35, 84, 137; Cuvier and, 144–6; ecological imagination and, 101, 112–13, 116–17; materiality and, 100, 119–22, 227n24; taxonomy and, 143–7; vegetarianism and, 82, 98–101, 105–22, 221n2, 223n14, 227n22; *Defence of Poetry*, 146; *Epipsychidion*, 67; *The Mask of Anarchy*, 113; 'Mont Blanc,' 99, 112, 118–19, 120, 144–7, 202; 'Ode to the West Wind,' 119–22, 143; *On the Vegetable System*, 99, 107, 110–17; *Prometheus Unbound*, 101, 113–14, 116, 143, 144; *Queen Mab*, 70, 99, 107, 108, 116, 117–18; *Refutation of Deism*, 107–10, 112; 'To a Skylark,' 63, 70, 84, 142; *A Vindication of Natural Diet*, 99, 104, 110–17, 122
Simpson, David, 10, 15, 17–19, 212n11, 213n14
Smellie, William, 103, 104–5, 106–10, 222n11
Smith, Jonathan, 212n9, 228n7
sociobiology, 66
species, 123–47: definition of, 123–7, 130–1, 144, 224n2, 224n4, 225n6; endangered, 123; hybrids, 123, 133, 139. *See also* animals

Spinoza, Benedict de, 117
Stafford, Barbara Maria, 155, 156
Sterne, Laurence, 161
Stevens, Wallace: 'The Snow Man,' 26–9, 205
Stoddart, John, 160–1
Stubbs, George, 70, 71–7; *Freeman, the Earl of Clarendon's Gamekeeper*, 71–7; *Gimcrack on Newmarket Heath*, 74; *The Grosvenor Hunt*, 74, 91; *Lord Grosvernor's Arabian*, 74; *Warren Hastings*, 74

Tarter, Jim, 124
Taylor, Paul W., 219n9
Taylor, Thomas, 220n15
taxonomy, 123–47, 204–5, 225n6; animal consciousness and, 138–9; anthropomorphism and, 138–9; empiricism and, 139, 143, 147; history of, 125–33; language and, 125; perception and, 129–31; race and, 136–7; representation and, 127–32, 147; romanticism and, 125
Tetreault, Ronald, 119
Thelwall, John, 215n12
Thomas, Keith, 75, 78
Thomson, James, 75, 103
Thoreau, Henry David, 18, 137, 209–10
Thornton, Col. T., 76–7
Todorov, Tzvetan, 149–50
travel writing, 36; audience and, 162, 166, 185; environmentalism and, 165; gender and, 180–1; genre and, 149–56, 180–1, 183–5; ideology and, 149–56, 163, 166, 174, 187; landscape and, 148–99; lyric and, 150–1, 165, 179; maps and, 164–5; materiality and, 148–99 passim, 228n1; narrative and, 149–50, 161–2, 183; nationalism and, 195–9; particularity and, 160–1, 165; perception and, 148–99 passim; picturesque and, 155–60, 165, 174, 181, 186, 189, 192, 195; romantic ideology and, 151–2, 153, 157, 186–7; wildness and, 198–9
Trotter, Thomas, 222n13
Turner, James, 75
Tweed, J., 221n6

USDA, 101, 221n5
US Wildlife Service, 123

Veblen, Thorsten, 91
vegetarianism, 224n20; animals and, 103–7; consciousness and, 112–13; disease and, 111, 113; history of, 101–7; materiality and, 100, 112; Shelley and, 82, 98–101, 105–22, 221n2, 223n14, 227n22; violence and, 114–16
Voltaire, 75

Wallis, George, 102
Walton, Isaak, 92
Watkins, Daniel, 176
Weiskel, Thomas, 4–5
Wellek, René, 133
Werner, Abraham, 50
West, Thomas, 159, 229n10
White, Gilbert, 18, 37, 38, 55, 79, 141; *Natural History of Selborne*, 137–9
White, Newman Ivey, 221n2
wildness, 198–9, 207–10
Willey, Basil, 108
Williams, Helen Maria, 155–6, 164
Williams, Raymond, 33, 153, 163
Williams, William Carlos, 24, 140

Index

Willich, A.F.M., 221n6
Wollstonecraft, Mary, 82, 181
Woodman, Ross, 227n23
Wordsworth, Dorothy, 16, 38, 166, 179–99; optical illusion and, 190–5; travel and, 179–99, 231n23, 231n27; *Alfoxden and Grasmere Journals*, 182–4; *Recollections of a Tour Made in Scotland*, 166, 181–99
Wordsworth, William, 9, 10, 12, 17, 18, 21, 24, 116, 120, 154; animals and, 88–97; childhood and, 205–6; Dorothy Wordsworth and, 180–1, 185–6, 192, 197–9; elegy and, 36, 39, 40–4, 48, 51, 54, 63–4; materiality and, 35, 37, 39, 41–64, 65, 98, 215n16; nature and, 30–64; picturesque and, 157–8; travel and, 166–79; 'Anecdote for Fathers,' 40, 89; 'Composed upon Westminster Bridge,' 51–2, 191; *Essay Supplementary to the Preface of 1815*, 14, 47; *The Excursion*, 71, 88; 'Fidelity,' 90; 'The Green Linnet,' 84, 90; *Guide to the Lakes*, 172–3; 'Hart-Leap Well,' 90–4, 97; 'I Wandered Lonely as a Cloud,' 177, 179; 'Incident Characteristic of a Favourite Dog,' 90; 'Intimations, Ode,' 35–6, 41, 205–6; 'The Kitten and the Falling Leaves,' 89; 'Michael,' 57, 58, 202; *Peter Bell*, 94, 196–7; 'The Pet Lamb: A Pastoral,' 88–9; *Preface* to *Lyrical Ballads*, 94; *Prospectus* to *The Recluse*, 43; 'Resolution and Independence,' 48–9, 51; *The Ruined Cottage*, 57–64, 202; 'She was a Phantom of Delight,' 176–7; 'Simon Lee,' 46–7, 49, 58, 90, 91, 94, 97; 'A Slumber Did My Spirit Seal,' 39–43, 58, 59; 'Solitary Reaper,' 177, 179; 'Stepping Westward,' 177–8; 'The Tables Turned,' 56; 'The Thorn,' 44–6; 'Tintern Abbey,' 16, 35, 47, 49, 52, 167; 'To a Butterfly,' 89; 'To a Cuckoo,' 90; 'To a Skylark,' 90; 'Tribute to the Memory of the Same Dog,' 90; 'We Are Seven,' 40, 89; *The White Doe of Rylstone*, 95–7; 'With Ships the Sea Was Sprinkled,' 174–6; 'The World Is Too Much with Us,' 51–2
– *The Prelude*: book 1, 54, 167; book 3, 61; book 5, 49–54, 89–90; book 6, 54–5, 169–71; book 7, 57; book 11, 157–8; book 12, 168; book 13, 171–2
Worster, Donald, 222n8
Wyatt, John, 152, 216n16, 216n20

Young, Thomas, 220n15

OHIO UNIVERSITY LIBRARY

Please return this book as soon as you have finished with it. In order to avoid a fine it must be returned by the latest date stamped below. All books are subject to recall after two weeks or immediately if needed for reserve.

CF